Strengthening the Responsibility to Protect

This book provides a systematic analysis of reform measures aimed at strengthening the implementation of the 'Responsibility to Protect' (R2P) doctrine, utilising a cosmopolitan lens.

In 2005, member states of the United Nations (UN) accepted a 'Responsibility to Protect' against four mass atrocity crimes: genocide, crimes against humanity, war crimes, and ethnic cleansing. Despite this commitment, mass atrocities remain a pervasive aspect of the international landscape. In addressing R2P reform, the book utilises a 'transitional cosmopolitan' lens. The aim of this transitional cosmopolitan approach is to promote incremental progress towards solving moral problems by operating within particular contexts and practical barriers to change. Three areas for reform are explored: the UN Security Council P5's power of veto, to prevent the veto obstructing timely and decisive R2P response action; the powers of the UN General Assembly as an alternative means for responding to mass atrocity situations; and the establishment of an 'R2P Commission' to hold states accountable for their R2P commitments. These are not advocated as the definitive areas for R2P reform. However, each of the recommendations made can contribute at least some positive progress towards a more cosmopolitan application of the R2P that would help in curbing mass atrocity and improving the protection of fundamental human rights.

This book will be of much interest to students of the Responsibility to Protect, genocide, humanitarian protection, and International Relations in general.

Richard Illingworth is a researcher working at the European Centre for the Responsibility to Protect, University of Leeds (UK) and has a PhD in Politics and International Studies.

Global Politics and the Responsibility to Protect

The aim of this book series is to gather the best new thinking about the Responsibility to Protect into a core set of volumes that provides a definitive account of the principle, its implementation, and its role in crises, that reflects a plurality of views and regional perspectives.

Series Editors: Alex J. Bellamy *University of Queensland,* Sara E. Davies, *Griffith University* and Monica Serrano *The City University of New York.*

Constructing the Responsibility to Protect
Contestation and Consolidation
Edited by Charles T. Hunt and Phil Orchard

Protecting the Global Civilian from Violence
UN Discourses and Practices in Fragile States
Timo Kivimäki

Covid-19 and Atrocity Prevention in East Asia
Edited by Mely Caballero-Anthony and Noel M. Morada

Advocacy Networks and the Responsibility to Protect
The Politics of Norm Circulation
Sarka Kolmasova

Regional Approaches to the Responsibility to Protect
Lessons from Europe and West Africa
Jochem Rietveld

Strengthening the Responsibility to Protect
A Transitional Cosmopolitan Approach
Richard Illingworth

For more information about this series, please visit: https://www.routledge.com/Global-Politics-and-the-Responsibility-to-Protect/book-series/GPRP

Strengthening the Responsibility to Protect

A Transitional Cosmopolitan Approach

Richard Illingworth

Routledge
Taylor & Francis Group

LONDON AND NEW YORK

First published 2024
by Routledge
4 Park Square, Milton Park, Abingdon, Oxon OX14 4RN

and by Routledge
605 Third Avenue, New York, NY 10158

Routledge is an imprint of the Taylor & Francis Group, an informa business

British Library Cataloguing-in-Publication Data
A catalogue record for this book is available from the British Library

Library of Congress Cataloging-in-Publication Data
Names: Illingworth, Richard, author.
Title: Strengthening the responsibility to protect : a transitional cosmopolitan approach / Richard Illingworth.
Description: Abingdon, Oxon [UK] ; New York, NY : Routledge, 2023. | Series: Global politics and the responsibility to protect | Includes bibliographical references and index.
Identifiers: LCCN 2023018439 (print) | LCCN 2023018440 (ebook) | ISBN 9781032494982 (hardback) | ISBN 9781032494999 (paperback) | ISBN 9781003394105 (ebook)
Subjects: LCSH: Responsibility to protect (International law) | Law reform. | United Nations. General Assembly. | United Nations. Security Council. | International obligations.
Classification: LCC KZ4082 .I45 2023 (print) | LCC KZ4082 (ebook) | DDC 341.4/8–dc23/eng/20230802
LC record available at https://lccn.loc.gov/2023018439
LC ebook record available at https://lccn.loc.gov/2023018440

ISBN: 978-1-032-49498-2 (hbk)
ISBN: 978-1-032-49499-9 (pbk)
ISBN: 978-1-003-39410-5 (ebk)

DOI: 10.4324/9781003394105

Typeset in Sabon
by Newgen Publishing UK

Contents

Acknowledgements

Formal Acknowledgements

I thank Brill for their permission to republish previously used content from *Global Responsibility to Protect* journal: Illingworth, R. 2020. 'Responsible Veto Restraint: A Transitional Cosmopolitan Reform Measure for the Responsibility to Protect'. *Global Responsibility to Protect* 12(4), pp. 385–414. https://doi.org/10.1163/1875-984X-01204008.

Personal Acknowledgements

In writing this section my mind cannot help but be drawn to *Father Ted's* 'Golden Cleric' acceptance speech. Nevertheless, I must thank those that have supported me both during the PhD, and before it began. First, I thank the University of Leeds for funding this research. Without a Leeds Doctoral Scholarship, there is no chance I would have been able to undertake doctoral study. I must also thank – including *all* persons therein who have been involved with this research, or its process, in some way or another – the University of Leeds Department of Politics and International Studies, the European Centre for the Responsibility to Protect, the British International Studies Association, and the BISA IR2P working group.

Of course, there must be special thanks given to my two PhD supervisors, Garrett W. Brown ('good cop') and Adrian Gallagher ('prepare for the worst cop'), whose sagely wisdom, praise, and criticism have guided me through the past 3+ years. This project would never have happened had I not wandered into Adrian's office back in 2017 to discuss the idea of PhD study. He should know that I will be eternally grateful for all he's done in getting this project from start to finish. Who knows what life would look like for me right now without his efforts? At the very least, I wouldn't have spent the last several years bashing out a hundred thousand words. For sure, my heart sank pretty much every time I opened Adrian's feedback on my chapter drafts, but it was all necessary pain. Garrett's 'ok, here's how you get around this' comments would also often help raise my heart back up again, if only by a little bit.

I would also like to extend my thanks to Jürgen Klopp for turning us Liverpool fans from doubters to believers. A sentiment I think I tried to carry into this book, battling against my own natural cynicism to remain committed to the potential for improving the world, even just a little bit. Klopp, I have no doubt, would be a firm supporter of the Responsibility to Protect.

To those closest to me, while you are definitely *not* too countless to refer to by individual names, I'm still not going to anyway. To my family, thank you for all you have done to get me here, even though I'm still pretty sure you have absolutely no idea what I do, or what this book is about. To my friends, I like less than half of you half as well as you deserve but thanks for being a constant bastion of witty, satirical, and cynical musings. Finally, to my cohabitants, I feel lucky every day to have you in my life.

Abbreviations

ACT Group	Accountability, Coherence and Transparency Group
BRICS	Group of Brazil, Russia, India, China, South Africa
CAR	Central African Republic
CNN	Cable News Network
CoI	Commission of Inquiry
GCR2P	Global Centre for the Responsibility to Protect
ICC	International Criminal Court
ICISS	International Commission on Intervention and State Sovereignty
ICJ	International Court of Justice
IIFFMM	Independent International Fact-Finding Mission on Myanmar
IIMM	International Investigative Mechanism for Myanmar
IMF	International Monetary Fund
NATO	North Atlantic Treaty Organization
NGO	Non-governmental organisation
OHCHR	Office of the United Nations High Commissioner for Human Rights
OCHA	United Nations Office for the Coordination of Humanitarian Affairs
P3	Permanent Three members of the UN Security Council – Britain, France, United States
P5	Permanent Five members of the UN Security Council – Britain, France, United States, Russia, and China
R2P	Responsibility to Protect
RVR	Responsible Veto Restraint
RwP	Responsibility while Protecting
UfP	Uniting for Peace
UN	United Nations
UNGA	United Nations General Assembly
UNHCR	United Nations High Commissioner for Refugees

UNHRC	United Nations Human Rights Council
UNSC	United Nations Security Council
UPR	Universal Periodic Review
US	United States of America
WSOD	World Summit Outcome Document

1 Introduction

The Responsibility to Protect and the Necessity of Reform

1.1 The Responsibility to Protect and a Human Protection Regime in Crisis

… if humanitarian intervention is, indeed, an unacceptable assault on sovereignty, how should we respond to a Rwanda, to a Srebrenica—to gross and systematic violations of human rights that offend every precept of our common humanity? (UN, 2000, p. 48).

It is over 20 years ago that former United Nations (UN) Secretary-General Kofi Annan posed this fundamental challenge to UN member states. Annan's question cut right to the core of the aspirational yet sometimes conflicting nature of the UN system: the question of whether it is state sovereignty and non-interference in the pursuit of international peace, or the protection of fundamental human rights at the potential cost of this peace that should be given precedence at times of grave crisis. It was Canada that responded to Annan's challenge, sponsoring the establishment of the International Commission on Intervention and State Sovereignty (ICISS) in September 2000, which put forward the concept of the 'Responsibility to Protect' (R2P) in its landmark 2001 report (ICISS, 2001).

Annan's challenge and the subsequent evolution of the R2P were a response to the mass violence and atrocity crimes committed in numerous conflicts throughout the 1990s. In particular, they were a reaction to the failures of the international community to adequately respond to the events in Rwanda and Kosovo. In Rwanda, in 1994, the international community had failed almost entirely to produce an international response to an unfolding genocide which led to the deaths of over 800,000 people (Human Rights Watch, 1999). Conversely, in the case of Kosovo, in 1999, a timely international response occurred but did so illegally through a NATO-led intervention that lacked authorisation from the UN (Independent International Commission on Kosovo, 2000).

Rwanda and Kosovo raised questions as to whether the UN was adequately placed to deal with the most egregious international crimes. In response, the R2P was devised by the ICISS as a means to avoid future inaction in

DOI: 10.4324/9781003394105-1

the face of mass human suffering, while also aiming to promote an international culture that prioritised mass atrocity prevention. Specifically, the R2P attempts to reframe the concept of state sovereignty from a perspective of responsibility, setting out to protect populations from four mass atrocity crimes: genocide, war crimes, crimes against humanity, and ethnic cleansing. These goals are framed under the R2P through multilateral and legal means in accordance with the UN Charter. Ultimately, the R2P is a moral and political commitment that concrete action must be taken to prevent atrocity crimes; that inaction is not an option when the most fundamental human freedoms are threatened.

A significantly shortened version of the ICISS's 91-page report was adopted by the UN General Assembly (UNGA) at the 2005 World Summit. Now boiled down to just two paragraphs of the 2005 World Summit Outcome Document (WSOD), paragraphs 138 and 139 (UNGA, 2005) read thus:

138. Each individual State has the responsibility to protect its populations from genocide, war crimes, ethnic cleansing and crimes against humanity. This responsibility entails the prevention of such crimes, including their incitement, through appropriate and necessary means. We accept that responsibility and will act in accordance with it. The international community should, as appropriate, encourage and help States to exercise this responsibility and support the United Nations in establishing an early warning capability.

139. The international community, through the United Nations, also has the responsibility to use appropriate diplomatic, humanitarian and other peaceful means, in accordance with Chapters VI and VIII of the Charter, to help protect populations from genocide, war crimes, ethnic cleansing and crimes against humanity. In this context, we are prepared to take collective action, in a timely and decisive manner, through the Security Council, in accordance with the Charter, including Chapter VII, on a case-by-case basis and in cooperation with relevant regional organizations as appropriate, should peaceful means be inadequate and national authorities are manifestly failing to protect their populations from genocide, war crimes, ethnic cleansing and crimes against humanity. We stress the need for the General Assembly to continue consideration of the responsibility to protect populations from genocide, war crimes, ethnic cleansing and crimes against humanity and its implications, bearing in mind the principles of the Charter and international law. We also intend to commit ourselves, as necessary and appropriate, to helping States build capacity to protect their populations from genocide, war crimes, ethnic cleansing and crimes against humanity and to assisting those which are under stress before crises and conflicts break out.

Later, in a 2009 report by then Secretary-General Ban-Ki Moon, the core ideas of the R2P contained in the above paragraphs were conceptualised into a 'three pillar' system as the R2P is understood today (UNGA, 2009). The three pillars cover both the prevention of mass atrocity crimes and the need for international response if and when they occur. Pillar One of the R2P concerns primary host state responsibility towards its own population vis-à-vis the prevention of the four listed mass atrocity crimes. Pillar Two refers to the responsibility of the international community in assisting and encouraging other states in meeting their primary responsibility. Finally, Pillar Three declares that the international community has a duty to at least consider taking action on a case-by-case basis when a state is 'manifestly failing' to meet its primary protection responsibility (UNGA, 2009).

The R2P has been explicitly invoked by the UN Security Council (UNSC) in 89 resolutions or Presidential Statements (GCR2P, 2022).[1] These resolutions and statements have mostly referenced ideas most closely associated with host state responsibility under R2P Pillar One, but they have contained the logic of international assistance measures under Pillar Two, and arguably, at times, robust enforcement under Pillar Three.[2] The UN Secretary-General has published annual thematic reports on R2P since 2009, which help provide conceptual clarity and political momentum for the doctrine (Šimonović, 2019, p. 252). These reports are drafted by the Special Adviser of the Secretary-General on the Responsibility to Protect, a post created by the Secretary-General in 2008 to lead 'the conceptual, political, institutional and operational development of the Responsibility to Protect principle and its implementation by the United Nations, Member States, regional arrangements and civil society' (UN, 2014, p. 4). The UNGA holds annual debates on the Secretary-General's reports. As of May 2021, following a 115-15 vote in favour (with 28 abstentions), discussion of the R2P is now also a formal matter included on the UNGA's annual agenda (UNGA, 2021). A significant civil society and academic movement follows developments on the R2P with keen interest, and states have institutionalised their commitment to the doctrine through mechanisms such as the 'R2P Group of Friends' (which has 56 member states), and by establishing 'R2P focal points' (more than 60 of these posts exist around the world) at the domestic level. These developments demonstrate that the R2P is a 'norm', meaning that it sets out widely shared expectations and standards of appropriate state behaviour (Finnemore and Sikkink, 1998). As Hunt and Orchard (2020, p. 7) put it, 'by any measure the evolution of the R2P has been impressive', with the doctrine having developed from a nascent conceptual ideal as 'sovereignty as responsibility' in the 1990s (Deng et al., 1996), into what is now a commitment institutionalised at the highest levels of politics.

Yet, while the R2P offered hope that the tension between state sovereignty and fundamental human rights protection had finally been resolved (Evans, 2008, p. 284), regrettably, since the R2P was adopted by the UN in 2005, mass violence has actually increased. At the time of writing, the Global Centre for the Responsibility to Protect (GCR2P) identifies 13 current atrocity crises around the world, with several others characterised as either at 'imminent risk' or 'serious concern' (GCR2P, n.d.). Violent conflict, while not exclusively the arena in which mass atrocities occur (UN, 2014, p. 10), has witnessed a surge from 2007 onwards – with stark human, social, and economic costs (World Bank Group, 2018). Uppsala Conflict Data (2022) show that 119,000 people were killed in organised violence in 2021, a rise of 46 per cent from 2020. Partly a result of this surge in conflict, refugee numbers are at their highest since the end of the Second World War (Šimonović, 2019, p. 253). Crisis Group (2022) observe that rapid human-induced climate change is 'exacerbating conflicts ... increasing human suffering ... [and] making the UN's day-to-day work harder' in countries that have experienced mass atrocities. Amnesty International (2022, p. x) note of 2021/22 that:

> conflict caused violations of international human rights and humanitarian law on a vast scale. In far too few instances did the needed international response come; in far too few cases were justice and accountability provided. Instead, conflict expanded. Extending over time, its impacts worsened.

Atrocities are evidently not being prevented consistently, and international response has often lacked where mass violence has emerged. Over Syria, for instance, the UNSC has seen 17 vetoed draft resolutions to date, which has greatly inhibited the international response to the crisis. This is despite the fact that events in Syria have left 6.7 million internally displaced, with a further 6.6 million refugees forced into exile (UNHCR, n.d.). Concerning Myanmar, the brutal military crackdown on Rohingya Muslims – which resulted in 1.3 million people needing humanitarian assistance (UNICEF) – never even made it onto the UNSC's formal agenda, while a military coup that occurred in February 2021, which has led to over 12,000 deaths from political violence in a situation regarded as a civil war (BBC, 2022), only drew a first UNSC resolution 22 months later in December 2022. The response to the persecution of Uyghur Muslims by the Chinese state has also been weak, despite actions which 'may constitute international crimes, in particular crimes against humanity' (OHCHR, 2022, p. 44), or even potentially genocide, as reportedly over a million ethnic Muslims have been arbitrary detained by the Chinese state, with evidence of torture, sexual violence, forced labour, and forced sterilisation (UK Foreign Affairs Committee, 2021).

Evidently then, the human protection regime is in a time of crisis (Glanville, 2021, p. 3). What this all suggests is that the *prevention* of, and *response* to, cases of mass atrocity violence has not been enhanced by the R2P in the way its proponents would have hoped.

1.2 Reform, Not Abandonment

Frequent failures of atrocity prevention and response are unacceptable when atrocities are understood as threatening the 'core dignity of human beings'

(UN, 2014, p. 1). There is then an urgent need to find ways to reform and strengthen the R2P in order to promote the goal of human protection. One of the main contributions of this book is to provide the first ever systematic study of reform measures for strengthening the responsibility to protect. It develops and applies transitional thinking as a means of overcoming some of the R2P's key implementation challenges. The book makes a novel contribution by tying together debates on international institutional reform and the R2P, exploring means through which mass atrocity prevention and response can be enhanced. It is argued here that without reform, progress toward the R2P's protection ideal is impossible. Reform, however, may offer the potential for incremental progress.

Suppressing atrocity crises is an aspirational goal, and the purpose of the R2P is to promote incremental progress towards that goal. However, as Gallagher (2015) draws to attention, many sceptics have misread the intention of the R2P. As he notes, too often the R2P has been decried for failing to halt mass violence entirely, something it could never feasibly achieve, particularly in its relatively miniscule lifespan. Further, many advocates have talked up the transformational power of the R2P as if it is *the* solution to the issue of mass violence. Indeed, Gallagher's critique holds sway by highlighting the need to 'manage expectations' over what the R2P can feasibly achieve. Indeed, as we highlight elsewhere, mass atrocity is likely to remain a permanent feature of the international landscape, for a multitude of complex reasons (Gallagher et al., forthcoming). While this book offers an analysis of reform proposals that can strengthen the R2P it acknowledges that these are unlikely to comprehensively solve the issue of mass atrocity.

As Bellamy (2019, p. 21) notes, there is currently a sense of foreboding about the future which is generating sentiments of 'xenophobia, nationalism, authoritarianism, and mercantilism'. This has led to the sucking of attention introvertedly towards domestic concerns over international obligations to the vulnerable. Contemporary problems faced by the international community regarding events such as the election of right-wing populists, persistent challenges to multilateral frameworks such as the UN and EU, and the effects of COVID-19 pandemic, point to the unfavourable environment in which the R2P currently occupies (Evans, 2020, pp. 363–365).

As Luck (2020, p. 383) observes, '[t]he path from aspiration to practice has been demanding and uncertain for R2P'. At the heart of this uncertainty remains contestation over the R2P and the promotion of human rights within large sections of the international community (Jacob, 2021). In particular, states such as Brazil, Russia, India, and China, in addition to regional groupings such as the Association of Southeast Asian Nations (ASEAN), remain divided over the R2P's relationship with the use of coercive military force under Pillar Three (Stuenkel, 2014; Rotmann, Kurtz, and Brockmeier, 2014). This became more pronounced in the wake of the perceived overstepping of the UNSC's 2011 intervention mandate in Libya (Morris, 2016).

Even if this opposition to the use of force is not entirely value-based, and rather bound up in a web of concealed self-interest, the Libya episode has at least provided a convenient argument for those wishing to shield regimes from unwanted intervention. The sudden withdrawal of US and Coalition forces from Afghanistan in August 2021 also sounds caution against an expectation that the US and its allies will champion the interventionist norm of the R2P. These themes point to a world in which the immediate future of the R2P seems bleak.

However, rather than simply conceding these points and abandoning hope that the R2P can rise to meet such challenges, proponents of human protection must remain committed to the potential for positive progress. It should be remembered that the R2P is a relatively new norm, and so we should therefore not be too quick to dismiss its value. This should especially be the case at a time of international normative regress, in which moral arguments need strengthening, not dismissing. Indeed, the whole point of aspirational norms of desired behaviour is that they set standards to improve on current practice. Pattison (2021) has recently hypothesised about what the future for the R2P would look like in a post-liberal world order. While writing that the R2P would see a diminished influence in a number of post-liberal scenarios (Pattison, 2021, pp. 5–7), he notably argues that this calls for a re-emphasis on the values of the international responsibility to protect, not a surrendering of the concept to the forces of nationalism and non-intervention (Pattison, 2021, p. 11).

Scholars such as Hehir and Murray (2017) have argued that fatalism is unacceptable in pursuing the goal of international human rights, but also that we should not be overly utopian about what we can hope to achieve. Hehir has also claimed that it may now be time to abandon the R2P, since it is not working as it was intended (Hehir, 2018, pp. 218–221). In calling for abandoning the R2P, however, Hehir seems to fall prey to the same fatalism he claims to decry. As Pattison (2015, p. 204) has noted, there is not a plausible rival candidate to the R2P. This would suggest that we must 'stick with what we've got', so to speak, and that pursuing alternatives would likely be politically unfeasible. Not only would alternatives likely be unfeasible, but pursuing them would be to discard the more than two decades of effort so far put into building the R2P's universal consensus. As Šimonović (2019, p. 256) stresses to us, sticking with the R2P prevents states from being able to backtrack on the commitments they have made, meaning we are able to scrutinise their practice in light of R2P's agreed principles. As Pattison (2015, p. 204) writes:

> For the last 10 years, and for the foreseeable future, R2P has largely framed the discussion of the tackling of mass atrocities. Adopting an alternative would require significant political will, which would most likely be better spent on promoting R2P.

Nevertheless, the current R2P approach *can* be strengthened, which calls for proactive recommendations on how to reform the R2P and its application for the better. As such, this book takes the position of 'critical friend' of the R2P, situating itself between those 'advocates' who emphasise the R2P's progressiveness, and those 'sceptics' who emphasise its failings.[3] This middle position accepts that a fully functioning R2P would contribute to a world better able to live up to duties of human protection, however, it also acknowledges that a fully functioning R2P is impossible without reform to relevant international structures.

As is developed more in Chapter 4 when discussing the concept of 'feasibility', we should never equate what is impossible with what is improbable (Gilabert and Lawford-Smith, 2012). Human capacity for adaptation and change makes it possible to achieve a more peaceful world (Bellamy, 2019, p. 8), and this has historical precedence (Glenn, 2013). While the potential for R2P reform is not as strong as we would perhaps wish, this does not mean that it is fundamentally impossible to achieve.

If reform measures can be adopted, then the efficacy of the R2P can be improved, promoting action that is consistent with duties of atrocity prevention and response. Critiquing the R2P is quite simple. Offering proactive recommendations on how to address its shortcomings, however, is significantly more challenging. Reform that can aid the R2P will be difficult to realise, but it is no more utopian than the idea that we can achieve human protection without long and arduous political struggle. It is the goal of this book to try and address these challenges proactively.

1.3 Cosmopolitanism and R2P Reform

To address the issue of R2P reform, this book utilises cosmopolitan theory. In general, cosmopolitanism holds that all human individuals possess an inherent moral worth (Brown and Held, 2010, p. 1); a moral worth that exists regardless of any particular characteristics an individual possesses, such as ethnicity, religious preferences, or national allegiances (Beardsworth, 2011, p. 20). In this way, cosmopolitanism promotes the concept of a common humanity, extending universally, transcending the limits of state boundaries. For cosmopolitans, this perception of universal human worth produces a concern for 'global justice' as a normative goal to aspire to. Exactly what global justice requires is contested within cosmopolitan literature. Nevertheless, if achieved, any meaningful form of global justice would promote the protection of individual human beings through the consistent fulfilment of universal moral duties.

While all cosmopolitan theory is, in essence, a normative and moral project, there are numerous different schools within the cosmopolitan literature. Moral cosmopolitans, for example Caney (2005) and Shue (1996), promote their ideas of what global justice demands in relation to the rights and duties held by and towards human beings. Legal cosmopolitans, such as Habermas (2008), call for the embedding of cosmopolitan rights and duties into constitutional systems of international law. Institutional cosmopolitans like Pogge

(2002b), argue that reform of the world's institutions is required in order to promote a more just international system that avoids the imposition of harm and the production of unequal outcomes. Political cosmopolitans, such as Archibugi (2008) and Held (2010) promote the cosmopolitanisation of global governance structures, to make world politics more inclusive, and in doing so, more just and democratic.

In this book, a moral, generally non-relational, cosmopolitan framework is applied, which seeks to interpret what obligations are owed to the world's vulnerable at risk of atrocity crimes. This moral cosmopolitan position is explored in detail in Chapter 2.

The choice to apply a cosmopolitan reading of the R2P in this book is a logical one. This is because the most consistent and morally rich reading of the R2P, if we take human life and human rights seriously, is via cosmopolitanism.[4] Both seek to place the value of human beings before the interests of the state, both promote the need to further obligations universally towards all peoples, and both strive to overcome inaction in the face of human suffering (Wyatt, 2019; Bellamy and Tacheva, 2019). The R2P is therefore *theoretically* linked with a cosmopolitan demand to secure the fundamental rights of the vulnerable as a moral imperative. As such, it would appear that the R2P is a *prima facie* expression of cosmopolitan sentiment at the international level, and of the moral demand to halt widescale mass harms (Linklater, 2001; Pogge, 2002a; Shapcott, 2008).[5] However, as will be drawn to attention, despite this theoretical connection, the current R2P approach is failing to achieve this cosmopolitan demand in practice, and as a consequence, is unable to promote the reduction of mass atrocity crimes in the way proponents would wish. As examined in Chapter 3, the current R2P approach fails to meet a cosmopolitan demand for acting on duties to both prevent and respond to cases of mass atrocity violence.

Cosmopolitanism is useful here because it offers guiding principles for human conduct (Brown, 2010, pp. 46–47), and therefore provides us with a normative lens to illuminate what is morally required of the R2P. This can allow us to critically analyse where the current R2P approach fails in meeting moral demands, and also in analysing how potential reforms can aid the R2P by bringing it more favourably towards achieving these demands.

A full chapterisation of the theoretical approach and the reforms explored in this book follows shortly. Three unique themes are inherent to the discussion and contained throughout. The first of these is the *transitional cosmopolitan* approach to R2P reform which is adopted in light of contemporary political challenges noted above. This transitional cosmopolitanism calls for incremental progress towards cosmopolitan conditions by operating within particular contexts and practical barriers to change. In doing so, the aim is to advocate cosmopolitan standards as an end point to work towards, which serves as a guiding ideal to address contemporary moral problems. However, this comes with the practical acknowledgement that this standard is not being advocated as an easily achievable goal – and instead likely requires compromise over what reforms are promoted – yet also acknowledges that moral progress can *only* be achieved by reform.

The transitional cosmopolitan approach aims to find a 'middle position' wherein some normative progress can be made, and where the possibility of future progress can be opened up. This transitional form of cosmopolitanism is developed in detail in Chapter 4.

In applying this transitional cosmopolitanism, the book seeks to explore and overcome feasibility constraints that stand in the way of R2P reform. In particular, it addresses how the UN-centred state system can adapt to provide a more cosmopolitan application of the R2P. As such, the book seeks to work among cutting-edge debates, by operating at the vanguard of cosmopolitan research which seeks to 'bring the state back in' (Beardsworth, Brown, and Shapcott, 2019). Overcoming the political obstacles that the R2P faces is imperative for creating a fully functioning norm of mass atrocity prevention. This calls for the incorporation of broadened cosmopolitan state responsibilities which are sensitive to the politics of international relations. In doing so, the book wishes to frame states as part of the solution to overcoming mass violence, highlighting that without such an approach, institutional reform will be unrealisable.

A second theme running through the book is the promotion of reform which can help impose a stronger duty to act in *response* to cases of mass atrocities. The book applies a cosmopolitan reading to show that there is a demand to always act in response to mass atrocities via ways that can help ameliorate crises, and to promote the means through which this can be achieved. To make progress toward this end, reforms will need to address institutional failings attached to the current R2P approach. For example, reform to international institutional structures such as the UNSC is needed in order to help overcome the barriers of R2P inaction. This necessitates, as one example, reform to the power of veto held by the UN Security Council's five permanent members (P5), which currently serves as a major obstacle in the way of implementing Pillar Three of the R2P. Another example is the need to improve the means of holding states accountable to their R2P commitment; to consistently highlight R2P breaches and prevent states from remaining unaccountable to both their domestic and international human protection responsibilities.

Cosmopolitan responsibilities also underpin the third theme running through the book, which is the call to promote a more coherent international practice of mass atrocity *prevention*. A coherent R2P approach demands that the international community works effectively towards the goal of atrocity prevention and that international actions do not conflict with this goal. As Bohm and Brown (2021) have noted, however, the current R2P approach focuses too much on the symptoms of conflict, without adequately addressing its longer-term structural causes. This reflects the failure to meet a cosmopolitan-based duty to act in the prevention of mass violence. Furthermore, the current R2P approach fails to acknowledge that the same international community charged with preventing mass violence is the same community that in-part contributes to its perpetuation (Bohm and Brown, 2021). Indeed, the harms facilitated by the international community (though indirect ones) in the form of things like political support for, and the sale of arms to, oppressive human right abusing regimes ought to be viewed as part of the problem of mass violence. These problems call for reform that can better promote the responsibility to prevent mass atrocity.

The research in this book highlights not just the importance of promoting human protection from a cosmopolitan perspective, but the importance of promoting a functioning international state system that allows for the promotion of universal security and the reduction of conflict and human suffering. Enacting cosmopolitan-based reform that seeks to alter the international system is an arduous task. However, a transitional cosmopolitan approach seeks to promote reform that is inclusive of international actors and sensitive to their interests. This transitional approach provides the best hope for overcoming the barriers that the R2P faces in its application.

1.4 Book Structure

Six substantive chapters and a conclusion follow from this introduction. The first three of these chapters set the theoretical basis for the book. Chapter 2 lays out the parameters of the book's normative-cosmopolitan underpinning (theory to practice), then Chapter 3 analyses the connection between this cosmopolitanism and the current state of the R2P (practice to theory). Chapter 4 espouses the approach to R2P reform that is later applied in Chapters 5 through 7. The approach to reform championed in Chapter 4 is necessarily underwritten by the previous two chapters as these serve to provide the normative compass for R2P progress; setting aspirational demands, then using these to measure the current state of real world practice, before an approach can then be set out to help us navigate the path toward positive change.

'What Cosmopolitanism Demands of the R2P' establishes the cosmopolitan and normative theoretical basis for the book. It sets the parameters for what a cosmopolitan approach to human protection ought to morally demand, providing a normative yardstick to later analyse the current state of the R2P. In this way, the chapter applies an analytical direction from theory to practice that begins the process of tracing the connection between cosmopolitan human protection and the R2P norm. This chapter first attempts to espouse a cosmopolitan moral framework centred on the value of a common humanity, which calls for positive and negative duties to secure the fundamental rights of all human beings. Taking these cosmopolitan duties into consideration, the chapter then argues that the R2P ought to be promoted as a cosmopolitan responsibility. A cosmopolitan application of the R2P would first demand an appropriate international response to all cases of mass atrocity, and to promote the conditions within which this is possible.

Second, it would demand meaningful commitments to prevent atrocity crises from arising in the first place. It is this cosmopolitan standard which is used to assess the current state of the R2P in Chapter 3, while also serving as the normative base to judge the value of measures recommended in later chapters.

'The R2P: A Faltering Cosmopolitan Aspiration' begins by explicating the theoretical links between the R2P and the cosmopolitan protection standard elaborated in Chapter 2. While Chapter 2 applied theory to practice to present an ideal cosmopolitical vision for the R2P, this chapter starts with the R2P as it is and moves to what a cosmopolitan approach would say about the doctrine in its current state. This first highlights a conceptual concomitance between the R2P and a cosmopolitan approach to human protection. The chapter then moves into an analysis of the actual implementation of the R2P in practice. This starts by arguing that the R2P is a norm with limited compliance pull, meaning that it does not have a necessarily desirable impact on state behaviour. This theme is then applied to an analysis of the application of cosmopolitan positive and negative duties in practice. This highlights the failures of the current R2P approach to meet a positive duty to *respond* to cases of mass atrocity violence, and failure to meet a positive and negative duty to *prevent* mass atrocity violence. Finally, the chapter explores the theme of the R2P's statist focus and why, combined with the weakness of institutionalised means for enforcing positive and negative duties, this has further contributed to the R2P's failure to live up to a cosmopolitan standard. In all, the chapter highlights why R2P reform is necessary, while setting up some of the reform debates examined in later chapters.

With the previous two chapters providing a dual reading of the R2P – establishing a cosmopolitan vision for the norm and highlighting the ways in which the R2P falls short of this vision – Chapter 4, 'A Transitional Cosmopolitan Approach to R2P Reform', grounds the moral demand for progress towards a cosmopolitan application of the R2P within a philosophy of what is being labelled as *transitional cosmopolitanism*. Conscious of the fact that the R2P operates in a world of competing sovereign prerogatives where aspirational cosmopolitan norms will always face tough challenges, this transitional cosmopolitan approach calls for tempered and politically sensitive progress towards a more robust form of cosmopolitics. The chapter promotes the criteria of effectiveness and feasibility as central to this approach of transitional cosmopolitics, and sets out a framework of tests used for analysing the effectiveness and feasibility of the reform measures examined in subsequent chapters. The chapter also argues that to promote the effectiveness and feasibility of proposed reform measures, we need to work among the reality of the current statist-focused international relations in order to have the best chance of overcoming barriers to reform.

Chapters 5 to 7 are dedicated to specific measures for strengthening the R2P. These chapters operate on a spectrum of increasingly radical suggestions for reform. Chapter 5 provides a recommendation that seeks to work within the boundaries of the current 2005 accepted and UNSC-centric R2P approach. Chapter 6 proposes a measure that looks to go beyond this UNSC-centric vision for R2P to instead explore the value of implementing R2P action through the UNGA. Finally, Chapter 7 offers an entirely new institutional UN body for assisting in the implementation of the R2P. This approach provides a logical progression through reform recommendations; one which allows the book to gradually explore more radical suggestions for R2P reform, and which may provide useful insight into the potential effectiveness and feasibility of making more or less radical reform suggestions. These proposals do not provide an exhaustive list of potential R2P reform measures and the core message is not to suggest that the adoption of these individual reform recommendations will allow for atrocity crimes to be outright halted. However, each of these recommendations can contribute at least some positive progress towards a more cosmopolitan application of the R2P that would improve the protection of fundamental human rights. Reform measures are not mutually exclusive with each other, and combining them together would likely be a positive step in the name of cosmopolitan human protection.

'Ending UNSC Paralysis: Responsible Veto Restraint' addresses one of the main institutional barriers to the R2P's implementation in practice: the UNSC P5's power of veto. The veto power has been heavily linked with episodes of R2P inaction. In response, veto restraint initiatives have garnered increasing support. This has included those of the Accountability, Coherence, and Transparency (ACT) group's Code of Conduct, and the France-Mexico joint initiative. This chapter analyses the desirability and political viability of these proposed measures from the transitional cosmopolitan perspective, determining that neither offer an effective nor feasible channel for transitional cosmopolitan progress to a more desirable application of the P5's veto. In response, the chapter offers its own version of veto restraint that is better aligned with transitional cosmopolitanism: 'Responsible Veto Restraint' (RVR). This is a new recommendation for informal P5 veto restraint which differs from previous veto restraint proposals in several key aspects. The RVR proposal provides that coercive measures such as sanctions, criminal prosecutorial mechanisms, and non-consensual military force should not apply to veto restraint. RVR also calls for the removal of subjective get-out clauses for the P5, and includes a more stringent trigger system for when veto restraint should become active. It is argued that by adopting these aspects, RVR can be a more effective and feasible measure for veto restraint than the ACT Code or the France-Mexico initiative. The final section of the chapter utilises Syria as a case study to demonstrate the potential value of RVR.

Given the difficulties of reforming the P5's veto, 'Overcoming the Authority Dilemma: Uniting for Peace Through the UN General Assembly' turns to the Uniting for Peace (UfP) mechanism and the powers of the UNGA as a means for enacting R2P response. The use of UfP would keep R2P response aligned with a legal and UN-centred collective international approach, allowing the

UNGA to recommend a host of potential measures that may be effective in addressing mass atrocity situations. The chapter argues, however, that some alterations to both UfP language and procedure could serve to further align the mechanism with transitional cosmopolitanism. The chapter recommends a nuanced alteration to the UfP mechanism's trigger procedure in order to reduce friction between the UN's two principle bodies (the UNSC and UNGA). It recommends that the UNSC be placed as the principle body for triggering UfP, except for in circumstances where the Council is not actively exercising its Charter responsibilities. To this end, it proposes some clear criteria for determining when the UNGA can rightly step in. This would maintain the UNSC's preponderance over matters of international peace and security, but not to the extent that it would prevent the UNGA from rightfully acting on its secondary responsibility to international peace and security under the UN Charter. The chapter also calls for the removal of the 'lack of P5 unanimity clause' in UfP; to emphasise that UfP is a response to UNSC failure and one that can rightfully be triggered in instances where there is no explicit indication of a lack of P5 unanimity. Finally, as a means of enhancing UfP's feasibility, the chapter also recommends that UfP language be altered to place less emphasis on the use of military force, and instead emphasise that there is a wealth of international and R2P-based responses at the disposal of the UNGA.

'Holding States to Account: An R2P Commission' explores the potential for establishing a new and supplementary institution for enhancing the R2P's implementation. Currently, there is a lack of accountability for state commitments made under the R2P, as states are under no enforced duty to act in response to instances of mass atrocities, nor do cases of state malpractice get highlighted in a consistent manner. The chapter first explores and rejects recommendations for the creation of an independent institution with the power to punish and enforce action in response to R2P breaches (Tesón, 2006; Archibugi, 2008; Hehir, 2012; Roff, 2013). The chapter then examines the UN Human Rights Council (UNHRC) as the body which may appear *prima facie* best suited to the role of holding states accountable to their R2P. However, the chapter argues that the UNHRC cannot serve as the solution to the R2P's accountability problem due to political biases inherent to its state makeup. Instead, to align with the transitional cosmopolitan approach, the chapter calls for the creation of an 'R2P Commission'. This is a suggestion for a body composed of elected experts that would serve in an independent capacity. The R2P Commission would scrutinise state practice across the R2P's three pillars via determinations of where manifest R2P failures have occurred, review of international practice vis-à-vis atrocity prevention and response, and recommendations for altering practice and potential state action.

Finally, the book's concluding chapter, 'The R2P – Let's Remain Critical Friends', serves to tie together the various strands of argument presented throughout the book. It also tries to respond as adequately as possible to some potential limitations of the study, before ending with a re-affirmation of the need to engage with the R2P as a 'critical friend'. It reminds readers that we cannot rely on the *current* R2P approach to serve the ends of cosmopolitan human protection. Instead of taking the position of outright positive advocacy, or outright cynical scepticism, those assessing the value of the R2P ought to assume the role of 'critical friend'. This means rejecting fatalism, rejecting the status quo, and instead pursuing a middle line that advocates positive change in the name of protecting human beings.

Notes

1 As of 1 January 2023.
2 Pillar Three has never been directly referenced within a UNSC resolution or Presidential Statement. Nonetheless, R2P tenets did arguably influence the Council's decision to pass resolution 1973 permitting 'all necessary measures' to protect Libyan civilians in 2011 (UNSC, 2011). The UNSC has also authorised numerous robust peacekeeping mandates in places such as Darfur, Mali, and the Central African Republic. These mandates, which apply Pillar Two logic, are often accompanied by direct R2P language. For example, UNSC resolution 2149 (2014) recalled the 'primary responsibility' of the Transitional Authorities to protect CAR's populations while also establishing the United Nations Multidimensional Integrated Stabilization Mission in the Central African Republic (MINUSCA) (UNSC, 2014).
3 This language of R2P 'advocates' and 'sceptics' is drawn from Gallagher and Ralph (2015).
4 An alternative reading may be to view R2P as a liberal project, rather than a cosmopolitan one. There are some key differences between both approaches which suggest, however, that cosmopolitanism is the more appropriate theoretical frame for R2P. First, liberalism tends to prioritise the value of the state, and although cosmopolitanism can have a statist element, with states having instrumental value, human beings are viewed as primary. Crucially, R2P is meant to be about the prioritisation of victims (individuals) and not interveners (states) (Bellamy and Luck, 2018, p. 21). Second, liberalism does not have the same commitment to distributive justice as cosmopolitanism. Liberalism is concerned mainly with negative duties between states, and not positive duties of distributive justice. R2P, however, is at least linked with goals of cosmopolitan distributive justice in its attempt to promote long-term structural prevention (Brown and Bohm, 2016, p. 909). Third, liberalism is deeply ingrained with democratic peace theory in a way that cosmopolitans are not (Archibugi, 2008, chap. 3). Rather than simply calling for the extension of democracy to all states, cosmopolitanism advocates for a wider universalism of human protection, which is also inherent to R2P theory. I am grateful to Garrett W. Brown for these points.
5 While cosmopolitanism is individualistic in nature and the R2P is aimed at securing the rights of 'populations', there may appear a theoretical tension between the two. However, this work does not seek to address this concern, or to separate the group-based crimes of R2P into individualistic consideration. For this project, it is a strong enough connection that R2P is aimed at protecting against mass crimes which greatly undermine security on both a group and individual level.

References

Amnesty International 2022. *Amnesty International Report 2021/22: The State of the World's Human Rights* [Online]. [Accessed 10 January 2023]. Available from: https://www.amnesty.org/en/documents/pol10/4870/2022/en/.

Archibugi, D. 2008. *The Global Commonwealth of Citizens: Toward Cosmopolitan Democracy*. Princeton, NJ: Princeton University Press.

BBC 2022. The Deadly Battles that Tipped Myanmar into Civil War. [Accessed 1 February 2022]. Available from: https://www.bbc.co.uk/news/world-asia-60144957.

Beardsworth, R. 2011. *Cosmopolitanism and International Relations Theory*. Cambridge: Polity Press.

Beardsworth, R., Brown, G.W. and Shapcott, R. (eds.). 2019. *The State and Cosmopolitan Responsibilities*. Oxford: Oxford University Press.

Bellamy, A.J. 2019. *World Peace (And How We Can Achieve It)*. Oxford: Oxford University Press.

Bellamy, A.J. and Luck, E.C. 2018. *The Responsibility to Protect: From Promise to Practice*. Cambridge: Polity Press.

Bellamy, A.J. and Tacheva, B. 2019. R2P and the Emergence of Responsibilities Across Borders *In*: R. Beardsworth, G.W. Brown and R. Shapcott, eds. *The State and Cosmopolitan Responsibilities*. Oxford: Oxford University Press, pp. 15–40.

Bohm, A. and Brown, G.W. 2021. R2P and Prevention: The International Community and Its Role in the Determinants of Mass Atrocity. *Global Responsibility to Protect*. **13**(1), pp. 60–95.

Brown, G.W. 2010. Kant's Cosmopolitanism *In*: Brown, G.W. and Held, D. eds. *The Cosmopolitanism Reader*. Cambridge: Polity Press, pp. 45–60.

Brown, G.W. and Bohm, A. 2016. Introducing Jus Ante Bellum as a Cosmopolitan Approach to Humanitarian Intervention. *European Journal of International Relations*. **22**(4), pp. 897–919.

Brown, G.W. and Held, D. (eds.). 2010. *The Cosmopolitanism Reader*. Cambridge: Polity Press.

Caney, S. 2005. *Justice Beyond Borders: A Global Political Theory*. Oxford: Oxford University Press.

Crisis Group 2022. Priorities for the UN's New Agenda for Peace. [Accessed 12 August 2022]. Available from: https://www.crisisgroup.org/global/priorities-uns-new-agenda-peace.

Deng, F.M., Kimaro, S., Lyons, T., Rothchild, D. and Zartman, I.W. 1996. *Sovereignty as Responsibility: Conflict Management in Africa* [Online]. Washington D.C.: Brookings Institution Press. [Accessed 27 November 2019]. Available from: https://books.google.co.uk/books/about/Sovereignty_as_Responsibility. html?id=EQR6DwAAQBAJ&source=kp_book_description&redir_esc=y.

Evans, G. 2008. The Responsibility to Protect: An Idea Whose Time Has Come … and Gone? *International Relations*. **22**(3), pp. 283–298.

Evans, G. 2020. The Dream and the Reality. *Global Responsibility to Protect*. **12**(4), pp. 363–365.

Finnemore, M. and Sikkink, K. 1998. International Norm Dynamics and Political Change. *International Organization*. **52**(4), pp. 887–917.

Gallagher, A. 2015. The Responsibility to Protect Ten Years On from the World Summit: A Call to Manage Expectations. *Global Responsibility to Protect*. **7**(3–4), pp. 254–274.

Gallagher, A. and Ralph, J. 2015. The Responsibility to Protect at Ten. *Global Responsibility to Protect.* 7(3–4), pp. 239–253.

Gilabert, P. and Lawford-Smith, H. 2012. Political Feasibility: A Conceptual Exploration. *Political Studies.* 60(4), pp. 809–825.

Glanville, L. 2021. *Sharing Responsibility: The History and Future of Protection from Atrocities.* Princeton, NJ: Princeton University Press.

Glenn, H.P. 2013. *The Cosmopolitan State.* Oxford: Oxford University Press.

Global Centre for the Responsibility to Protect n.d. Populations at Risk. [Accessed 1 January 2023]. Available from: http://www.globalr2p.org/regions/.

Global Centre for the Responsibility to Protect n.d. UN Security Council Resolutions and Presidential Statements Referencing R2P. [Accessed 1 January 2023]. Available from: http://www.globalr2p.org/resources/335.

Habermas, J. 2008. *Between Naturalism and Religion: Philosophical Essays.* London: Polity Press.

Hehir, A. 2012. *The Responsibility to Protect: Rhetoric, Reality and the Future of Humanitarian Intervention.* Basingstoke: Palgrave Macmillan.

Hehir, A. 2018. *Hollow Norms and the Responsibility to Protect.* London: Palgrave Macmillan.

Hehir, A. and Murray, R.W. 2017. *Protecting Human Rights in the 21st Century* [Online]. London: Routledge. [Accessed 10 December 2018]. Available from: https://www.routledge.com/Protecting-Human-Rights-in-the-21st-Century-1st-Edition/Hehir-Murray/p/book/9781138218932.

Held, D. 2010. Reframing Global Governance: Apocalypse Soon or Reform *In*: G.W. Brown and D. Held, eds. *The Cosmopolitanism Reader.* Cambridge: Polity Press, pp. 293–311.

Human Rights Watch 1999. *Leave None to Tell the Story: Genocide in Rwanda* [Online]. [Accessed 29 April 2019]. Available from: https://www.hrw.org/reports/1999/rwanda/index.htm#TopOfPage.

Hunt, C.T. and Orchard, P. 2020. Introduction: Consolidation and Contestation of the Responsibility to Protect *In*: Hunt, C.T. and Orchard, P. eds. *Constructing the Responsibility to Protect: Contestation and Consolidation.* London: Routledge, pp. 1–27.

Independent International Commission on Kosovo 2000. *The Kosovo Report: Conflict, International Response, Lessons Learned.* Oxford: Oxford University Press.

International Commission on Intervention and State Sovereignty 2001. The Responsibility to Protect: Report of the International Commission on Intervention and State Sovereignty. [Accessed 14 December 2018]. Available from: http://responsibilitytoprotect.org/ICISS%20Report.pdf.

Jacob, C. 2021. Institutionalizing Prevention at the UN: International Organization Reform as a Site of Norm Contestation. *Global Governance: A Review of Multilateralism and International Organizations.* 27(2), pp. 179–201.

Linklater, A. 2001. Citizenship, Humanity, and Cosmopolitan Harm Conventions. *International Political Science Review.* 22(3), pp. 261–277.

Luck, E.C. 2020. The Adolescent: R2P at Fifteen. *Global Responsibility to Protect.* 12(4), pp. 381–383.

Morris, J. 2016. The Responsibility to Protect and the Use of Force: Remaking the Procrustean bed? *Cooperation and Conflict.* 51(2), pp. 200–215.

OHCHR 2022. *OHCHR Assessment of Human Rights Concerns in the Xinjiang Uyghur Autonomous Region, People's Republic of China* [Online]. [Accessed 1

September 2022]. Available from: https://www.ohchr.org/sites/default/files/docume nts/countries/2022-08-31/22-08-31-final-assesment.pdf.

Pattison, J. 2015. Mapping the Responsibilities to Protect: A Typology of inter- national Duties. *Global Responsibility to Protect.* 7(2), pp. 190–210.

Pattison, J. 2021. The International Responsibility to Protect in a Post-Liberal Order. *International Studies Quarterly.*

Pogge, T.W. 2002a. Cosmopolitanism: A Defence. *Critical Review of International Social and Political Philosophy.* 5(3), pp. 86–91.

Pogge, T.W. 2002b. *World Poverty and Human Rights.* Cambridge: Polity.

Roff, H. 2013. *Global Justice, Kant and the Responsibility to Protect: A Provisional Duty.* London: Routledge.

Rotmann, P., Kurtz, G., and Brockmeier, S. 2014. Major Powers and the Contested Evolution of a Responsibility to Protect. *Conflict, Security & Development.* 14(4), pp. 355–377.

Shapcott, R. 2008. Anti-cosmopolitanism, Pluralism and the Cosmopolitan Harm Principle. *Review of International Studies.* 34(2), pp. 185–205.

Shue, H. 1996. *Basic Rights: Subsistence, Affluence, and US Foreign Policy.* Princeton, NJ: Princeton University Press.

Šimonović, I. 2019. R2P at a Crossroads: Implementation or Marginalization *In*: C. Jacob and M. Mennecke, eds. *Implementing the Responsibility to Protect: A Future Agenda.* London: Routledge, pp. 251–267.

Stuenkel, O. 2014. The BRICS and the Future of R2P: Was Syria or Libya the Exception? *Global Responsibility to Protect.* 6(1), pp. 3–28.

Tesón, F.R. 2006. The Vexing Problem of Authority in Humanitarian Intervention: A Proposal. *Wisconsin International Law Journal.* 24, pp. 761–772.

UK Foreign Affairs Committee 2021. *Never Again: The UK's Responsibility to Act on Atrocities in Xinjiang and Beyond* [Online]. [Accessed 8 July 2021]. Available from: https://committees.parliament.uk/publications/6624/documents/71430/default/.

UN 2000. *We the Peoples: The Role of the United Nations in the 21st Century.*

UN 2014. *Framework of Analysis for Atrocity Crimes: A Tool for Prevention* [Online]. Available from: http://www.un.org/en/genocideprevention/documents/about-us/ Doc.3_Framework%20of%20Analysis%20for%20Atrocity%20Crimes_EN.pdf.

UNGA 2005. Resolution adopted by the General Assembly on 16 September 2005. A/RES/60/1. [Accessed 15 November 2018]. Available from: http://www.un.org/ en/development/desa/population/migration/generalassembly/docs/globalcompact/ A_RES_60_1.pdf.

UNGA 2009. Implementing the Responsibility to Protect Report of the Secretary- General. A/63/677. [Accessed 3 December 2018]. Available from: https://undocs. org/A/63/677.

UNGA 2021. The Responsibility to Protect and the Prevention of Genocide, War Crimes, Ethnic Cleansing and Crimes Against Humanity. A/75/L.82. [Accessed 5 July 2021]. Available from: https://undocs.org/en/A/75/L.82.

UNHCR n.d. Syria Emergency. [Accessed 31 August 2021]. Available from: https:// www.unhcr.org/uk/syria-emergency.html.

UNICEF n.d. Rohingya Crisis. [Accessed 18 May 2021]. Available from: https:// www.unicef.org/emergencies/rohingya-crisis.

UNSC 2011. Resolution 1973. S/RES/1973. [Accessed 3 January 2020]. Available from: https://www.nato.int/nato_static/assets/pdf/pdf_2011_03/20110927_110 311-UNSCR-1973.pdf.

UNSC 2014. Resolution 2149. S/RES/2149. [Accessed 15 August 2021]. Available from: https://www.securitycouncilreport.org/atf/cf/%7B65BFCF9B-6D27-4E9C-8CD3-CF6E4FF96FF9%7D/s_res_2149.pdf.

Uppsala 2022. Major Increase in Conflict-related Deaths. [Accessed 10 January 2023]. Available from: www.uu.se/en/news/article/?id=19098&typ=artikel.

World Bank Group 2018. Pathways for Peace: Inclusive Approaches to Preventing Violent Conflict.

Wyatt, S.J. 2019. *The Responsibility to Protect and a Cosmopolitan Approach to Human Protection*. London: Palgrave Macmillan.

2 What Cosmopolitanism Demands of the R2P

2.1 Introduction

There is a *prima facie* link between the R2P, as a commitment to curb mass atrocities, and cosmopolitan aspirations for the protection of fundamental human rights. What this suggests is that there may be conceptual value in linking the two ideas together as a means of understanding what the R2P ought to, as a moral norm, promote. Yet, the relationship between the R2P and cosmopolitanism is one which remains under-theorised within the literature (Brown and Bohm, 2016).

Cosmopolitanism provides a useful lens to illuminate what is required of the R2P as a norm of human protection. What this normative lens allows is for us to critically analyse where the current R2P approach fails in meeting moral demands, and therefore in analysing how potential reforms can aid the R2P by bringing it more favourably towards achieving these demands (the subject taken up in Chapters 5–7). Before a cosmopolitan-based analysis of the current state of the R2P can take place then, there is first a need to understand what a cosmopolitan approach requires of efforts to stop mass atrocity. This chapter argues that a cosmopolitan application of the R2P – conceptualising what the R2P demands of domestic and international actors in efforts to curb mass atrocity – necessitates positive and negative duties to secure the fundamental rights of the vulnerable. If the R2P is to succeed in achieving its lofty goals of human protection, then it ought to promote the standards set out by this cosmopolitan vision.

The chapter begins in section 2.2 by addressing what a cosmopolitan view of human protection obliges from actors operating at the international level, arguing that a cosmopolitan view of global justice espouses the existence of both positive and negative duties to secure fundamental rights at a universal level. Section 2.3 then argues that if actors hold these positive and negative duties to secure fundamental rights, they must by extension hold a duty to intervene in other states in order to secure the fundamental rights of that target state's population. This section argues that, ideally, this duty should be met with non-forceful measures, but that if this is not possible, then it may be permissible to exercise this duty via the use of coercion, potentially including

DOI: 10.4324/9781003394105-2

military force. Having supported the existence of cosmopolitan duties, section 2.4 attempts to relate these duties to the R2P norm. This section argues that the R2P, if viewed through a cosmopolitan lens, ought to be predicated on the universal obligation to secure people's fundamental rights to be free from egregious harm. This cosmopolitan reading is i) a demand for an appropriate international response to any given mass atrocity case, and to promote the conditions within which this is possible, and ii) a responsibility to take meaningful commitments to prevent atrocity cases from arising in the first place. It is this cosmopolitan standard which is used to critique the current state of the R2P in Chapter 3.

2.2 Cosmopolitan Rights and Duties

This chapter focuses on what appropriate behaviour towards others (including those distant) demands from a cosmopolitan perspective. Beginning with the foundations: cosmopolitanism is the view that members of humankind are bound by a shared sense of moral equality, regardless of the characteristics that make individual human beings unique. The foundations of a cosmopolitan ethic are rooted in its appreciation for homo sapiens as the ultimate units of moral worth. A cosmopolitan view sees all human individuals as in possession of an essentially equal and intrinsic moral value, meaning that we are all united by a sense of common humanity (Linklater, 2001, p. 264). Flowing naturally from this, cosmopolitans view national boundaries and state borders as having an arbitrary moral value that should not automatically be taken as intrinsically significant (Caney, 2008, pp. 505–506). For the cosmopolitan, state borders and an individual's location within them is an outcome purely of chance, meaning that these artificially drawn boundaries do not automatically relate to the value of their contents. The state, from the cosmopolitan perspective, should not automatically be viewed as possessing moral value separate from its actual population (Benhabib, 2008, p. 19). Crucially then, cosmopolitans perceive a common value of all peoples which permeates beyond borders, uniting different groups, and as Beardsworth (2011, p. 20) notes, focuses 'on a common humanity beyond ethnic, religious, class, or gender particularities'. Consequently, cosmopolitans see the world not as a set of closed and separate political communities, but one of globalised and interlinked societies where universal conceptions of morality and justice penetrate (Held, 1999).

Together, these values generate the three fundamental principles of a moral ethic grounding all cosmopolitan scholarship. These are the base criteria of *individualism*, *egalitarianism*, and *universalism*. First, cosmopolitan-based *individualism* views all human beings as the ultimate unit of moral concern, meaning that all individuals possess fundamental needs and deserve the ability to autonomously lead their lives separate from the pressures of unwarranted coercion. States and other institutionalised collectives can only be viewed as valuable to the extent that they promote the wellbeing of individuals residing within them. States, as a result, have an instrumental value if appropriately ordered in a way that benefits their populations, but they do not have an intrinsic value in and of itself, as is often argued by neo-sovereigntists. Second, cosmopolitan *egalitarianism* views every human being as having an inherently equal value. This means that, from a cosmopolitan perspective, it is morally impermissible to prioritise the fundamental needs of a group of individuals at the expense of another group of individuals. Consequently, a cosmopolitan would say that actors, like states, cannot deprive any populations of their fundamental needs in order to promote advantages to other populations. Finally, cosmopolitan *universalism* views the moral status of individuals as generating an ethical demand to be concerned with the welfare of others. Ultimately, this demand can be taken as a normative stipulation that humanity must work towards the betterment of all human beings. This is a requirement that cannot be ignored simply because of distance between peoples and lack of close proximity, or the absence/limited nature of social and/or political connection between these groups (see Pogge, 1994; Barry, 1995; Beitz, 1999; Moellendorf, 2002; Caney, 2005).

Individualism, egalitarianism, and universalism underpin all cosmopolitical thought. For instance, Held's (2010) normative approach views these principles as constituting a cosmopolitan demand for both autonomy and impartiality within a political order. For Held (2010, p. 236), autonomy refers to the principle wherein measures of social protection are required to ensure egalitarian principles. Essentially this is a view that individuals should exist in a state of freedom where their fundamental needs are protected, and that it is the affected individuals that ought to be the ones to influence life altering decisions. While impartiality, Held (2010, pp. 237–238) argues, is a moral frame of reference for specifying rules and principles that can hold a genuine universalisability; political outcomes are only fair if they are equally applied and are acceptable for everyone. For Beitz (2010, pp. 93–96), universalism is a necessary moral principle as world communities now exist in shared forms of coercion, wherein close economic ties and institutionalised means of cooperation and exploitation are in abundance. For Beitz, it is these relationships which call for egalitarian justice and a need to rectify harms so that all individuals can prosper. Similarly, Barry's (2010, p. 102) conception of justice speaks to individualism by calling for fundamental rights to be upheld, egalitarianism in that inequality can only be justifiable when it is the result of autonomous choice, and universalism in that there are obligations to help those who are 'victims of misfortune'.

Critics of expansive cosmopolitan universalism, such as Nagel (2005) and Miller (2007), argue that we hold different relationships with those to whom we are closer. For these scholars, this includes fellow nationals that we live alongside in shared systems of coercion and cooperation, including through institutions like taxation and national law. For Miller (2010, pp. 384–385), nations are linked by a shared sense of identity, culture, and belonging, which hold a real and significant moral value. Similarly, Kymlicka (2010, p. 437) argues that nation-states still share a belief in their own independent 'communities of fate', meaning that national citizens care about each other's fate and want to share in this fate as a nation. Miller (2002, p. 83) argues that while global obligations do exist, these should be differentiated from, and are perhaps weaker than those we hold to compatriots (see also Miller, 1998; Blake, 2001).

Yet, undoubtedly globalisation has changed the way different peoples interact, bringing new forms of shared coercion as well as new threats. Such changes support the view that some form of cosmopolitan universalism is now a moral necessity. Increased interconnectivity between peoples and states in the form of shared institutions, political and economic relationships, and membership of international organisations mean that relationships of moral concern are now exercised between states and not just within them (Archibugi, 2008, p. 53; Valentini, 2011, p. 54). For instance, all states have ceded at least part of their sovereign control to international organisations, and all states are bound up in complicated webs of global supply and trade. Such relationships mean that, as Kant (1795) highlighted as far back as the 18th century, the effects of something that occurs on one side of the globe can often be felt on the other. For instance, climate change represents a 'global process leading to the production of benefits (those who benefit from activities producing greenhouse gases) and burdens (dangerous climate change)' (Caney, 2008, p. 497). The COVID-19 crisis, its direct impact on public health as well as its damage caused to global supply chains, is also testament to the way in which contemporary security threats permeate beyond borders and affect all peoples as a matter of global concern (Brock, 2020; Maulaya and Jasuma, 2021). For cosmopolitans, these forms of shared coercion and shared susceptibility to security threats demand universalised normative concern. As Onora O'Neill (2010, p. 64) puts it, 'if complex, reasoned communication and association breach boundaries, why should not principles of justice do so too?'.

For all cosmopolitans, taken together, the three fundamental cosmopolitan principles of individualism, egalitarianism, and universalism must facilitate a concern for 'global justice' as a goal for humankind to pursue. Justice, understood from a cosmopolitan view, can be rooted in a more minimalist (or thin) standard (the position adopted in this book) which takes a less stringent and minimal demand for the basic requirements of human life as owed to all individuals. This standard is based on the need to secure everyone's *fundamental rights* to a minimum standard of the good-life (see Shue, 2020). Alternatively, cosmopolitan justice can be rooted in a more maximalist (or thick) standard which demands that we attain autonomy and equality for all the world's individuals (see Caney, 2008). Regardless of which view is taken, cosmopolitanism demands normative progress towards justice, which by its cosmopolitan nature must exist at the global level.

The proviso of justice lies in the creation of rights and obligations held by and towards fellow human beings. The inherent needs which are held by humans as creatures of 'finite, needy being' (O'Neill, 2010, p. 73) – from a cosmopolitan perspective which views differences between peoples as morally irrelevant – gives rise to moral demands in the form of human rights. Human rights exist as a claim to a good, a claim made between the rights holder and the agents charged with upholding the right. Human rights serve to protect the fundamental interests of the holder (Pogge, 2002, pp. 56–58) and act as a kind of accountability system to make incumbent upon those charged with upholding those protections that they have a responsibility to protect those rights (Breau, 2016, p. 94). For cosmopolitans, such as Nickel (2005, p. 391), these human rights exist in both social and economic forms, which, at their crux, are concerned with maintaining individuals' claim to have a life, to lead their own life, and to avoid the imposition of cruel or unfair treatment. These rights, held by all human beings, impose upon the agents of justice (whether they be other human beings, states, or institutions charged with generating and exercising human protection) universalised duties to uphold the rights of individuals. If someone is said to possess a right, it is morally impermissible to deprive them of the ability to meet this right (Fabre, 2012, p. 24).

The cosmopolitan demand to uphold the fundamental human rights of all individuals is said to exist in both 'negative' and 'positive' forms of duties (Nickel, 2005, p. 392). These duties are maintained as general obligations held by all, to all.

The 'negative' form of cosmopolitan obligations holds that there is a duty to avoid acting in certain ways; to avoid causing harm to others that would infringe upon their rights (Pogge, 2002, chap. 2). This is largely predicated on the notion that an ethical imperative to value all human life equally creates a fundamental demand to avoid imposing cruelty upon others (Linklater, 2001, p. 265). Drawing on Linklater's work, Shapcott (2008, pp. 195–196) refers to this idea as the 'harm principle', which identifies a cosmopolitan recognition of moral respect for the value of others, appreciating that the harms we cause to others must be minimised as a moral imperative. These negative duties are not biased towards any particular group, nor do they impose upon agents a specific demand of action to be followed. Rather, these duties simply appreciate that there is a duty to *not* act in ways which could either knowingly or unknowingly facilitate harm. Negative duties are universal, for they can easily be applied to all peoples; despite the wide array of ethical worldviews which exist between different cultures, it is generally accepted that harm and cruelty should be minimised (Shapcott, 2008, p. 199). Theoretically then, negative duties to avoid harming others should be easier to meet than positive duties, for (if properly met) they do not necessitate direct action to secure other's rights which may be viewed as overly demanding, but rather require the preclusion of harmful actions.

The 'positive' form of moral cosmopolitan obligations holds that there are duties to take certain actions; to actively support others in achieving their rights by providing help and assistance in whatever ways are appropriate. Note that this positive duty does not hold that better-off individuals must sacrifice their own basic needs and rights for the sake of others (Fabre, 2012, p. 22; Singer 1972), for such a position would be too demanding.[1] However, cosmopolitan positive obligations do demand support for, and the implementation of, just institutions, laws, and policies which can aid others in meeting their right to freedoms and resources which they need in order to lead (at least) a minimally decent life (Fabre, 2012, p. 33). There is then, under the cosmopolitan view, a demand to take positive action with the aim of bettering the human condition.

It is important to note that both positive and negative duties cannot in practice be viewed as entirely separate from one-another. As Pogge (2002, pp. 68–70) argues, if negative duties are to be successfully met, then they impose a requirement not just to omit certain actions which facilitate harm, but also to take action to end harms which *already* exist. This view of negative duties takes a non-ideal reading and attests to the reality that negative duty violations do occur in practice. Due to this fact, negative duties cannot simply be viewed in purely abstract terms as the omission of harm. The successful fulfilment of rights, as Pogge (2002, p. 65) notes, stems not just from avoiding direct violations of those rights, but also from successfully securing a basic standard of enjoyment to begin with. If this basic standard is not met, then it is impossible to say that agents are taking their negative duties seriously, as they are in effect permitting the existence of a harm.

The result is that positive and negative duties must interact together. If negative duties to avoid harm are taken seriously, then there are also positive duties to take action where necessary to secure the rights of all peoples. Under this cosmopolitan view then, international institutions must be designed in such a way as to serve needs and reduce vulnerabilities (O'Neill, 2010, p. 78). Furthermore, it would also seem conceptually flawed to suggest that it is permissible to violate one type of duty if the other is being successfully met. For instance, if a state upholds an economic policy which damages the livelihood of foreign populations and infringes on their rights, this does not become permissible simply because the violating state is simultaneously proffering foreign aid to the other state. Cosmopolitanism therefore demands that both positive and negative duties be met in order for any moral standard of global justice to be upheld.

2.3 The Cosmopolitan Duty to Intervene

Having argued that a cosmopolitan view calls for the provision of positive and negative duties as a means of securing fundamental rights and promoting (some kind of) standard of universal justice, we now need to understand how this relates to a demand for international intervention in cases of gross human rights violations (as per the four mass atrocity crimes listed under the R2P). This discussion is important, for its logic lies at the heart of the R2P's ambitious international element. That is, the attempt to promote international responsibilities of assistance in atrocity prevention by noting that '[t]he international community should, as appropriate, encourage and help States to exercise this responsibility', as well as the controversial stipulation that the international community may respond to atrocities through coercive means, being 'prepared to take collective action, in a timely and decisive manner … on a case-by-case basis … should peaceful means be inadequate and national authorities are manifestly failing to protect their populations' (UNGA, 2005, paras 138–139). It is argued here that if duties do indeed exist to aid in the fulfilment of other's basic rights, then there is, by extension, a cosmopolitan duty to intervene (coercively and militarily if necessary) in order to secure the fundamental rights of exogenous populations at risk of mass atrocities. As Fabre (2012, p. 183) argues:

> Generally, and subject to costs and to considerations of allocative fairness, individuals can be held under a duty to step into the breach when the primary duty-bearers are no longer able or willing to protect those whom they must protect. At the bar of cosmopolitan justice, the duty extends across borders as well.

If one accepts the cosmopolitan notion that all individuals have the right to (at least) a minimal standard of the good-life (Shue, 2020), then there are duties to secure the fundamental rights of others which entails a demand to act and halt cases of widescale suffering. In other words, there exists a moral duty towards basic human protection which necessitates external intervention by the international community in cases where the fundamental rights of populations are threatened to such an egregious level that this represents the violation of a universal moral minimalism (see Gallagher, 2013, pp. 73–78).

Intervention efforts towards alleviating this mass suffering would, in any ideal case, be achievable through non-military means alone. Military action is fraught with moral dilemmas and undesirable consequences (Brown, 2012, p. 80; Hunt, 2017) that force policy-makers to 'get their hands dirty' (Walzer, 1973; Edyvane and Souter, 2019, p. 49). This includes the likelihood of civilian casualties, serious damage to local infrastructure, in addition to the death of military personnel. The logical argument would therefore seem to be in favour of non-military modes of international intervention, such as economic sanctions, criminal prosecution, diplomatic pressure, or humanitarian aid, if such measures can help in securing the fundamental rights of the vulnerable. However, it is worth noting that even these non-military measures are themselves fraught with ethical conundrums and so recourse to them is not as straight forward as is often claimed (see Pattison, 2018). It is also critical to acknowledge that in some cases (such as the Rwandan genocide, or the war against Nazi Germany) military measures are simply a necessity to halt mass atrocity (Bellamy, 2022).

In contrast to this latter point, Dunford and Neu (2019) posit that the underlying logic of a perceived necessity for military intervention is inherently flawed. They argue that supporting a norm of international military action to halt atrocity crimes legitimises a militaristic attitude that portrays would-be interveners as virtuous responders to gross human rights problems which have originated *elsewhere*. In reality, as will be argued in Chapter 3, those same would-be interveners are already engaging in damaging structural practices that help facilitate the very same forms of mass violence they claim to be acting to halt (see Jones, 1995; Levene, 2005). In Dunford and Neu's (2019, p. 1095) words, '[i]n hiding from view already existing intervention [practices which contribute to cases of mass violence] and simultaneously justifying military intervention, the R2P contributes to a climate in which violence for the alleged purpose of protection comes to be perceived as just, civilised and virtuous'.

Dunford and Neu's critique is an important one, which highlights issues with the international community's failure to meet negative duties of atrocity protection. However, it does leave a key problem unaddressed. Their argument does not help us when we are faced with those most hard-line of ongoing atrocity cases where timely and decisive response is essential to saving lives. Instead, their argument brings us back full-circle back to the world before the R2P, when Kofi Annan (UN, 2000, p. 48) questioned what is to be done when the international community is faced with a Rwanda or a Kosovo. The problem with Dunford and Neu's stance is that without a complete universal commitment to pacifism, there will always be aggressors who can take advantage of those unwilling to stand-up to them (Bellamy, 2019, pp. 95–96). In a world occupied by imperfect, generally self-serving, or at least, altruism-wary human beings (Valentini, 2011, p. 180), universal pacifism is an unrealistic and potentially dangerous thing to advocate. If perpetrators of mass atrocities know that a military response from the international community is guaranteed to be off the table, there is likely nothing else that will deter them from committing such crimes (Bellamy, 2022, pp. 279–280). The argument here then is that it must be possible to both justify and implement the use of military means in some specific circumstances where the goal of human protection cannot be achieved by non-military measures. Here, war is taken as sometimes (though regrettably) necessary based on Pattison's (2018) reading of Just War Theory's criteria of necessity and last resort. This views military measures as necessary in cases where such measures would be both i) better than doing nothing at all and ii) better than the alternatives to military measures. If these criteria are met, then military force can be justified as a response to supreme humanitarian emergency, as it would be the only potential form of intervention to have efficacy in redressing the situation.

But how can a cosmopolitan position align with the idea (inherent to the concept of the R2P) that there is sometimes a demand to intervene, by the application of deadly force, to save the population of a target state from suffering mass harm? In other words, how can a moral framework that espouses the fundamental right to human life simultaneously justify depriving some individuals of this right to life? Such a position would seem *prima facie* a contradictory one. However, it is possible to defend such a claim. To argue in favour of this idea, the following analysis draws largely from Cécile Fabre's notion of 'Cosmopolitan War' (2012).

To justify depriving human life in certain circumstances, Fabre draws on the ideas of self and other-defence. She argues that if an individual is attacked, unjustly and without cause, and as a result their fundamental rights are threatened, then they are permitted to exercise lethal force in their own self-defence, and therefore, are permitted to value their own life above that of their attacker (Fabre, 2012, p. 60). To forbid self-defence in such an instance would be tantamount to arguing that the victim ought not to place significant enough value on their own life to defend themselves. This idea is not partial to any factors specific to the attacker or defender, such as their ethnic, religious, nationality, or gender status. It is rather a universal right held by all individuals that they are permitted to prioritise their own fundamental interests when they are unjustly threatened.

Logically flowing from this premise – and situated within a cosmopolitan understanding of duties outlined above – Fabre argues that the right to self-defence can be extended to others in the form of a positive duty to come to their aid (in defence of the other). This notion of 'other-defence' appreciates that agents possess a positive duty to protect those that are unjustly attacked and whom have their fundamental interests threatened. This therefore permits an intervening party to use deadly force against the attackers if this is a necessary step in order to protect the fundamental interests of the victims (Fabre, 2012, p. 62). This is because, if a person has a right to life, and a right to protect their own life against unjust threat, then under a cosmopolitan understanding of positive duties, third parties logically have an obligation to protect that right to life too. In contrast, however, the attacker, by carrying out an unwarranted and unjust action, has forfeited their own right to not be harmed. Under these circumstances, the attacker so becomes a legitimate target of deadly action. This is the case even for cosmopolitans that see inherent moral value in humanity, though notably it rejects a totally deontological view of human life.[2]

The position taken here argues that there is a duty to intervene militarily under circumstances of mass atrocity violence, if this is the best way to secure the fundamental rights of the victims. This position therefore must reject a pacifist stance, such as is adopted by Moses (2017) when he calls for the removal of forceful elements from the current R2P approach.[3] The removal of the R2P's forceful aspects would damage the moral imperative to act on cases of egregious harm, which will *sometimes* necessitate the use of lethal military force in order to secure the fundamental rights of vulnerable peoples. While Moses argues that a separation of the use of force from the R2P would shift greater focus onto its preventive aspects, this idea misses the fact, as outlined by Bellamy and Luck (2018), that prevention is double-faceted; prevention includes longer-term structural prevention methods, but also *reactive* operational prevention in the form of timely and decisive response to halt emerging cases of mass atrocities, which in some cases does necessitate a timely and decisive military response.[4]

This account of a necessary duty to intervene (sometimes militarily) in cases of mass violence still leaves some issues unresolved. For it is relatively straightforward to see how that in isolated cases of individuals being attacked there is a positive duty resting on third parties to intervene. In cases of widescale mass atrocity violence, however, it becomes significantly more complex to know *who* holds the duty to act and who can justifiably be *harmed*. Questions remain on how, from a moral cosmopolitan perspective, military interventions ought to be implemented. Who can rightfully be targeted during military interventions and who must incur the risks associated with a military intervention?

Starting less controversially, it seems fair to suggest, as Pattison (2015, p. 201) does, that all actors capable of making a contribution have a general responsibility to do so. This means that the costs associated with an intervention ought to be split among all states with the capability to act. Those states that are materially weaker can still contribute towards meeting their duty with troop support, intelligence assistance, or simply through diplomatic backing for the intervention within international political fora. The more materially stronger states, on the other hand, can contribute significantly more, such as by shouldering the majority of the financial burden and in supplying the necessary military hardware.

While all states possess a general responsibility to support a justifiable military intervention, special responsibilities become incumbent upon the parties engaged directly in military action (Pattison, 2015, p. 209). For ultimately, it is these states (or more specifically, the military personnel from them) who shoulder the duty to use lethal military force, and therefore become the specific actors capable of either protecting or ending human lives. Following from the concept of other-defence espoused above, lethal force can be justifiably applied by intervening forces against combatants that resist a just intervention. Combatants that resist (such as state security forces) become complicit in the atrocity crimes orchestrated by their regime. This applies even if they have not directly taken part in any atrocity crimes themselves. In turn, they assume moral responsibility upon themselves for the violation of fundamental rights occurring in their territory. As a result, and flowing from the idea of self and other-defence, these individuals lose their right to not be killed and therefore become legitimate targets for intervening forces (Fabre, 2012, p. 193). Though notably, they only remain legitimate targets so long as they continue to resist the intervention.

The situation becomes more ethically complex, however, when non-combatants are factored into the equation. Indeed, the application of military force will unfortunately always jeopardise the fundamental interests of some innocent individuals, as the use of force will always carry with it unintended consequences (Hunt, 2017, p. 114; Edyvane and Souter, 2019, p. 49) by *doing harm*, which is often argued in moral philosophy as being worse than allowing harm (Pattison, 2019, p. 28). However, *unintended* deaths of non-combatants can be morally justified within the context of an intervention to protect the fundamental rights of the vulnerable. This justification flows from the idea that if all non-combatants are viewed as being of equal value, then there does not need to be a choice of whom exactly to save (Fabre, 2012, p. 202). If there is, as argued here, a moral value in saving victims, then that goal must be pursued, even if unintentional civilian deaths will result. To not pursue this course of action would be tantamount to condemning *all* non-combatants to their fate and therefore a failure to fulfil an agent's positive duty to act. As Fabre claims, if potential victims stand a higher chance of having their fundamental rights protected by an intervention than if no intervention were to take place,[5] then they are *ex ante* beneficiaries of military action, and hence if they are (unintentionally) killed during its campaign then this is a morally justifiable harm, regardless of any potential 'undesirable consequences'.[6]

However, Fabre also notes that the fact that non-combatants are potential beneficiaries of a military intervention does not always permit interveners to shift harm onto them (Fabre, 2012, p. 204). This argument is taken further here to suggest that cosmopolitan morality demands that harm not be shifted to non-combatants in order to protect the intervening parties. The fact that *potential* victims are also *potential* beneficiaries seems too weak a reason to justify exposing them to more risk in order to benefit the survival chances of the intervening party. To do so is to treat the intervening forces as possessing greater moral worth than the supposed beneficiaries of an intervention; a standard inconsistent with a cosmopolitan disposition. If, for example, a pilot of a plane from an intervening state conducting an aerial assault on legitimate combatant targets can reduce her chance of being shot down by flying at a higher altitude, but by doing so would significantly increase the chance of killing civilians with a misplaced attack, then this seems morally worse than the pilot exposing themselves to higher risk and their own potential death.[7] If the intervening party *is* (as it is claimed here they are) under a duty to intervene, and also *in bello* possessing of a special responsibility towards that target state's population, then they are *prima facie* also under a duty to expose themselves to necessary risk. If interveners refuse to expose themselves to risk at the expense of the intended beneficiaries of the intervention, then they undermine the very duty that they hold to begin with, de-valuing the lives of the supposed beneficiaries. This would also serve to undermine positive outcomes of protection by placing civilians in harm's way (Archibugi, 2008, p. 199).

The implementation of an intervention must reflect an equal moral standing of both beneficiaries and interveners. There is then a moral imperative to preserve the lives of innocents wherever possible. This, however, can become even more morally complex if a bombing campaign carried out by intervening forces is essential for halting further widescale harm down the line. In these circumstances, therefore, the pilots, lives being saved may serve an overall greater purpose, even if a number of civilian casualties were incurred in the process. This is likely even more complex when one factors in the 'body bag' effect, that servicepersons being killed in action is likely to turn domestic opinion in intervening states against the intervention effort and thus undermine the overall campaign to save innocents. Evidently, this would require much more detailed theorising and exploration of specific examples, to which space here does not permit. For now, it is sufficient to say that taken *prima facie*, combatants must do, or be made to prioritise the reduction of collateral damage, at least to the extent that it does not severely impinge their military effort in bringing about the end to the widescale harms the military effort is purportedly aiming to address.

Following Gilmore (2015), to place interveners on an even moral level with intended beneficiaries requires more direct engagement on the ground during interventions. Gilmore argues that intervening forces need to engage more with the communities they purport to be serving the interests of, for example, by engaging more in on-foot patrols and reducing dependency on tactics of aerial warfare (Gilmore, 2015, p. 111). The use of aerial warfare has attempted to distance the risk of the soldier, but it maintains the risk for the civilian on the ground, creating an asymmetry between the moral value of the solider and the foreign civilian (Gilmore, 2015, pp. 75–76). This results in undermining a moral cosmopolitan standard while simultaneously serving to jeopardise the goals of the intervention and a long-term peace. This is not simply to suggest that the prioritisation of the lives of intervening forces over intended beneficiaries is morally wrong in itself, but also that it leads to outcomes which run anathema to the very purpose of the intervention.

2.4 What Cosmopolitanism Demands of the R2P

The previous two sections laid out fundamental cosmopolitan demands relating to the goal of human protection. This section now attempts to frame these cosmopolitan demands in the context of the R2P. It is argued here that a cosmopolitan view of the R2P demands that it be taken as a responsibility to act on positive and negative duties; duties to both respond to ongoing instances of mass atrocity, and to take concerted efforts to prevent such crises from emerging in the first place.

The successful implementation of cosmopolitan duties would lead to more favourable outcomes of protection. In other words, meeting a cosmopolitan standard would result in international actors consistently taking action to respond to cases of mass atrocity violence, while also leading to actions consistent with the goal of preventing atrocities from arising. This is not to suggest that a more cosmopolitan application of the R2P will automatically lead to the end of mass violence, but merely that actions consistent with a cosmopolitan moral ethic can contribute to the alleviation of such violence and, consequently, progress towards curbing some of the most egregious acts of violence that continue to plague the human condition.

Stymying atrocity crises is the *sine qua non* for the R2P. This requires a coherent approach that demands action in response to mass atrocity crises, and promotes atrocity prevention in a logical way. As Crossley (2020, p. 444) puts it, '[c]oherence is a precondition for both principled protection practices, as well as tenacious and invariable protection practice. Without a coherent framework, and without coherent principles, rules, and norms, it is difficult for protection agents to meet protection responsibilities in a principled way'. Without a clear understanding of what the R2P demands of relevant actors, it seems unlikely that it could serve the goal of protection against mass atrocity crimes.

To re-state, a cosmopolitan demand for human protection requires both negative duties to avoid imposing harm, as well as positive duties to actively work to secure other's fundamental rights. If the R2P is to have maximum practical utility in meeting the goal of the alleviation of mass human suffering – and to promote these goals through a coherent approach – then it must be deployed as a cosmopolitan responsibility. Measures to help progress towards a cosmopolitan standard can aid in overcoming the R2P's problems and promote the goals of human protection. This should contribute to the R2P being better implemented, better enforced, and better regulated in the political realm of international politics.

This cosmopolitan interpretation of the R2P is, first, about promoting a demand for an appropriate international response to any given mass atrocity case. The R2P should serve the cosmopolitan duty to act on the moral imperative to protect vulnerable populations from suffering mass atrocities. In its reactive aspect, the R2P ought to be about generating the will and conditions in which an international response for *every* mass atrocity case is possible. This goes beyond simply demanding a responsibility for the international community to try and do *something* in the face of mass violence, to demand that it be possible for all avenues of potential response under the R2P toolkit to be considered in every R2P case, and for the action which is chosen to be the justifiable one (Pattison, 2022, p. 108). Brown (2010, p. 314) argues that '[a]trocities are allowed to happen not because there is no appropriate legal framework to prevent them, but because … those states that could act do not believe it is in their interests so to do'. The influence of politics on decisions of whether to intervene is not disputed here. However, this cosmopolitan vision for the R2P attempts to address the point that, currently, avenues of response to mass atrocities are closed-off by present international institutional and political realities, even though there are a wealth of options available to states for discharging their positive duty (UN, 2012). A cosmopolitan responsibility to act therefore demands a response to every mass atrocity case and to promote the conditions within which this is possible. This is the only way that it can be possible for the international community to meet its reactive responsibility under the R2P. Crucially, this is something that can only be achieved by reform.

Second, it is imperative to emphasise that for the R2P to be coherent, it must not solely refer to the demand to respond to cases of mass suffering, but also that it should enshrine the responsibility to take meaningful commitments to prevent such cases from arising in the first place. If states are serious about preventing mass atrocity crimes and human suffering, then they must invest in both short-term mechanisms of operational prevention, as well as long-term strategies to address the structural conditions underwriting mass atrocity. Part of this latter requirement means that states will need to reframe how they currently understand prevention, as their cosmopolitan responsibilities necessitate them acting to halt their own harms committed against outside populations that help facilitate mass atrocity violence. If states continue to facilitate harms, then they are not demonstrating a willingness to support human protection, and therefore are guilty of failing to meet the duties associated with a cosmopolitan position.

If the R2P is to meet these cosmopolitan demands for the protection of vulnerable populations from mass atrocity crimes, it therefore ought to enshrine the following duties.[8] First, all states in the international community ought to uphold a *negative* duty towards atrocity *prevention* by avoiding the imposition of harms upon others which may contribute to the perpetuation of mass violence. These include direct harms such as the application of mass violence against one's own population. These also include more indirect harms which might include but are not limited to: the sale of arms to known human rights abusing regimes; protectionist trade policy measures which damage the economic livelihoods of those in poor producer countries; and political ties to regimes who exploit their country's wealth for their own gain (Bohm and Brown, 2021). These are what Pattison (2015, p. 202) refers to as 'responsibilities not to act', which also include the duty to not take action that would exacerbate mass violence in progress. These duties apply universally and consistently upon all states, regardless of their international status or material power.[9]

Second, all states have a *positive* duty to contribute to the *prevention* of mass violence. These include Pillar One duties to implement domestic practices which support the preventive agenda of the R2P such as applying an 'atrocity prevention lens' to government policy, Pillar Two actions such as preventative diplomacy measures, capacity building of effective judiciaries, security service reform, and the development of early warning mechanisms, and Pillar Three reactive prevention measures to halt impending mass crimes before they become widespread and/or systematic (UN, 2009). Crucially, these also include the need to take action to halt practices which facilitate harm, such as those just described above. Hence, positive and negative duties must interplay in practice. While the richest states in the international community ought to shoulder the greatest financial burden in these pursuits due to their enhanced capacity, there may also be a duty of reparative justice resting on those states which have contributed to previous failures of human protection through past harms inflicted, such as former colonial powers (Glanville,

2021, p. 94). However, all states, at the least, hold a duty to support others in their prevention efforts in whichever way is appropriate (Pattison, 2015, pp. 200–201), for example by offering localised support in an area situated geographically close to them, or through diplomatic encouragement.

Third, all states in the international community hold a positive duty to act in *response* to cases of mass atrocity violence in whatever ways are best appropriate to that case, including through robust action when necessary. This includes actions of reactive prevention in response to impending atrocity violence, as well as reaction to cases where mass crimes have become widespread and/or systematic. Response can be coercive and/or incentivising, both through military and non-military means under Chapters VI, VII, and VIII of the UN Charter, while invoking (or at least implicitly relating to) Pillar Three of the R2P (UNGA, 2009; UN, 2014). This can include actions such as diplomatic pressure, humanitarian aid, asset freezing, targeted sanctions, and criminal prosecution. This also calls for a duty to intervene militarily if this course of action is the best way to halt atrocity violence. While the most powerful states ought to shoulder the greatest burdens in intervention action – and hence also assume the special responsibilities to the populations of the target state during an intervention – all states ought to contribute in whichever ways they feasibly can to an intervention. Notably, capacity to act does not refer solely to a state's material power. There is also an expectation that states with particular proximity or ties with a state experiencing atrocity crimes may hold a special responsibility to act (Miller, 2001, p. 462; Welsh, 2012, p. 107).[10] Once again, there is also a compelling responsibility on particular states if they were complicit in the outbreak of mass violence. The 2003 illegal and illegitimate intervention in Iraq, for instance, created a sense of culpable responsibility for states intervening to combat the threat of ISIS from 2014 onward (Glanville, 2021, p. 94). Nonetheless, regardless of any special responsibility for a particular case, all other states should offer political support and not attempt to stop action,[11] ought to offer troop and resource support, and should also offer logistical aid where necessary. At the least, this duty demands that international actors respond in legitimate ways that appreciate their duty to uphold the fundamental rights of all the world's populations. Clear cases of inaction and a failure to respond to mass violence would represent illegitimate action and a failure to meet cosmopolitan obligations towards human protection. It is worth noting, as Pattison (2018, p. 1) does, that there is always *something* that can be done in the face of mass atrocity violence and so there should always be an international response to any given R2P case, even though the particular means of response must be context-specific.[12]

Finally, and crucially, there is also a duty to *reform* to improve the application of the R2P (Pattison, 2015, p. 205). This includes a duty to actively support reforms which can aid the R2P in meeting the previous three duties. The duty of reform is therefore about facilitating the conditions within which a cosmopolitan vision for the R2P can be successfully met, and ought to facilitate the more consistent meeting of these duties. For example, if, as is often argued, the UNSC shoulders the greatest burden in implementing a positive duty to act in response to mass violence, then reform ought to aid the UNSC in being able to more consistently meet this obligation. Reform is essentially about promoting a more consistent application of the R2P; to facilitate the will and conditions within which the prevention of and response to cases of mass atrocity crimes is successfully promoted.

2.5 Conclusion

This chapter has provided the cosmopolitan normative base for the rest of this book. It has laid out the moral cosmopolitan position that is used to assess the current state of the R2P in Chapter 3, and that provides a normative compass to direct proposals for international reform explored in Chapters 5–7.

A cosmopolitan position emphasises the moral value of all human beings. As a result, it proposes that all individuals have rights which must be upheld as a matter of human protection. These rights in turn generate duties upon agents. These include both negative duties to avoid harming and depriving others of their rights, and also positive duties to actively pursue the fulfilment of the rights of others. These duties are consistent with the position that there is a moral demand to intervene to halt cases of mass violence, using whatever means are most appropriate, including military means if necessary. The application of military force, despite serving to deprive some individuals of their lives, has been argued here as justifiable in the context of an intervention to secure the fundamental rights of a threatened population, if this is the best way their fundamental rights can be secured. Using these demands generated by a cosmopolitan position, it was argued that the R2P norm ought to promote cosmopolitan demands for both positive and negative duties to secure the fundamental rights of all individuals through prevention of, and response to, mass atrocity.

As will be elaborated more in the following chapter, cosmopolitan obligations are largely theoretically aligned with the values of the R2P, even if these goals are often unmet in current practice. Cosmopolitan thought is useful for understanding where and why the R2P currently fails to live up to its objectives. Cosmopolitan thought also serves the dual purpose of identifying how potential reforms can strengthen the R2P by moving the doctrine more favourably in the direction of cosmopolitan aims, and therefore in serving the R2P's ultimate goal of protecting populations from mass atrocity crimes.

Notes

1 There is, however, in this author's view, a special responsibility held by military forces in cases of humanitarian intervention to risk their own lives for the good of others.

2 Note, this is not to permit deadly response to any infringement upon people's rights, but only in cases where their fundamental rights are unjustly threatened. Response must be proportionate to the harm caused.

3 Morris (2016) makes a similar call for the removal of force from the R2P's third pillar. Though his argument is predicated on the claim that this would enhance the R2P's political appeal, and he does not wish to see military intervention entirely ruled out as a response to mass atrocity.

4 This is in no way to downplay the importance of structural prevention methods, which from a cosmopolitan perspective also imposes duties to act in ways to address structural causes of mass violence. However, it merely takes the practical view that it is not possible to prevent *all* cases of mass violence without the occasional need to apply military force in some specific circumstances.

5 It is worth reiterating that this of course depends on whether military force is an appropriate measure for helping to realise the goal of human protection against mass atrocities. Hence it is not permissible to carry out a mass-scale military campaign if the goal of protection could be better achieved by other non-military means that would result in less harm to innocents (see Pattison, 2018).

6 The phrase 'undesirable consequences' is used here for want of a better one. It is not wished for this to be interpreted as trivialising the tragic loss of human life.

7 This example is particularly relevant to the NATO bombing campaign against the Federal Republic of Yugoslavia in 1999, which was conducted with the aim to protect Kosovar Albanians. There NATO was accused of conducting a 'zero-casualties' war that resulted in around 500 civilian deaths. Voon (2000, p. 1112) argues that NATO gave 'absolute precedence to the lives of its forces over those of the civilian population, including the Kosovar Albanians it was fighting to protect. Thus, in several incidents the primary beneficiaries of NATO's precision weapons technology were the aircrew, who were able to direct attacks from higher altitudes at lower risk to themselves, rather than the civilians'.

8 These duties draw largely from Pattison's (2015) article on a typology of R2P duties.

9 Note, if taken seriously, this negative duty also calls for positive action to end current instances of where this duty is being failed.

10 Though focusing solely on the crime of genocide, the ICJ (2007) found in the *Bosnia and Herzegovina v. Serbia and Montenegro* case that Serbia had violated its legal duty to prevent genocide in Srebrenica by not taking the necessary measures. Here, the court found that Serbia failed in its duty of conduct to prevent genocide, as the state held particular financial, military, and political influence in Bosnia and Herzegovina and so 'manifestly failed to take all measures that were within its power' (Mennecke, 2021, p. 335).

11 Although there is a duty to stop action if the actions proposed would contribute more harm than good, as Pattison (2015, p. 202) notes, there will almost always be *something* that can be done to help alleviate mass suffering in cases of atrocity crimes.

12 This account does leave unaddressed questions, recently raised (Glanville and Pattison, 2021), of where to prioritise protection efforts where multiple atrocity cases exist. Such questions are pertinent given the challenges faced in a world increasingly marred by diminishing cosmopolitan impulses. Here though it is merely emphasised that there is a moral duty to act coherently in the name of atrocity prevention, and to consistently act in response to outbreaks of atrocity violence through context-appropriate means.

References

Archibugi, D. 2008. *The Global Commonwealth of Citizens: Toward Cosmopolitan Democracy*. Princeton, NJ: Princeton University Press.

Barry, B. 2010. International Society from a Cosmopolitan Perspective *In*: G.W. Brown and D. Held, eds. *The Cosmopolitanism Reader*. Cambridge: Polity Press, pp. 100–113.

Barry, B.M. 1995. *Justice as Impartiality: A Treatise on Social Justice, Volume II*. Oxford: Oxford University Press.

Beardsworth, R. 2011. *Cosmopolitanism and International Relations Theory*. Cambridge: Polity Press.

Beitz, C.R. 1999. *Political Theory and International Relations*. Princeton, NJ: Princeton University Press.

Beitz, C.R. 2010. Justice and International Relations *In*: G.W. Brown and D. Held, eds. *The Cosmopolitanism Reader*. Cambridge: Polity Press, pp. 85–99.

Bellamy, A.J. 2019. *World Peace (And How We Can Achieve It)*. Oxford: Oxford University Press.

Bellamy, A.J. 2022. R2P and the Use of Force. *Global Responsibility to Protect*. **14**(3), pp. 277–280.

Bellamy, A.J. and Luck, E.C. 2018. *The Responsibility to Protect: From Promise to Practice*. Cambridge: Polity Press.

Benhabib, S. 2008. *Another Cosmopolitanism*. Oxford: Oxford University Press.

Blake, M. 2001. Distributive Justice, State Coercion, and Autonomy. *Philosophy & Public Affairs*. **30**(3), pp. 257–296.

Bohm, A. and Brown, G.W. 2021. R2P and Prevention: The International Community and Its Role in the Determinants of Mass Atrocity. *Global Responsibility to Protect*. **13**(1), pp. 60–95.

Breau, S. 2016. *The Responsibility to Protect in International Law: An Emerging Paradigm Shift*. London: Routledge.

Brock, G. 2020. Cosmopolitanism, Nationalism and Closed Borders in the Covid-19 Era. [Accessed 6 August 2020]. Available from: www.cambridgeblog.org/2020/06/cosmopolitanism-nationalism-and-closed-borders-in-the-covid-19-era/.

Brown, C. 2010. On Gareth Evans, The Responsibility to Protect: Ending Mass Atrocity Crimes Once and For All. *Global Responsibility to Protect*. **2**(3), pp. 310–314.

Brown, C. 2012. Tragedy, 'Tragic Choices' and Contemporary International Political Theory. *In*: T. Erskine and R.N. Lebow, eds. *Tragedy and International Relations*. Basingstoke: Palgrave Macmillan, pp. 75–85.

Brown, G.W. and Bohm, A. 2016. Introducing Jus Ante Bellum as a Cosmopolitan Approach to Humanitarian Intervention. *European Journal of International Relations*. **22**(4), pp. 897–919.

Caney, S. 2005. *Justice Beyond Borders: A Global Political Theory*. Oxford: Oxford Univeristy Press.

Caney, S. 2008. Global Distributive Justice and the State. *Political Studies*. **56**(3), pp. 487–518.

Crossley, N. 2020. Conceptualising Consistency: Coherence, Principles, and the Practice of Human Protection. *Global Responsibility to Protect*. **12**(4), pp. 440–463.

Dunford, R. and Neu, M. 2019. The Responsibility to Protect in a World of Already Existing Intervention. *European Journal of International Relations*. **25**(4), pp. 1080–1102.

Edyvane, D. and Souter, J. 2019. Good International Citizenship and Cosmopolitan Responsibilities to Protect: Balancing Responsibilities and Dirty Hands *In*: R. Beardsworth, G.W. Brown and R. Shapcott, eds. *The State and Cosmopolitan Responsibilities*. Oxford: Oxford University Press, pp. 41–60.

Fabre, C. 2012. *Cosmopolitan War*. Oxford: Oxford University Press.

Gallagher, A. 2013. *Genocide and its Threat to Contemporary International Order*. London: Palgrave Macmillan.

Gilmore, J. 2015. *The Cosmopolitan Military: Armed Forces and Human Security in the 21st Century*. London: Palgrave Macmillan.

Glanville, L. 2021. *Sharing Responsibility: The History and Future of Protection from Atrocities*. Princeton, NJ: Princeton University Press.

Glanville, L. and Pattison, J. 2021. Where to Protect? Prioritization and the Responsibility to Protect. *Ethics & International Affairs*. **35**(2), pp. 213–225.

Held, D. 1999. The Changing Contours of Political Community: Rethinking Democracy in the Context of Globalisation. *Theoria: A Journal of Social and Political Theory*. (94), pp. 30–47.

Held, D. 2010. Principles of Cosmopolitan Order *In*: G.W. Brown and D. Held, eds. *The Cosmopolitanism Reader*. Cambridge: Polity Press, pp. 229–247.

Hunt, C.T. 2017. All Necessary Means to What Ends? The Unintended Consequences of the 'Robust Turn' in UN peace Operations. *International Peacekeeping*. **24**(1), pp. 108–131.

International Court of Justice 2007. Case Concerning Application of the Convention on the Prevention and Punishment of the Crime of Genocide (Bosnia and Herzegovina b. Serbia and Montengro). [Accessed 21 July 2021]. Available from: www.icj-cij. org/public/files/case-related/91/091-20070226-JUD-01-00-EN.pdf.

Jones, R.W. 1995. 'Message in a Bottle'? Theory and Praxis in Critical Security Studies. *Contemporary Security Policy*. **16**(3).

Kant, I. 1795. Perpetual Peace: A Philosophical Sketch.

Kymlicka, W. 2010. Citizenship in an Era of Globalization *In*: G. W. Brown and D. Held, eds. *The Cosmopolitanism Reader*. Cambridge: Polity Press, pp. 435–443.

Levene, M. 2005. *Genocide in the Age of the Nation State, vol. 2: The Rise of the West and the Coming of Genocide*. London: IB Tauris.

Linklater, A. 2001. Citizenship, Humanity, and cosmopolitan Harm Conventions. *International Political Science Review*. **22**(3), pp. 261–277.

Maulaya, M. and Jasuma, N.B. 2021. COVID-19: Cosmopolitanism's Criticism and Proposals. *PCD Journal*. **9**(1), pp. 1–21.

Mennecke, M. 2021. The International Court of Justice and the Responsibility to Protect: Learning from the Case of The Gambia v. Myanmar. *Global Responsibility to Protect*. **13**(2–3), pp. 1–25.

Miller, D. 2001. Distributing Responsibilities. *Journal of political philosophy*. **9**(4), pp. 453–471.

Miller, D. 2002. Cosmopolitanism: A Critique. *Critical Review of International Social and Political Philosophy*. **5**(3), pp. 80–85.

Miller, D. 2007. *National Responsibility and Global Justice*. Oxford: Oxford University Press.

Miller, D. 2010. Cosmopolitanism *In*: G.W. Brown and D. Held, eds. *The Cosmopolitanism Reader*. Cambridge: Polity Press, pp. 377–392.

Miller, R.W. 1998. Cosmopolitan Respect and Patriotic Concern. *Philosophy & Public Affairs*. **27**(3), pp. 202–224.

Moellendorf, D. 2002. *Cosmopolitan Justice*. Boulder, CO: Westview Press.

Morris, J. 2016. The Responsibility to Protect and the Use of Force: Remaking the Procrustean Bed? *Cooperation and conflict*. **51**(2), pp. 200–215.

Moses, J. 2017. The Limits of R2P and the Case for Pacifism *In*: A. Hehir and R.W. Murray, eds. *Protecting Human Rights in the 21st Century*. London: Routledge, pp. 215–230.

Nagel, T. 2005. The Problem of Global Justice. *Philosophy & Public Affairs*. **33**(2), pp. 113–147.

Nickel, J.W. 2005. Poverty and Rights. *The Philosophical Quarterly*. **55**(220), pp. 385–402.

O'Neill, O. 2010. A Kantian Approach to Transnational Justice *In*: G.W. Brown and D. Held, eds. *The Cosmopolitanism Reader*. Cambridge: Polity Press, pp. 61–80.

Pattison, J. 2015. Mapping the Responsibilities to Protect: A Typology of International Duties. *Global Responsibility to Protect*. **7**(2), pp. 190–210.

Pattison, J. 2018. *The Alternatives to War: From Sanctions to Nonviolence*. Oxford: Oxford University Press.

Pattison, J. 2019. The Ethics of Foreign Policy: A Framework. *SAIS Review of International Affairs*. **39**(1), pp. 21–35.

Pattison, J. 2022. Beyond Imperfection: The Demands of the International Responsibility to Protect. *Global Responsibility to Protect*. **14**(1), pp. 105–108.

Pogge, T.W. 1994. An Egalitarian Law of Peoples. *Philosophy & Public Affairs*. **23**(3), pp. 195–224.

Pogge, T.W. 2002. *World Poverty and Human Rights*. Cambridge: Polity.

Shapcott, R. 2008. Anti-cosmopolitanism, Pluralism and the Cosmopolitan Harm Principle. *Review of International Studies*. **34**(2), pp. 185–205.

Shue, H. 2020. *Basic Rights: Subsistence, Affluence, and US Foreign Policy*, 3rd ed. Princeton, NJ: Princeton University Press.

UN 2000. *We the Peoples: The Role of the United Nations in the 21st Century*.

UN 2012. Responsibility to Protect: Timely and Decisive Response. Report of the Secretary-General. A/66/874–S/2012/578. [Accessed 30 April 2019]. Available from: https://undocs.org/A/66/874.

UN 2014. Fulfilling Our Collective Responsibility: International Assistance and the Responsibility to Protect. Report of the Secretary-General. A/68/947–S/2014/449. Available from: http://responsibilitytoprotect.org/N1446379.pdf.

UNGA 2005. Resolution adopted by the General Assembly on 16 September 2005. A/RES/60/1. [Accessed 15 November 2018]. Available from: http://www.un.org/en/development/desa/population/migration/generalassembly/docs/globalcompact/A_RES_60_1.pdf.

UNGA 2009. Implementing the Responsibility to Protect: Report of the Secretary-General. A/63/677. [Accessed 3 December 2018]. Available from: https://undocs.org/A/63/677.

Valentini, L. 2011. *Justice in a Globalized World: A Normative Framework*. Oxford: Oxford University Press.

Voon, T. 2000. Pointing the Finger: Civilian Casualties of NATO Bombing in the Kosovo Conflict. *American University International Law Review*. **16**, pp. 1083–1113.

Walzer, M. 1973. Political Action: The Problem of Dirty Hands. *Philosophy & Public Affairs*. pp. 160–180.

Welsh, J.M. 2012. Who Should Act? Collective Responsibility and the Responsibility to Protect *In*: Knight, A.W. and Egerton, F. *The Routledge Handbook of the Responsibility to Protect*. London: Routledge, pp. 117–128.

3   The R2P

A Faltering Cosmopolitan Aspiration

3.1 Introduction

To appreciate why the current R2P approach is in need of reform, this chapter uses the cosmopolitan demands laid out in Chapter 2 as a benchmark[1] to measure the state of mass atrocity prevention efforts, as understood in the mainstream through the R2P. This enables us to understand the weaknesses of mass atrocity prevention efforts and, importantly, what cosmopolitan elements are missing which can be brought in to critique and reinforce the R2P doctrine via reform. The argument put forward here is that the R2P is a norm that aims to set a 'standard of appropriate behaviour' (Katzenstein, 1996, p. 5; Finnemore and Sikkink, 1998, p. 891) in relation to tackling atrocity crimes, and is therefore representative of having what could be considered a cosmopolitan goal. However, the related aspects of the current R2P approach analysed here reflect failings which stand in the way of the R2P meeting a cosmopolitan standard. These obstruct cosmopolitan positive and negative duties to halt mass atrocities and secure the fundamental rights of the vulnerable. Consequently, it is argued that reform is required which can enhance the R2P's connection with cosmopolitanism, and therefore strengthen mass atrocity prevention efforts.

First, in section 3.2, the chapter assesses the extent to which the R2P holds a theoretical connection with the demands of cosmopolitanism. This serves the purpose of highlighting the conceptual links between the R2P and a cosmopolitan position on both a basic level, in addition to a deeper cosmopolitan understanding of human protection and cosmopolitan duties. Section 3.3 provides an overview of debates surrounding the R2P's norm status. This discussion is important, for it lies as the heart of what the R2P is in terms of a norm aimed at influencing state practice. Determining here that the R2P represents a norm with weak compliance pull, the chapter then applies this idea to the failing implementation of the R2P in realising cosmopolitan demands in practice. This examines the failure of R2P practice to consistently meet the positive duty to respond to mass violence (section 3.4), the positive duty to prevent mass violence (section 3.5), and the negative duty to prevent mass violence (section 3.6). Finally, section 3.7 addresses the issue of the

DOI: 10.4324/9781003394105-3

R2P's statist focus and whether this issue underpins current failures. As the R2P is predicated on the rights of individuals and not the rights of states, it is important to understand whether this tenet is actually reflected in practice. While some have decried the R2P's statist approach, this chapter argues that this is not inherently destructive to the R2P's purposes; what is required is institutional reform that can better enforce and regulate state's cosmopolitan duties under the R2P.

3.2 The R2P and Cosmopolitanism: Exploring the Theoretical Link

3.2.1 Basic Cosmopolitan Demands

The R2P sets out widely shared expectations about how the international community ought to work towards ending atrocity crimes (Bellamy and Luck, 2018, p. 38). The four crimes listed under the 2005 iteration of the R2P (genocide, war crimes, crimes against humanity, and ethnic cleansing) can be understood as ones that directly threaten the fundamental right of human beings to a minimally decent life. The R2P, therefore, at the very least, represents the acknowledgement of a cosmopolitan duty premised on both the negative duty not to inflict harms upon one's own population (Pillar One),[2] and a humanitarian-based positive duty to assist the most vulnerable in securing their fundamental rights to live and lead their lives (Pillar Two and Pillar Three). These cosmopolitan obligations recognise that there is a universal equal standing of all human beings and that this imposes a responsibility to protect or assist those who are in dire need, regardless of their location, national allegiance, or any other morally arbitrary factor.

The R2P would appear then to hold a relationship with the three basic cosmopolitan criteria of individualism, egalitarianism, and universalism highlighted in Chapter 2. First, in its focus on the victims of mass violence, the R2P is premised on the prioritisation of victims above the preferences of intervening powers, aiming to protect peoples from mass violence rather than seeking to simply enshrine a state's right to act (or not) (Evans, 2008). The R2P is meant to be about framing mass atrocities from the perspective of victims, not those who may be considering intervening (Bellamy and Luck, 2018, p. 21). Hence, its focus is on the protection of individuals as the ultimate units of moral concern, rather than states. Second, the R2P promotes an egalitarian ethic as it concerns all individuals as equal, giving no stated preference to any particular region, state, or culture. Obligations to outsiders as understood through the R2P's second and third pillars are, in theory, to exist independent from obligations to members of one's own political community. Third, the R2P meets the category of universality as it promotes a moral concern of human protection as a matter of concern for all. This is evident in its reference to the wider international community's role in fulfilling the responsibilities that it proscribes (UNGA, 2005, paras 138–139). As Bellamy and Tacheva (2019, p. 18) have claimed, the R2P commands a global normative consensus that mass violence is incompatible with the interests of international society. Hence, the R2P can be conceived as cosmopolitan in nature and not simply a Western concept promoting Western interests.[3] In fulfilling the three basic criteria of individualism, egalitarianism, and universalism, the R2P can be seen to hold at least a *prima facie* connection with fundamental cosmopolitan tenets.

3.2.2 The Positive Duty to Respond to Mass Atrocity

Beyond those simpler cosmopolitan tenets, the R2P's relationship with the deeper requirements of cosmopolitan human protection need to be understood before we can make a judgement on where reform may be required. Wyatt's (2019) analysis, highlighting the connection between the R2P and a cosmopolitan positive duty to respond to mass atrocity crimes, is useful in this discussion. His argument is that the R2P holds a connection to cosmopolitan maxims of conditional state sovereignty, collective security, and delineates criteria for when intervention can be understood as a legitimate response to human suffering. For Wyatt (2019, pp. 27–35), these criteria lay out a cosmopolitan typology for human protection, which at its heart is concerned with the legitimacy of a positive duty for international intervention in cases of extreme humanitarian emergency. His criteria, again in theory, point to the R2P as further promoting the demands of a (thin) cosmopolitan ethic premised on the positive duty to act to alleviate mass-scale suffering, as they seek to set a standard for a cosmopolitan ethos premised on the need to halt wide-scale harms to human populations which threaten their fundamental needs.

Regarding his first criteria, *conditional state sovereignty*, Wyatt (2019, p. 103) argues that the R2P limits the actions a sovereign can commit to within its territory. This coheres with Pillar One of the R2P and the responsibility of a state to protect its populations from four mass atrocity crimes (genocide, war crimes, crimes against humanity, and ethnic cleansing), with the R2P lying 'first and foremost' with the host state (UNGA, 2009, para. 11a). The R2P sets a very clear duty for states to not commit acts of mass atrocity against the populations that reside there. Should a state fail in this duty, Pillar Three of the R2P implies that the sovereign right to non-intervention can legitimately be breached in cases that can be considered supreme humanitarian emergencies (Walzer, 1977, pp. 251–255). If a state is manifestly failing to protect its populations, the international community should (ideally) 'respond collectively in a timely and decisive manner', in accordance with the UN Charter (UNGA, 2009, para. 11c). This includes the potential use of coercive measures against a sovereign government's will under Chapter VII of the UN Charter. This theoretically serves to limit sovereignty as conditional upon meeting R2P Pillar One responsibilities.

Regarding his second criteria, *collective security*, Wyatt (2019, pp. 103–105) argues that the R2P invokes a universal and collective duty, with residual responsibility placed on outside states to both assist others in meeting their obligations under Pillar One, and to act on cases of supreme emergency to halt mass-scale suffering. This argument is consistent with Pillar Two and Pillar Three of the R2P. 'Pillar two is the commitment of the international community to assist States in meeting those obligations [of host state responsibility]' (UNGA, 2009, para. 11b). This denotes a universal duty incumbent on all members of the international community. Further, Pillar Three's reference to the need for 'timely and decisive' action (UNGA, 2009, para. 11c) denotes a collective duty on the wider international community to at least *consider* taking action in cases where Pillar One responsibilities have been breached. These duties delineate the remedial duty bearers under the R2P, placing a cosmopolitan duty on the international community, whether it considers acting upon it or not.

Finally, regarding his third criteria, *delineating criteria for intervention*, Wyatt (2019, p. 106) argues that the R2P's narrow scope on four mass atrocity crimes fits a cosmopolitan typology for the necessity of military force. Pillar One sets criteria for meeting obligations under the remit of protecting against the four mass atrocity crimes (UNGA, 2009, para. 11a), while Pillar Three suggests that if these crimes are committed, intervention can be a legitimate response. Due to the egregious nature of these acts, these criteria confer with a cosmopolitan positive duty to take action to halt mass atrocity crimes, which can include the need for military force in cases of extreme humanitarian emergency (see Chapter 2).

In essence, the R2P appears to hold a theoretical relationship with cosmopolitanism through a positive duty to respond to mass atrocity violence. As Dahl-Eriksen notes, the R2P is essentially about the violation of human rights on a mass scale and is therefore 'consistent with the expectations of a thin cosmopolitan community for an applied moral universalism beyond the morality of states' (Dahl-Eriksen, 2016, p. 127). The R2P is premised on the idea that the protection of the extremely vulnerable ought to generate a moral imperative to take action where mass-scale atrocity violence is occurring, and as a result, the traditional understanding of sovereignty as a right to non-interference can be cast aside in favour of action to protect a state's vulnerable populations.

3.2.3 The Positive and Negative Duty to Prevent Mass Atrocity

The R2P, in its 2005 UN World Summit form, speaks to tackling four mass atrocity crimes, and in practice this is understood to incorporate a broad understanding of atrocity prevention. In this sense, the R2P can be, at least conceptually, linked with cosmopolitan aims of the *prevention* of mass harm. The R2P is understood as a deep doctrine and does not view mass atrocity crimes in isolation from wider human rights issues. According to former Secretary-General Ban-Ki Moon, the R2P's 'implementation will be broad, and encompasses a full range of UN atrocity prevention activities'

(UNGA, 2009). For Bellamy and McLoughlin (2018, p. 187) this approach is evident in the international community's 'broad and deep' approach to human protection which focuses not just on intervention after the fact, but also incorporates an array of norms and institutions that focus on preventing atrocities from occurring in the first place.

The R2P has attempted to be more than a doctrine for intervention in response to mass crises, with economic, political, and legal commitments also incorporated into its framework for prevention (Brown and Bohm, 2016, p. 909). In his comments at the June 2018 UNGA formal dialogue on R2P, Secretary-General Antonio Gutteres remarked that prevention is 'the core of the Responsibility to Protect' (UN, 2018). Gutteres' subsequent reports in 2019–2021 were similarly centred on the issue of prevention (UN, 2019; UN, 2020; UN, 2021), and this underscores the general favourability that UN and state actors have shown towards the notion of prevention, at least in a rhetorical sense. The UN Framework of Analysis for Atrocity Crimes (2014), for instance, identifies 14 risk factors and 143 indicators which speak to underlying root causes of atrocity, as well as more specific triggering episodes, and in doing so provides a frame of reference to actors for identifying atrocity risk, but also areas for preventive efforts to target. This preventive focus appreciates both that (potential) perpetrators can be influenced before atrocities become widespread and / or systematic, and that conditions can be altered to reduce the risk of the commission of such acts.

Reike, Sharma, and Welsh (2015, pp. 32–33) identify a three-stage process in which the atrocity crimes listed under the R2P tend to escalate: i) the presence of risk factors, such as those of a history of atrocity, economic and societal instability, and an exclusionary ideology;[4] ii) upheaval and mobilisation, often the result of a particular crisis event; and iii) an imminent emergency characterised by increasing levels of violence. For them, addressing the first stage calls for long-term, systemic strategies, while addressing the latter two stages requires more timely and specific action (Reike, Sharma, and Welsh, 2015, p. 33).

These long-term, systemic strategies, as well as more timely and specific action, can be identified in the R2P's preventive focus, which exists at the *operational* and *structural* levels (Bohm and Brown, 2021, p. 61). Operational level prevention refers to the strengthening of local and international capacity for what could be classified as 'reactive-prevention'; that is, efforts aimed at promoting capacity for rapid preventive action in response to emerging crises. This overlap with the R2P's reactive focus underscores the fact that prevention is, as Bellamy and Luck (2018, p. 141) note, multifaceted and containing both the prevention of longer term causes as well as early-violence response. Operational level prevention has a particularly institutionalised focus, including aspects such as early-warning capacity building, institution building, and technical assistance. This level of prevention should also include what Reike, Sharma, and Welsh (2015, pp. 27–28) have referred to as 'targeted' preventive efforts aimed at changing the incentives of those contemplating atrocity, or to change the vulnerability of potential victims.

Structural-level prevention, on the other hand, refers to attempts at addressing the underlying root causes of mass violence (McLoughlin, 2019, p. 143). At the structural level, methods include those such as humanitarian aid, supporting grassroots political movements like women's and minority's rights groups (UN, 2018), while also working to tackle longer term issues such as history of human rights violations, discrimination, and radicalisation (UN, 2021). At the structural level, the R2P hints at a cosmopolitan understanding of the need to secure the rights of others by preventing what Linklater (2001, p. 273) refers to as 'abstract' harms that facilitate conditions which perpetuate mass violence. These manifest in the R2P concept as an understanding of the need to halt structural drivers of mass violence, including efforts such as developmental assistance to tackle societal poverty, the promotion of basic rights, political participation, justice, and security (Bellamy and Luck, 2018, pp. 117–120). Wyatt (2019, p. 132) has similarly made the connection between the R2P and cosmopolitan distributive justice, claiming that the R2P connects with cosmopolitan socio-economic themes of global justice. For him, the R2P's connection to the poverty-causation model – by acknowledging the role of socio-economic factors in the perpetuation of mass violence – helps to bridge the gap between cosmopolitan distributive justice and cosmopolitan human protection. In this sense, the R2P is meant to be taken as a proactive understanding of the need to tackle deeper human rights issues to improve the efficacy of the prevention of mass violence (Hehir, 2018, p. 48).

Crucially, however, for this focus on structural-level prevention to be coherent, the R2P would also need to be linked with the negative duties associated with the preventive concept of the cosmopolitan 'harm principle'. This negative form of obligations holds that there is a duty to avoid causing harm to others that would infringe on their rights and negatively impact their life chances (Pogge, 2002, chap. 2). This is largely predicated on the notion that an ethical imperative to value all human life equally creates a fundamental demand to avoid imposing cruelty upon others (Linklater, 2001, p. 265).

Bellamy and Tacheva (2019) have claimed that the R2P meets the standards of the cosmopolitan harm principle. They argue that the R2P represents 'a general agreement that, despite global cultural differences, some forms of systematic large-scale violence are universally deemed abhorrent and should be prohibited' (Bellamy and Tacheva, 2019, p. 17). They see the R2P as a nascent cosmopolitan principle, one focused on the protection of individuals and groups from the mass harms of atrocity, promoting a consensus that states owe protection responsibilities to those not just within their own borders, but also universally to those that dwell outside their territory as well (Bellamy and Tacheva, 2019, pp. 17–18).

As noted above, the R2P does hold a connection with cosmopolitan principles and does enshrine an element of the harm principle as it is aimed at reducing 'concrete harm' – that is the harm that particular human agents intentionally inflict on specific others (Linklater, 2001, p. 269) – which is clearly evident in its noted focus on preventing mass atrocity crimes. Notably though, this only exists *explicitly* as a Pillar One domestic responsibility which the sovereign power holds towards its own populations, rather than an explicit acknowledgement of the duty to avoid harming outside populations. The duty to avoid harming others could possibly be taken as implied from the positive duty conferred on the international community to prevent and react to atrocity crimes. However, as discussed below, the failure to make this duty explicit would seem to undermine the R2P's preventive agenda.

3.3 The R2P's Weak Compliance Pull

The above analysis establishes theoretical links between the R2P and cosmopolitanism, which is important in conceptualising the normative value of the R2P. Yet, it is clear that we must go beyond simply establishing theoretical concomitance between the R2P and cosmopolitan values, and also assess whether cosmopolitan duties are met in the realities of state practice. To assist with this it is worth spending some time here first evaluating the R2P as a 'norm' of appropriate state behaviour. Utilising constructivist scholarship, the argument made in this section is that the R2P represents a norm with weak compliance pull, and as a consequence, has a limited influence on state practice.

Norms are social patterns that exist to regulate the behaviour of actors by setting a standard for what action *ought* to be followed. The R2P attempts to set standards of appropriate behaviour vis-à-vis halting mass atrocities by legitimising a shift in what constitutes appropriate state behaviour; mobilising will to act, raising the political costs of inaction, and, as discussed above, promoting the development of tools to both prevent and respond to atrocity crimes (Welsh, 2019, p. 56).

The classic model of the 'norm life-cycle' from Finnemore and Sikkink (1998) is a useful starting point for understanding how norms might affect actors like states. They suggest that an international norm goes through three distinct stages during its adoption. The first stage is norm emergence, where the norm is promoted by a select few key actors or 'norm entrepreneurs'. The second stage is the norm cascade, where the norm becomes accepted by a 'critical mass' of states. The final stage is 'norm internalisation' where the norm assumes a 'taken for granted' quality and finds its implementation routine, with violations consistently punished. Wyatt has argued that the R2P confers with at least the second stage of Finnemore and Sikkink's life-cycle model because through years of negotiation it has now become accepted by a critical mass of states (Wyatt, 2019, p. 158); this is clearly reflected in the R2P's unanimous adoption at the UN in 2005. Wyatt goes as far as to suggest that the norm may be internalised and cohere with Finnemore and Sikkink's third stage due to the increasing normalisation of references made to it within the UNSC (Wyatt, 2019, p. 159). Bellamy takes a similar line here when reflecting on the R2P's normative acceptance, claiming that the R2P's 'habitual' references in international political fora (especially the UNSC, UNGA, and UNHRC) point to its increased acceptance as an international norm, reflective of a positive development in practice (Bellamy, 2015, p. 161; Bellamy and Tacheva, 2019). With Edward Luck, Bellamy has also claimed that the 'R2P's normative arguments have prevailed' with the next focus on working it into practice (Bellamy and Luck, 2018, p. 1).

While core principles of the R2P are universally accepted (i.e., that mass atrocity is intolerable and there is a duty to prevent it), the doctrine does not have a set and static meaning to all international actors (Hunt and Orchard, 2020, p. 18). More recent work on norm theory has effectively argued that the meaning of a norm is never fixed, with norms operating in a continuous state of contestation and re-interpretation by actors (Acharya, 2004; Wiener, 2009; Panke and Petersohn, 2012; Wiener, 2018; Deitelhoff and Zimmermann, 2020; Jacob, 2021; Mulford, 2022). While contestation does not automatically equate to the weakening of a norm (Badescu and Weiss, 2010; Deitelhoff and Zimmermann, 2020), it can nevertheless lead to backsliding, where norms can be re-interpreted in such a way that differs from the original intentions of the norm's original entrepreneurs (Welsh, 2013, p. 380). Hence, even if a norm is accepted by a 'critical mass' of states (to use Finnemore and Sikkink's language), it is still subject to contestation and a potential change in meaning.

For Welsh (2013, pp. 383–384), the R2P has been prone to contestation on both procedural accounts, based on who controls the R2P debate, and also substantive contestation over the precise actions that the R2P should convey. As a result, she argues that the R2P exists as a 'complex norm', multi-layered in how it confers both domestic and international responsibilities (Welsh, 2014, p. 133). As norms involving positive duties are more open to contestation – since they require proactive behavioural change (Deitelhoff and Zimmermann, 2020, p. 57) – this makes the R2P particularly prone to contestation over what actions it requires of states. Glanville (2021, pp. 6–8) contends that the R2P's international responsibilities reflect an 'imperfect duty' because they are subject to the judgement of each state when debating on whether to take action, fall on no particular state, meaning that no specific duty bearer is identified, and provide no guidance on where to prioritise protection in a world where multiple instances of mass atrocity are likely occurring at any given instance. The result is that the R2P's international duties are prone to inconsistency in their practical application.

Welsh (2013, p. 387) argues, in relation to its international reactive aspect, that the R2P is a 'duty of conduct', existing as a 'responsibility to consider' whether a case is one of mass atrocity and whether international response should occur through Pillar Three. Yet such an understanding is not acceptable when viewed within the cosmopolitan framework of duties to human protection outlined in Chapter 2. A duty to simply 'consider' leaves too much room for inaction and, consequently, opens up the possibility for shirking cosmopolitan duties of prevention and response. More promisingly, Bellamy and Luck (2014, p. 72; 2018, pp. 55–58) have spoken of the R2P as enshrining a 'responsibility to try'. Like Welsh, they rightly note that a lack of military intervention in response to mass atrocity is not indicative of failure given the complexities of this action, in addition to the range of other potential responses available under the R2P (Bellamy and Luck, 2018, p. 55). For them, the R2P requires deliberation over action, with intent to protect, and that states ought to furnish material support for such action (Bellamy and Luck, 2018, p. 58).

However, a responsibility to try arguably also falls short of the standards called for by a cosmopolitan reading of the norm. A responsibility to try and fulfil the R2P suggests that states can claim that they are 'trying' to curb mass violence, while in reality they may avoid employing action that could be more efficacious in addressing a situation (Hehir, 2018, p. 169), and which would be the most justifiable course of action in regards to actually serving the R2P's protection agenda (Pattison, 2022, p. 108). The notion of a responsibility to try and fulfil the R2P also implies that states will display limited appetite for promoting action over what ought to be a clear mass atrocity case (Butchard, 2020, pp. 44–52). A responsibility to try, therefore, also leaves open room for inaction. Such a standard would serve to reinforce inconsistent practice, which is anathema to the R2P's purpose. A responsibility to try seems somewhat status quo. It suggests that the current R2P approach works, does not need strengthening, and permits states to continue doing what they are doing. The responsibility to try consequently would not seem to demand reform of international structures to better promote atrocity prevention, or reform to promote context-appropriate responses in all cases where atrocity violence has occurred, such as is required by a cosmopolitan interpretation of the R2P's demands.

It is worth remembering of course that a key reason as to why the R2P was even adopted by the international community in 2005 was that the ambiguity in the R2P's international protection duties represented a political compromise at the time; a compromise which purposely left short any obligatory responsibility to act (Glanville and Widmaier, 2020, pp. 58–60). While the 2001 ICISS report on the R2P sought to change the way that response to atrocity crimes occurs by fostering greater accountability for P5 states and tackling institutional barriers to humanitarian action (Bellamy, 2006, p. 146), the accepted 2005 UN World Summit version of the R2P offered no legal or institutional alternatives to the way atrocity crimes should be tackled. The version of the R2P that was adopted in 2005 is a much watered-down version of that proposed by the ICISS in 2001, removing aspects such as P5 veto restraint, criteria for the implementation of the use of force, and the call for action to be taken outside the UNSC when it is deadlocked. The 2005 agreement is also ambiguous in the sense that it fails to specify exactly what is required of the international community, and precisely when these duties become active. It is a non-binding commitment representing a form of 'R2P-lite' as Thomas Weiss (2006) referred to it. The R2P builds on established frameworks and legal precedents such as the 1948 Genocide Convention, the international laws of war, and the 1998 Rome Statute of the International Criminal Court, as well as placing the UN (particularly the UNSC) as central to the norm's implementation (Gholiagha and Loges, 2020, p. 74). So, rather than establishing a brand new set of obligations, the R2P is more a political clarification of pre-existing duties held by states (Reike and Bellamy, 2010). This has helped in packaging demands for atrocity prevention into a politically useful conceptual framework; successfully moving the international community away from 'sovereignty as right' to 'sovereignty as responsibility' (Orchard, 2020, p. 33). However, what the R2P hasn't done is effectively overcome problems of inconsistency in responding to mass atrocity. To be clear, it is not claimed here that the R2P *should* have successfully done this in the less than 20 years since its adoption; the problems of R2P implementation are complex, multifaceted, and necessitate transitional thinking if they are to be overcome. However, the point to highlight here is that the R2P norm does promote inconsistency, and this in turn contributes to protection failures.

Welsh, however, acknowledges the inconsistency 'built into the very fabric of R2P' and uses this fact to claim that individual case failings are not indicative of the R2P's failure (Welsh, 2013, p. 388). In the sense of the R2P as an aspirational norm this is correct, for a few failures in application do not present the death of a norm (Glanville, 2016; Deitelhoff and Zimmermann, 2020). Deitelhoff (2019, p. 161) argues that the R2P norm maintains its validity, that is, belief in its moral appropriateness, despite cases of applicatory contestation and inaction. Similarly, Welsh (2019) argues that the R2P has been shown to be quite robust, as while certain aspects (particularly the use of coercive intervention under Pillar Three) are divisive, the general validity and acceptance of a norm to work towards halting cases of mass atrocity violence remains throughout the international community. Further, Russo (2020, p. 232) argues that 'the fact that R2P has continued to move ahead despite a dysfunctional Security Council, flagrant violations by powerful states, and ongoing friction with the norm of state sovereignty, is a testament to just how strong the norm is'.

Yet, as was noted in the Introduction, the debate surrounding the R2P's normative status is highly polarised. According Hehir's (2018, p. 77) account, the R2P exists as a 'hollow norm' due to its malleable character and proneness to contestation, weakness in enforcement, and the fact that it is regulated by those it seeks to constrain (independent sovereign states). This suggests that, in practice, states are not held accountable to their 2005 commitment and are able to pursue policies which ignore their R2P responsibilities. This is particularly relevant regarding the R2P's more contentious third pillar, for while Pillar One and Pillar Two have been readily accepted by the international community – reflected in the 89 UNSC resolutions and presidential statements referencing R2P to date[5] – Pillar Three has remained contentious, having never been directly invoked in a UNSC resolution.[6] This is problematic since Pillar Three is the most ambitious and transformative element of the R2P doctrine (Hehir, 2018, p. 70). While Pillar One and Two concern host state responsibility and consensual international assistance, respectively, it is Pillar Three which has the potential to realise external enforcement of the R2P in cases where it has been breached. While inaction or weak responses under Pillar Three may not be an absolute failure in terms of the R2P's 'norm life cycle', they are, however, indicative of a failure to consistently meet cosmopolitan protection standards.

The fact that the R2P is not made irrelevant by examples of failings is no cause for great celebration in itself. Hehir (2018, p. 100) posits that the contestation over Pillar Three has led to the R2P becoming co-opted by states to reinforce non-intervention; practice which is anathema to the R2P's original purpose of generating the political will to respond to and halt mass atrocities. Similarly, Tacheva and Brown (2015, p. 454) have claimed that the R2P represents at the least a 'stalled', if not a 'degenerating' norm, noting that 'there is limited institutional capacity and/or normative willingness to promote it further' (stalled) with its meaning having been diluted over time since its original ICISS inception in 2001 (degenerating). Despite highlighting the R2P norm's overall robustness, Welsh (2019, pp. 68–69) and Deitelhoff (2019, p. 170) do also observe that continued contestation over Pillar Three has the potential to derail the R2P's long-term effectiveness.

As is outlined in subsequent sections, the implementation of the R2P often fails to meet cosmopolitan duties of human protection as responsibilities can be avoided where states interpret their interests as clashing with their cosmopolitan duties. This means that states are able to claim they are 'doing something' in the face of mass violence when in reality there may be more efficacious action that ought to be pursued. States are also able to undermine their R2P commitments by pursuing damaging policies at the international level which exacerbate cases of mass violence. Further, limited appetite by states to act on clear mass atrocity cases is often evident, meaning that some situations become effectively cast aside. As such, the argument made in this chapter is that while the R2P theoretically sets out duties which ought to be morally fulfilled, the norm is not applied in accordance with cosmopolitan standards in practice.

These factors point to the weak compliance pull of the R2P norm, highlighting that the current R2P approach is too weak for generating action consistent with the cosmopolitan ethic promoted in Chapter 2. As Newman (2016, p. 34) has highlighted, a 'more demanding, definition of a norm places more emphasis upon the practice of states in upholding and implementing principles and commitments'. Bloomfield (2017, pp. 167–168) argues that in order for a norm to be entrenched it requires a consistency in practice, supported by punishment for violations. Given the inherent contestation that surrounds the R2P as an international norm (Jarvis, 2022), to understand its strength as a norm of cosmopolitan human protection, we must look to examine R2P practice, rather than simply accepting rhetorical invocations as reflective of progressiveness. When the former is examined, the weakness of the current R2P approach for realising cosmopolitan obligations, and of the need for reform, becomes pressingly apparent.

3.4 The Positive Duty to Respond in Practice

The cosmopolitan positive duty to respond to instances of mass atrocity is often unmet in practice, as the international community often fails to undertake direct action when a manifest failing of R2P Pillar One occurs (Pattison, 2015, p. 197). To illustrate this, we can return to Wyatt's three criteria suggesting a theoretical link between the R2P and a positive cosmopolitan duty (conditional state sovereignty, collective responsibility, and delineation of criteria for when intervention is permissible). Contrary to the positive links that Wyatt wishes to demonstrate, these criteria actually show how a cosmopolitan duty to respond to mass atrocity violence is in-fact lacking in practice. In all, this helps to illustrate why R2P reform is necessary.

First, the fact that there is no guarantee of punishment for committing atrocities means that the duties associated with the cosmopolitan maxim of *conditional state sovereignty* are not successfully met. Wyatt's argument (2019, p. 111) that the R2P successfully confers a primary responsibility to protect is therefore difficult to accept at face value. The states most likely to commit atrocity crimes and human rights abuses have often still been able to commit them, and so evidently they have not had to alter their behaviour in line with a conditional understanding of sovereignty. Hence, we might say that it is possible for states to affirm commitment to the R2P without cost, reflecting the R2P norm's weakness in compliance pull (either in host state action or the responsibility of the international community). This is evident in how states can affirm support for the R2P in official rhetoric but can simultaneously continue to commit violence against their populations. For example, the case of Bahrain is illustrative, a state which has affirmed support for the R2P in discourse yet is widely known to continue committing human rights abuses in practice (Hehir, 2018, p. 159). Human Rights Watch's World Report (2021) has identified Bahrain's human rights situation as 'not improving', with the regular imprisonment and torture of protestors, censure of the press, and denial of access to the Office of the UN High Commissioner for Human Rights.

Further, the UNSC's preference for referencing those responsibilities most clearly attached to Pillar One and Pillar Two of the R2P reflects a deferral of a responsibility to intervene (Hehir, 2018, p. 135). The limited reference to or implementation of Pillar Three measures makes it difficult to declare that the R2P has created a conditional understanding of sovereignty in practice. As

Bloomfield notes, Pillar Three only imparts a 'permissive' standard on states to act on a case-by-case basis, which sustains a weakness in responding to cases of mass violence (Bloomfield, 2017, pp. 172–176).

It is important to highlight here that the problem is not that the same actions are not followed in each case of mass atrocities. Rather, the problem is that the current R2P approach permits inconsistency in whether action is taken *at all* (Paris, 2014, p. 578). While those such as Hehir (2013) have decried the R2P for the inconsistency in the way that it is implemented, drawing on Wheeler's (2000) distinction between consistency and coherence, Gallagher (2015, p. 272) argues that inconsistency in the way that the R2P is applied is not something inherently problematic. Gallagher differentiates between legitimate and illegitimate consistency, where the former means that 'complexities of the crisis dictate that there is no consensus on what action should be taken' and the latter being 'cases when the Great Powers are evading their responsibility or even participating in it themselves' (Gallagher, 2015, p. 271). Such an understanding seems logical, for it should not be the case that the same actions are followed in every instance of mass atrocities. The 'case-by-case' (UNGA, 2005) basis of the R2P is not inherently problematic, as different cases will likely always require differentiated responses. Indeed, in complex cases such as Syria, it is not immediately clear what international action ought to be taken.

The problem, however, is that the current R2P approach often does not even result in minimal action in a timely and decisive manner. There are a wealth of options available to respond to mass atrocity under Pillar Three of the R2P (UN, 2012), but the international community often fails to employ them. In the case of Syria, for instance, while the complexities of a military response are clear, probably denoting what Gallagher would describe as 'legitimate inconsistency',[7] on the other hand, the failure of the UNSC to even pass a rhetorical condemnation of the actions of the Assad regime at the outbreak of violence appears a clear case of 'illegitimate inconsistency' and would point towards the weakness of the current R2P approach. While those such as Paris (2014, p. 578) rightly argue that there are epistemic uncertainties as to whether *military* intervention should take place in a given case of mass atrocities, there is *always* some form of international response that should occur, even if this is only in the form of 'amelioration' efforts like humanitarian aid and the granting of refuge (Glanville and Pattison, 2021, p. 222).

Russo (2020) argues that violations of the R2P by the inability or unwillingness of the UNSC to act do not make the R2P worthless, as the international community has found novel ways of acting on its Pillar Three commitment where the UNSC has been deadlocked, such as through establishing fact-finding missions and promoting legal accountability. However, while making this point she also appreciates that secondary action through bodies like the UNGA or UNHRC are not as ideal as action taken through the UNSC as the primary duty bearer under the R2P's third pillar (Russo, 2020, p. 230).

Mass atrocity crises necessitate timely and decisive response, and the current R2P approach means that this is never guaranteed. This problem reflects the weakness of the UNSC as an institution for consistently implementing such a duty of response. Cases like Syria, Myanmar, and China demonstrate this, where wide-scale atrocities have often been met with an entirely dysfunctional UNSC. The Uyghur crisis in China, for instance, has failed to even make it onto the UNSC's agenda despite reports that the 'Chinese government is responsible for the mass detention of more than a million Uyghurs, for forcing them into industrial-scale forced labour programmes, and for attempting to wipe out Uyghur and Islamic culture in the region' (UK Foreign Affairs Committee, 2021, p. 3).

Second, in relation to the concept of *collective responsibility*, as noted, the R2P does recognise that meeting duties under Pillar Two requires placing agency in the hands of the entire international community. However, the duty react under Pillar Three, as per the 2005 iteration of the R2P, belongs explicitly to the UNSC (UNGA, 2005, para. 139). Bellamy and Tacheva (2019, p. 22) claim that this duty bestowed upon the UNSC represents a cosmopolitan responsibility which has made it more difficult for the UNSC to do nothing in the face of mass violence. As such, they claim a weak form of accountability has been generated between the UNSC and the wider UN membership (Bellamy and Tacheva, 2019, pp. 22–23), with '[t]he positioning of the Security Council as bearing special responsibilities … [aligning] with the cosmopolitan vision for the allocation of universal responsibilities' (Bellamy and Tacheva, 2019, p. 27). They support this with evidence that in 13 mass atrocity crises identified from 2011–2019, the UNSC acted in response to 11 (Bellamy and Tacheva, 2019, p. 31).

Some cases are acted on, others are not. Yet even when the UNSC does 'act', it may not do so in an effective way. As Hehir (2018, p. 135) notes, in its response to the crises highlighted by Bellamy and Tacheva, the UNSC has (mostly) focused on Pillar One and Two of the R2P.[8] In doing so, the more contentious third pillar has often been avoided. This has led to collective responsibility effectively being shirked in cases where the UNSC has distanced itself from actions against the sovereign will of a target state. The UNSC instead tends to emphasise that the host state holds the responsibility to stop the suffering and that only consensual elements can be employed in the international response. This defers responsibility to the host state, leaving the wider international community as a support mechanism.[9] The UNSC has evidently been unable or unwilling to meet its responsibility under the R2P where the interests of its members have clashed with its cosmopolitan duty. This is reflective of the politicised nature of the UNSC and the weakness this imposes when attempting to institutionalise a cosmopolitan duty of a responsibility to act on cases of mass atrocities.

Directly related to this, the veto power of the UNSC has remained near unchanged since 1945 and continues to impinge on the Council's response to mass violence where Pillar Three measures are concerned. Over Syria, for instance, 17 draft resolutions have been vetoed since 2011 despite the fact that Syria represents one of the clearest cases of manifest failing as understood under the R2P. Both Russia and China have often called for a 'political settlement' to the crisis while utilising their veto power to prevent the passage of robust measures aimed at holding perpetrators to account.[10] The veto power reflects a barrier standing in the way of the R2P's progress, and though Bellamy and Tacheva (2019) argue that the UNSC is now expected to act on mass atrocity, the continued presence of the veto undermines the accountability of the UNSC. While the veto power remains in place, collective responsibility is undermined as UNSC action is all but impossible in any case where a P5 member perceives its vital interests as at stake. As Vilmer (2018) has noted, veto restraint measures continue to be disputed among the P5 members. Reform of the veto would seem integral for there to be any chance of the UNSC being able to consistently meet its responsibilities under Pillar Three (the subject of veto reform is taken up in Chapter 5). However, such reform will be difficult and requires the support of all the P5 members. If the UNSC cannot be reformed to more effectively implement Pillar Three then other avenues of R2P response will need to be explored (the prospects for undertaking Pillar Three response via the UNGA is examined in Chapter 6).

Finally, regarding the R2P's promotion of *criteria for when intervention can be deemed legitimate*, the practice again falls short of cosmopolitan standards. In theory, the criteria for legitimate intervention are clearly stated in the R2P (under the four mass crimes) and align with a cosmopolitan demand for a positive duty to intervene (militarily if necessary) under circumstances where fundamental human rights are threatened by the advent of mass atrocity. However, it is evident that the practical interpretation of these criteria is inherently politicised. As such, the R2P cannot be said to realise a cosmopolitan duty of action where these criteria are met, as despite the moral demand for action, states are often reticent about intervening.

Take for example the case of Myanmar, where since 2016 state security forces have been widely reported as carrying out a campaign of atrocity crimes against Myanmar's Rohingya population. In August 2018 a UN fact-finding mission declared that 'senior generals of the Myanmar military should be investigated and prosecuted in an international criminal tribunal for genocide, crimes against humanity and war crimes' (UNHRC, 2018). The Gambia has since filed an official case against Myanmar in the ICJ for genocidal acts which remains ongoing. Despite crimes being committed that fall within legally understood definitions of atrocity crimes, the UN's response to the crisis has been limited. Indeed, the UNSC only referred to the Rohingya persecution in a single presidential statement made in November 2017 (UNSC, 2017). Following a coup by the military in February 2021, the UNSC failed to adopt a formal resolution until December 2022; that was 22 months after the coup occurred (UNSC, 2022).

Further, it has been widely commentated that contextual factors are crucial to any consideration by the UNSC to act on a case of mass atrocity

(Bellamy and Williams, 2011, p. 826). In the Libya situation, for instance, the influence of the League of Arab states in pushing for action against the Gaddafi regime has been noted as crucial in influencing Russia and China's decision not to veto UNSC resolution 1973 (Morris, 2013; Hehir, 2013). The continued importance of contextual and political factors would seem to undermine the idea that it is cosmopolitan moral standards of protection that are of a significant influence in practical responses to R2P crises. Alternatively, it seems the case that rather than the extent of mass crimes being committed, the political factors conducive to intervention are more likely to influence whether action occurs or not. Hence, it cannot be declared that the criteria for intervention as set out in the R2P are applied consistently. This is problematic from the perspective of the cosmopolitan positive duty to respond, for it suggests that state interest often supersedes the moral imperative to protect populations from mass violence. The point here is not that we should strive for the entire de-politicisation of R2P response. Such a demand would be overly utopian. The point here is simply to highlight that international response is often weak where the R2P's criteria have been met, and that there is a moral demand to strengthen this response in order to make progress toward a more cosmopolitan application of the norm.

A final point to add to this problem of contextualism is that a hierarchy seems to exist within the four mass crimes themselves. For instance, the use of chemical weapons, as a war crime, appears to carry a stronger normative intolerance within the international community than other mass crimes. In the case of Syria, while the response was never explicitly linked with the R2P (Orchard, 2020, p. 42), the use of chemical weapons crossed an international 'red-line' with Obama referring to it as a 'game changer' (BBC, 2013) which helped, in September 2013, to generate the first substantial international action in response to war crimes in Syria when the UNSC passed resolution 2118 that endorsed the (consensual) destruction of Syria's chemical weapons stockpile (Bellamy, 2022, p. 141). When chemical weapons were again used in 2017 and 2018, the US, along with military and/or diplomatic support from France and the UK, deployed targeted missile attacks on Syrian state installations with President Trump having referred to the 'beautiful babies' of Syria as a motivation for the US response (VOX, 2017).[11] When it came to chemical weapons these states were prepared to form a 'coalition of the willing', absent a UNSC mandate, yet have not been willing to in response to other systematic mass atrocity crimes in Syria. This seems to suggest that the taboo of chemical weapons carries more pull than actual civilian deaths, even when the death and destruction incurred through other atrocity crimes has *far* outnumbered those caused by chemical weapons.

It must be noted that each of the four crimes do carry differing levels of legal and practical applicability (Hubert and Blätter, 2012; Reike, Sharma, and Welsh, 2015, pp. 22–23). Yet ultimately, an inconsistency in acting in response to some crimes over others points to practice which is inconsistent with the ethos of the R2P and its cosmopolitan aspiration of halting atrocity. Inconsistency means that certain mass crimes are implicitly deemed 'less abhorrent' than others, and are essentially permissible if they don't contravene the interests of states strongly enough to generate a response. This is incompatible with a positive duty to take action to secure the fundamental rights of others; this demand ought to exist in any case of mass violence where fundamental rights are threatened, and not simply, for example, the application of chemical weapons. This further points to a need for reform to achieve a stronger institutionalisation of the responsibility to take appropriate action in cases where the R2P is breached.

3.5 The Positive Duty to Prevent in Practice

As highlighted in section 3.2.3, the R2P is not just about responding to mass atrocity violence that has already become widespread and/or systematic. The R2P is also about improving the prevention of mass atrocities via *operational* and *structural* mechanisms.

Attempts have clearly been made to institutionalise mass atrocity prevention since the adoption of the R2P. The UN has developed a 'Framework of Analysis for Atrocity Crimes' (UN, 2014a) which sets out current understandings of risk factors conducive to the occurrence of mass atrocities. A number of states have themselves established an 'R2P focal point': an institutional creation 'envisaged to encourage states to fulfil their national and international R2P responsibilities' (Serrano, 2015, p. 90). The joint UN office on the prevention of Genocide and the R2P also has an important advisory function to the UN Secretary-General in helping to bring attention to impending atrocity cases (UN, 2021). As noted, a number of the Secretary-General's recent R2P reports (UN, 2018; 2019; 2020; 2021) have also specifically focused on the issue of prevention, demonstrating that the notion is understood as intrinsic to the R2P's implementation.

Yet it is debatable as to the extent of whether these institutional advances have affected atrocity prevention efforts for the better. Regarding R2P focal points, for instance, while those such as Serrano (2015, p. 100; also McLoughlin, 2019, p. 152) have argued that establishing an R2P focal point 'could help improve the response capacity of states and international organizations, and over time help shape their institutional behaviour towards more routinized forms of R2P response', others, such as Hehir (2018, p. 184), observe that establishing a focal point has been one way for abusive states to deflect criticism of their own human rights practices, with focal points not influencing whether these states actually implement R2P-based policies. At the UN level, Strauss (2015, p. 81) argues that the UN's prevention-based mechanisms are constrained by a lack of joint understanding between member states, UN entities, and civil society as to what are the causes of mass atrocity violence, as well as the specific challenges mass atrocity presents in terms of required preventive action. This lack of a coherent understanding of atrocity prevention matters given that the UN is the most significant international actor in the context of co-ordinating the positive duty to prevent atrocity.

Others, such as Brown and Bohm (2016; Bohm and Brown, 2021), have highlighted the failure of the R2P to successfully move the international community in the direction of prevention. For them, the R2P remains a 'response to symptoms, not causes' of conflict (Brown and Bohm, 2016, p. 908). They argue this is characteristic of the R2P's inability to posit a language of duties, and the way the current R2P approach fails to address underlying structural causes of violence.

Establishing a causal link between structural risk factors and the outbreak of atrocity is not straightforward, however, and there are numerous instances where risk factors have existed, but atrocities have not occurred (Harff, 2003; McLoughlin, 2014 and 2019; Gallagher, 2022). Yet, this shouldn't undermine the fact that underlying structural risk factors can, at the very least, contribute to some instances of atrocity violence occurring; McLoughlin (2019, p. 149), for instance, notes that 'few, if any, cases of mass atrocities have occurred in the absence of such long-term structural risk factors'. Risk factors may include economic and social instability (Reike, Sharma, and Welsh, 2015, p. 30), or the proliferation of human rights abuses as a prelude to mass violence (Cederman, Weidmann, and Gleditsch, 2011; Ainley, 2017, p. 254). Where states fail to act on the positive duty to alleviate the structural conditions of mass violence, there is the potential for atrocity crimes to follow.

The evidence suggests that translating the R2P's theoretical preventive focus into practice has been difficult. The sheer number of cases of mass violence which have occurred since the R2P was adopted is testament to this (see GCR2P). It is of course not possible in the space here to cover each individual case, nevertheless, we can draw on some examples to highlight failures of prevention. In the case of Myanmar, for instance, risk factors conducive to mass violence – such as a long history of persecution for its Rohingya population (Nishikawa, 2020, pp. 95–96) – were clear and known for years prior to the campaign of ethnic cleansing which occurred in 2017 (Butchard, 2020, p. 47; Stensrud, 2021, p. 228). As Pedersen (2021, pp. 359–360) puts it, 'for anyone familiar with the tragic history of the Rohingya in Myanmar, every aspect of this most recent crisis, including the root causes, the execution, and the, so far, failed efforts to resolve it, will give a strong sense of déjà vu'. The Myanmar case suggests that clear warning does not necessarily translate into effective and actionable international prevention practice.

The case of persistent violence in the Central African Republic (CAR) serves as an illustrative example of both operational and structural prevention failures. Civilian targeting has been a common theme during the events in CAR, leading to a major humanitarian crisis. The UN Office for the Coordination of Humanitarian Affairs (OCHA) estimates that 3.4 million people (56 per cent of the population) will need humanitarian assistance in the year 2023, while there are 516,000 people internally displaced (OCHA, 2023). Mars notes that while CAR is often considered a neglected case, multiple interventions have in-fact been carried out by French, African, and UN forces since the country gained its independence in 1960 (Mars, 2015, p. 7). This suggests that the international community *has* attempted to play a role in preventing atrocities. However, international engagement with CAR has been reactionary, with concerns for short-term stabilisation trumping long-term investment in addressing underlying structural causes of violence. Experts argue that external actors have prioritised 'quick-fix solutions' (Carayannis and Lombard, 2015a, p. 324), with a desire to 'run for the exits' (Carayannis and Fowlis, 2017, p. 231) once armed conflict has subsided. This engagement has focused on the pursuit of elections before the structural needs (such as health, education, poverty) of the state as a whole. For Mars (2015, p. 7), the failure to prevent mass atrocity crimes in the 2012 uprising 'is a symptom of decades of ineffective engagement with the country'. This is representative of the failing of current international approaches to atrocity prevention to adequately address underlying factors which help perpetuate mass violence. One of the key flaws here has been the failure to appreciate how state actors themselves have perpetuated violence within CAR's melting pot of violence. Indeed, state actors have consistently maintained ties with armed groups within CAR, yet international assistance to the country in the context of Pillar Two has continued to be focused on strengthening the position of state actors (Collins, 2021). For example, international efforts have looked to restore CAR's state military, even though the army has been a source of insecurity for CAR's population for decades (Carayannis and Lombard, 2015a, p. 324).

Further, despite the number of international interventions directed at CAR in recent history, it is notable that the country remains beset by societal poverty. The World Bank (2022) notes that:

> With a population of over six million, the Central African Republic ranks at the bottom of the Human Capital and Human Development Indices. Its institutions are weak, citizens have limited access to basic services, infrastructure is woefully inadequate, gender-based violence is widespread, and the social fabric has been eroded.

The sheer number of interventions carried out in CAR suggests a potential connection between socio-economic factors and perpetual conditions of violence, while also reflecting the failure of international interventions to adequately aid in the alleviation of underlying structural conditions of violence. Of course, it is not simply that socio-economic factors contribute to the violence in CAR. Among many factors (see Carayannis and Lombard, 2015b), decades-old religious tensions were brought to the fore during the crisis of 2012–13 (Mars, 2015, p. 10), and the ruling elites were responsible for wide-scale accountability failures, purposely reducing their control over organised violence by allowing local militias to flourish, and a general unwillingness to live up to their R2P (Mars, 2015, p. 15; De Vries and Mehler, 2019, pp. 314–315). However, the case is reflective of the problem with an atrocity prevention focus that is fixated on dealing with short-term symptoms of conflict without properly attempting to address long-term underlying causes.

Moreover, when deadly violence broke out in 2012, despite the numerous cases of violence which had occurred previously leading to an international response, it took two years before the UN finally seized control of peace enforcement from competing African coalitions (Mars, 2015, p. 14). Notably, this meant that deployment of peacekeepers only occurred after many of the worst atrocities had already happened (Carayannis and Lombard, 2015a, p. 323). This has highlighted the problem of the international community's inability to work proactively to prevent violence from becoming widespread and systematic. In this sense, the CAR case is also reflective of the operational problem identified by Bellamy and Lupel (2015) of the short-term failure to consistently turn early warnings of impending atrocities into effective action and further demonstrative of the failings of the current R2P preventive approach.

The failure to act on the cosmopolitan demand to prevent mass violence from erupting in the first instance, and the failure to act preventatively to stop violence becoming widespread and systematic, further points to the need for reform to strengthen the R2P. The ways in which the international community acts to engage in atrocity prevention must be improved, as must the speed at which timely and decisive response is delivered in impending crises.

3.6 The Negative Duty to Prevent in Practice

The R2P may hold an implied connection with the cosmopolitan harm principle in its attempt to espouse a duty of prevention. However, in contrast to Bellamy and Tacheva (2019), it is argued here that the R2P cannot yet be fully recognised as a global harm convention since global harm conventions, as understood by Linklater (2001) and Shapcott (2008), refer to the duty to not harm *outsiders* as well as populations within one's own borders. While the R2P reinforces the negative responsibility of states to not inflict mass abuses against their own populations (Pillar One), it does not contain any direct acknowledgement of negative responsibilities to avoid harming outside populations. Instead, the R2P stipulates a positive duty to aid in the prevention of atrocities (Pillar Two) and a duty to consider responding should this fail (Pillar Three). In essence, these latter two duties are understood as humanitarian duties to alleviate suffering within an outside state, and fail to recognise any connection between the actions of outside state actors, and the occurrence of atrocities within a state.

To be clear, positive duties are important for reinforcing negative duties to not facilitate harm upon others (Pogge, 2002), and the positive duties present in the R2P do perhaps reflect an implicit appreciation that a duty of prevention includes a duty not to harm. However, somewhat paradoxically, the R2P fails to *explicitly* recognise that harms often stem, in part, from the same international community that the R2P charges with the duty of preventing them. In this way, the current R2P approach effectively legitimises international assistance from states who are themselves complicit in damaging practices of intervention in states where human rights abuses are rampant, and where atrocities have the potential to occur. This paradox and the absence of an explicit reference to negative duties towards others within the three pillar R2P framework presents a significant conceptual flaw. It leaves aside a vital element of a cosmopolitan approach to human protection that undermines the R2P agenda's preventive logic. A coherent R2P approach would oblige states to avoid imposing harms (as well as to actively work to halt current harms) which contribute to mass violence, and thus would better justify the logic of charging international state actors with assistance duties under the R2P.

It is in the context of *indirect* harms that the hypocrisy of the international community and the failure of the R2P to enshrine negative duties towards outsiders becomes evident. Linklater refers to abstract harm as an indirect form of harm resulting from the actions of transnational economic and political institutions (Linklater, 2001, p. 273). While promoting the concept of atrocity prevention, states simultaneously facilitate abstract harm upon outside populations (Getachew, 2019, pp. 235–236). This problem is reflective of a lack of political will to prioritise an intent to protect vulnerable peoples above that of national interest and the failure to apply a cosmopolitan standard that treats the 'self' as morally equivalent to the 'other'. This theme is well highlighted in the work of Brown and Bohm (2016, p. 909) who argue that the R2P is 'insufficiently cosmopolitan' because it locates the blame for mass violence with the government of the state, without paying heed to wider international causes.

The UN Secretary-General's 2014 (UN, 2014b, para. 17) report on Pillar Two of the R2P claims that 'poorly designed international assistance can inadvertently create or exacerbate social cleavages', yet fails to acknowledge that other means of engagement by the international community also exacerbate these same 'social cleavages'. Further, while the 11th report on the R2P by Secretary-General Guterres' (UN, 2019) on 'Lessons learned for prevention' makes a host of recommendations which speak to 'root cause' elements of atrocity prevention, the recommendations for international assistance in prevention efforts are more short term and 'operational' in their framing. Crucially, it doesn't seem to acknowledge that the *international* can be related to root cause elements. Evidently, there are still more lessons to be learned.

As Martin Shaw (2012) highlights, almost all genocidal actions – rather than simply being the result of 'bad' regimes and 'evil' leaders – have an international influence which stems from internationally supported structures of violence. Bohm and Brown (2021, p. 72) similarly argue that the R2P has generally ignored long-term systemic prevention because it is assumed that atrocities occur because of local factors, while global intervention is viewed as benign or positive. In reality, they argue, global actors have undermined atrocity prevention through a number of damaging policies such as International Monetary Fund (IMF) conditional assistance; unbalanced trade relationships; and driving demand for industries linked with the perpetuation of violence (see Bohm and Brown, 2021, pp. 82–87). As one example, they point to the actions of the IMF's 1990-91 'structural adjustment' programme in Rwanda and how this increased poverty and horizontal inequality as a prelude to the 1994 genocide (Bohm and Brown, 2021, p. 83). When it comes to driving demand for industries linked with atrocity, we might note, for instance, that 84 per cent of China's cotton is supplied from Xinjiang province, where an estimated 570,000 Uyghur Muslims have been forced to work as cotton pickers (UK Foreign Affairs Committee, 2021, p. 16). China supplies a quarter of the world's cotton, which means that the world's textile market is bound up in events occurring in Xinjiang (Anti-Slavery International and the CORE Coalition, 2020). Such examples highlight the complicity of international actors in underwriting local conditions of mass violence.

In alignment with these claims, Dunford and Neu (2019, p. 1083) contend that the R2P equates the problem of mass violence as one which simply exists *over there*: 'R2P does not bring into the picture potentially damaging practices of intervention that exist already. Members of the international community continue to be presented as helpers or bystanders, not as potential contributors to humanitarian crises'. According to Dunford and Neu (2019, p. 1090), most states fail to the meet the standard of good international citizens, as they themselves undertake irresponsible international actions that contribute to the commission of atrocity crimes. For instance, they argue that Western interference in the Middle-East has sought to stoke sectarian tensions for the self-interest of these Western states (Dunford and Neu, 2019, p. 1084). This has been evident, for example, in US and UK support for the Saudi Arabian regime as a balancer against Iranian influence in the region. Notably, this has helped fuel conflict via the civil war in Yemen, where a clash of the Sunni regime with Shia-based rebels has contributed to a major ongoing humanitarian crisis that has left an estimated 21.6 million people in need of humanitarian assistance (ReliefWeb, 2023).

Dunford and Neu also highlight the problem of the international arms trade as a contributor to cases of mass violence. They note, for instance, that the UK's involvement in the 2011 intervention in Libya came after a major surge in UK arms exports to Libya in the run-up year (Dunford and Neu, 2019, p. 1084). This is a practice that the UK continues to engage in. Evidence for this is supplied by the Campaign Against Arms Trade (CAAT), who note that, as of May 2022 published data, the UK has sold £7.1 billion worth of arms to Saudi Arabia since it began its campaign of bombing of Yemen in 2015; although CAAT estimates that this figure is more likely around £23 billion (CAAT, 2022).

A further case reflective of this is that of the Philippines. There the 'war on drugs' waged by authoritarian former leader Rodrigo Duterte has evidently been a clear case of crimes against humanity as understood under the 1998 Rome Statute, with systematic killings occurring against the members of the Philippine's population (Gallagher, Raffle, and Maulana, 2019, pp. 6–15). This has occurred against a backdrop of continued P5 state support for Duterte. For instance, the UK completed an arms deal with the regime worth £1.7 million in 2016 (Gallagher, Raffle, and Maulana, 2019, p. 17). While clearly the UK is not directly culpable for atrocity crimes committed in the Philippines, it nonetheless acted as an enabler for the Duterte regime by prioritising its own economic gains over considerations for stemming systematic violence in the Philippines.[12] This effectively suggests that systematic violence in the Philippines is perceived as acceptable if it provides the UK with economic benefits and therefore is reflective of the UK government's failure to respect the moral value of Philippine populations as equal to that of UK populations.[13]

A further example of negative harm violations comes from that of Chinese arms exports to Myanmar. In 2018, Myanmar was China's second largest arms export destination, receiving 105 million units from China (CNBC, 2019). Notably, this has occurred against the backdrop of what may be an ongoing campaign of genocide and ethnic cleansing in Myanmar against its Rohingya population; one which has left thousands dead and an estimated 700,000 displaced (BBC, 2020). This case provides another example of a state prioritising its own economic interests by holding close ties with a genocidal state – with China prioritising its global development strategy through the 'Belt and Road Initiative' – above a concern for promoting norms of human protection and fundamental rights.

Another example relating to Myanmar comes from a September 2020 report by Amnesty International which highlights global links between Myanmar Economic Holdings Limited (MEHL) and major international companies such as Japan-based Kirin Holdings, the company which brews the beer 'San Miguel' (Amnesty International, 2020a). MEHL is a business conglomerate directed and owned by Myanmar military personnel, including units and individuals under the Western Command: the regional command covering and overseeing operations in Rakhine State, including atrocities committed against the Rohingya population. Amnesty's Head of Business, Security and Human Rights, Mark Dummett, claims that MEHL shareholder records 'provide new evidence of how the Myanmar military benefits from MEHL's vast business empire and make clear that the military and MEHL are inextricably linked' (Amnesty International, 2020b). Yadanar Maung, spokesperson for civil society group 'Justice For Myanmar', notes that '[i]n providing this funding to military units, MEHL is boosting their resources and financing their operations which include crimes against humanity and war crimes' (Amnesty International, 2020b). Any company with global ties to MEHL has therefore funded atrocity crimes and failed to meet the negative duty to prevent atrocities and protect outsiders.

Arms deals, political, and economic ties between abusive regimes and other actors grant such actors a degree of legitimacy in the international sphere and provides a sense of diplomatic impunity from redress for their international crimes. They also directly enable systematic killing and violation of human rights by allowing regimes to fund and utilise arms supplied to them as instruments of harm. These ties are representative of an indirect form of harm that contributes to the perpetuation of mass violence and breaches of the R2P norm (Bohm and Brown, 2021).

Further, is it worth nothing that the sale of arms to oppressive states is a breach of international law as understood through Article 6 of the Arms Trade Treaty, which emphasises prohibitions on the sale of arms that would be used to facilitate violations of international humanitarian law, including crimes under the R2P (UN, 2013). While the treaty is not fully ratified (and notably not by the US), it represents emerging *opinio juris* on the need to halt arms sales to oppressive regimes (Pattison, 2017, p. 208). In this regard, the example above suggests that the UK is in violation of international law for its sale of arms to the Duterte and Saudi Arabian regimes (Perlo-Freeman, 2020). As Pattison (2017, p. 210) suggests, stronger mechanisms for stymying arms sales to oppressive regimes need to be established. This is a necessary step if states are to meet their negative duties to atrocity prevention. Such measures need to include greater efficacy in preventing sales, and punishment for those that violate prohibitions. Interestingly, the Secretary-General's 2014 (UN, 2014b, para. 60) report on the R2P highlights that '[i]nternational and regional actors should cooperate to stem the flow of small arms and light weapons, illicit financing and other forms of illegal trafficking, especially by strengthening cross-border customs cooperation and information sharing networks'. Yet the report fails to acknowledge that not only is this something the international community is weak at addressing, but that key global powers are some of the main actors involved in its proliferation.

The damage caused by indirect harms and the persistence of negative duty violations reflects a failure of mass atrocity prevention efforts. The failure to adopt cosmopolitan values by enshrining a standard provided for by the harm principle means that, currently, the R2P's approach to atrocity prevention ignores a key contributing factor to atrocities. This points to the need for reform to strengthen efforts to hold states accountable for their actions of harm which contravene their R2P (one such proposal is taken up in Chapter 7). Such reform can help the R2P in meeting a coherent standard of atrocity prevention, moving us beyond the portrayal of R2P crises as simply the result of 'bad' regimes and 'evil' leaders (Shaw, 2012) towards an approach that recognises that mass atrocities are bound up in global webs of state policy and therefore require concerted international action to avoid the imposition of harm.

3.7 The Statist Focus of the R2P

A final question to address in this chapter is whether it is the R2P's statist focus that is the underlying cause of the problems highlighted above. The relationship between the R2P and statism is important, for as noted in section 3.2, the R2P was intended to focus on the rights of individuals to be free from harm. If the R2P has lost this ethic to instead focus too much on the rights of states, then it may have lost its cosmopolitan purpose. If so, then the R2P will simply be reinforcing a state's right to shirk its responsibilities to vulnerable populations.

As noted earlier, the three pillar R2P system has in practice had its consensual elements prioritised by states. This is reflective of the fact that while Pillar One and Two were built out of strong stone – decades-old universal understandings of appropriate/legal state behaviour and a right of states to give and accept consensual international assistance – Pillar Three, on the other hand, was crafted from significantly weaker material, existing in a constant state of contention with well-enshrined norms of legal egalitarianism and non-intervention (Reike and Bellamy, 2010). For Hehir (2018, p. 100), this preference for consensual elements is problematic as 'the concept's contours have been moulded in a particular way so as to actually reaffirm practices and principles that are anathema to R2P's original normative agenda'. The consensus surrounding Pillar One has meant that the state-centric aspect of the R2P has been reinforced (Hehir, 2018, p. 104). As Welsh (2013, p. 373) notes, states have been supportive of the R2P because it does not demand a radical transformation of existing practice. China, for instance, while not outright rejecting the R2P's core tenets, has sought to emphasise the norm's consensual and state-based elements as a means of downplaying its interventionist aspects (Fung, 2019, pp. 135–141).

Moreover, this focus on the primary role of the host state has arguably allowed the norm to be co-opted for instrumental purposes (Hehir, 2018). For example, the Syrian regime has been able to declare that 'every state has an exclusive responsibility to protect its population against mass atrocities' (Syria, 2014) while it simultaneously continued an unpunished campaign of crimes against humanity and war crimes against its own population. Another ironic example comes from the case of Qatar, which exists as a member of R2P Group of Friends despite being widely reported as committing human rights abuses against its population: including the detaining of critics, acts of torture, and the continued repression of women (Amnesty, 2022). The lip-service paid to the R2P by states who carry out systematic human rights abuses is indicative of the fact that the R2P norm remains a matter of self-regulation by states. This problem is symptomatic of the failure to establish institutional structures to effectively regulate and hold states accountable to their R2P, while also failing to overcome the political barriers in motivating states to act on R2P principles. This further enhances the argument that reform is required which can serve to weaken the ability of states to shirk their R2P responsibilities.

Welsh (2016, p. 986) has also argued that the R2P, as taken in its 2001 ICISS iteration, presents a more ambitious and cosmopolitan goal of human protection. She claims this approach has subsequently been moved away from, evident in the R2P's 2005 World Summit form and consequent interpretation by states. Axworthy (2016, p. 973) has similarly argued that the World Summit outcome moved the R2P away from its original focus on human protection, wasting too much attention on debates over the right for humanitarian intervention. Such an argument further points towards the R2P's failure to prioritise concerns for individual's security with its detachment from this principle being a result of its continued preference for state's rights. In a similar vein, Cunliffe (2017) has drawn attention to the R2P's focus as a doctrine of 'exceptionalism'. For Cunliffe (2017, pp. 471–476), the R2P's strong reassertion of the state has normed intervention as exceptional in character and has contributed it its rapid acceptance by states. This practice of exceptionalism has meant that no action is expected of states to respond to cases of mass atrocities, for the R2P serves to enhance the 'discretionary power of the state' (Cunliffe, 2017, p. 477). This appears problematic from a cosmopolitan perspective, as it suggests that states' duties to act are superseded by states' right to not need to act. Indeed, this problem is reflected in how the 2005 version of R2P moved away from the ICISS criteria of a state being 'unable or unwilling' to protect its population from atrocities (ICISS, 2001, p. 29) to a criterion of 'manifestly failing' (UNGA, 2005, para. 139), which opens a greater level of ambiguity for when international action is required (Gallagher, 2014).

Despite these points however, a statist focus does not automatically diminish the R2P's cosmopolitan element. As noted previously, the R2P still attempts to invoke a sense of universality and the need to stop the most egregious of harms even in a world of diverse, pluralist, morally differentiated political communities. Further, and as is drawn out in more in section 4.5 of Chapter 4, the reality is that states are the most likely medium through which human protection can be realised in practice (Beardsworth, 2011). As Bellamy (2019, p. 97) argues when discussing the role of the state in promoting world peace, 'the state – for all its faults and all its violence – is indispensable to the cause of world peace'. Consequently, states need to be viewed as part of the solution and not simply the problem of mass violence (Bellamy and Luck, 2018, p. 33; Beardsworth, Brown, and Shapcott, 2019).

Indeed, the political reality of inconsistent R2P implementation is really indicative of the weaknesses of institutionalised means for implementing the R2P and holding states accountable to their commitments in practice, rather than its statist focus itself. This again points to the necessity of reform which can help enshrine a cosmopolitan standard of human protection, promoting a coherent approach to atrocity prevention, and consistently generating a response from states to act on cases of mass violence and human suffering.

Such reform requires a top-down and statist focus. This point may rile those who wish to move R2P debates away from the agenda of high politics, to instead focus on the local level and grassroots protection agendas (see Welsh, 2013; 2016; Ferguson and Carver, 2021). But the actions of states are vital to meeting the goals set out under the R2P. As such, enforcing states to follow appropriate behaviour via top-down external regulation is a crucial component of the R2P agenda.

In contrast, Welsh (2016, p. 989) argues that we should focus on bottom-up approaches over top-down ones, claiming that macro-level structural reform – regarding institutional change to bodies such as the UN Security Council – should be moved away from, with a focus instead on implementing micro-level policies at the intrastate level. Welsh argues that the contestation surrounding the R2P's potential undermining of the longstanding norm of sovereign equality has led to attempts to downplay the remedial duty of the international responsibility to act on matters of R2P concern (Welsh, 2013, p. 394). For her, this leads to a recommendation to avoid the 'spectre of hierarchy and external enforcement' (Welsh, 2013, p. 395) and in doing so, she implies that any potential reform measures should not focus on improving the external enforcement of the R2P norm.

However, to disregard the idea of external enforcement in favour of micro-level measures would serve to reinforce current untenable practice. Focusing solely on the domestic level implementation of the R2P would maintain conceptual misgivings regarding atrocity prevention, as well as the selective imperative of states to act on R2P crises. As a result, this would promote practice which runs antithetical to a cosmopolitan standard to act on the moral imperative to alleviate mass human suffering.

To clarify, this is not at all to suggest that bottom-up micro-level changes – such as the role of NGOs and local peacebuilding networks – are unimportant. Bellamy and Luck (2018, Chap. 5) for instance have highlighted the domestic factors which contribute to the cause of atrocity crimes, and the importance of domestic level actors in preventing their occurrence. Such factors are indeed vital for atrocity prevention, particularly in the context of structural prevention methods at the domestic level as the way to help address underlying causes of atrocity crimes.[14] However, what we should emphasise is that micro-level actions need to run alongside calls for top-down reforms, and can't act as a substitute for them.

As the above sections of this chapter have demonstrated, external factors and international-based reform are imperative for creating a fully functioning R2P norm. At the conceptual level, disregarding external enforcement is problematic, for it ignores the international and external based factors which partly account for cases of mass atrocity violence. It also ignores the failings at the international level of states to meet their moral obligations, such as failures to act to address crises of vulnerable refugees fleeing atrocities. At the practical level, a disregard for external enforcement is also problematic, as top-down reform will be important for enforcing accountability for R2P commitments.

One weakness of the current R2P approach is that it essentially exists as a self-regulating mechanism, which is least likely to be effective on the states most likely to commit atrocity crimes and human rights abuses. States that commit atrocities do so out of rational cost-benefit calculations. Such cases tend to involve autocratic regimes committing atrocity crimes as a rational calculation based on their wish to preserve their own survival above all else (Hehir, 2018, p. 161; Bellamy and Luck, 2018, pp. 116–120) and the knowledge that they can get away with committing atrocities without fear of reprisal (Bellamy and McLoughlin, 2018, p. 200). Further, cost-benefit calculations also exist within those states considering whether to intervene externally or whether to pursue certain policies at the international level. For these states, the R2P competes with both normative and moral interests concerning the likes of the UNSC's responsibility to international peace and security (Morris, 2013); and also, with instrumental interests, such as their ties with oppressive regimes, or domestic duties (Bellamy and Luck, 2018, pp. 76–77). At its heart, these problems are reflective of what Bellamy and Luck (2018, p. 107) refer to as the greatest barrier to R2P implementation, decision-making, sovereignty. That is, the wish of sovereign powers to maintain control over their own decision-making powers which has led to weakness in response to atrocity crises where their interests are not deemed to be at stake.

It is in part external enforcement and regulation via top-down reforms that is necessary to rework states' cost-benefit calculations in regard to consistently implementing their R2P at the domestic and international level. This requires enforcement of the R2P by states in their response to atrocity crises abroad, as well as means for enforcing behaviour consistent with the goal of atrocity prevention. This points to the need for the creation of new, or reform to existing institutional structures, that can successfully hold states accountable, while aiding them in acting on their R2P obligations.

3.8 Conclusion

The R2P is cosmopolitan in aim and is reflective of (thin) cosmopolitical tenets in its promotion of human protection. The R2P aligns with general cosmopolitan requirements of individualism, egalitarianism, and universality. Beyond this, the R2P also holds a deeper theoretical connection with cosmopolitan human protection through its attempt to promote duties of atrocity prevention and response. Though while the R2P holds a theoretical relationship with a cosmopolitan duty to secure the fundamental rights of the vulnerable, the actual practice of the R2P's implementation fails to enmesh this into a consistent empirical reality wherein protection against mass atrocity crimes is assured.

As outlined in Chapter 2, cosmopolitanism demands a responsibility to act to alleviate the suffering of others. This chapter has argued, however, that the current R2P approach holds weak compliance pull as it fails to promote a demand to respond to cases of mass violence, or to promote international action which is conducive to the goal of atrocity prevention. The R2P remains largely a response to symptoms of atrocity crimes rather than its causes, and also fails to meet the standard of the cosmopolitan harm principle.

The weakness of institutionalised means for implementing the R2P has meant that the doctrine has served as a matter of self-regulation for states. This has upheld the discretionary power of the state to act on cases of mass atrocities as it sees fit. Further, as the R2P has been interpreted to preference its consensual elements, this has in practice served to undermine the very purpose of the R2P and has led to states being able to pay lip-service to cosmopolitan values while simultaneously committing mass human rights abuses at home. This does not highlight a conceptual fallacy of the R2P per se, as ultimately states are required for realising the R2P's cosmopolitan goals. However, it does highlight the need for reform to overcome inaction by better institutionalising the means for acting on cosmopolitan protection duties, in addition to better means for holding states accountable to their 2005 commitments.

Together these factors point to what Hehir (2017) has called the 'logical necessity' of reform. The R2P is representative of what could be considered a cosmopolitan purpose in attempting to overcome the problem of mass atrocity violence, but evidently, in practice, this cosmopolitan goal is not being realised. This points toward the need for reform that can aid in overcoming the R2P's challenges. Reinforcing the cosmopolitan elements of the R2P framework can help move it in the direction of achieving its purpose of stymying mass atrocity crimes. This will require reform of relevant international structures that can serve to better implement cosmopolitan responsibilities under the R2P. Any reforms will also have to attempt to address the political barriers which stand in the way of enhancing the R2P.

This is a difficult task. However, the aim here is to achieve modest gains, which at the very least can promote reform to work *incrementally* towards the aim of meeting the cosmopolitan demand for duties towards securing the fundamental rights of the most vulnerable. It is to the question of how this can be achieved that the following chapter now turns.

Notes

1 A cosmopolitan demand to secure the fundamental rights of all human individuals via the application of positive and negative duties.
2 As part of this Pillar One responsibility there is logically an implicit assumption that the duty not to inflict atrocities extends to outside populations as well.
3 To claim that the R2P is a Western concept ignores the crucial role that non-Western actors have played in shaping the concept. For instance, the R2P's atrocity crimes

criteria stems in-part from the African Union's 2000 Constitutive Act, Article 4(h). One of the ICISS co-chairs was an Algerian diplomat, Mohamed Sahnoun. And it was Ghanaian UN Secretary-General, Kofi Annan, that pushed the concept onto the UN's agenda despite opposition from his advisors (see Stefan, 2021).

4 See for instance, Harff (2003), Midlarsky (2005), and Bellamy (2012) for works addressing atrocity risk factors.

5 As of 1 January 2023.

6 Arguably, the intervention in Libya, mandated through UNSC resolution 1973, was an example of where R2P Pillar Three logic presented itself in real-world practice (Glanville, 2021, pp. 141–143).

7 Bellamy (2022) has argued, however, that the idea that force could not have been used to good effect in Syria is a shibboleth.

8 The international community does generally meet its collective responsibility in relation to Pillar Two positive assistance. As of the latest data (31 October 2022), there are 87,000+ personnel deployed across 12 peacekeeping operations (UN, 2022). The UNSC resolutions mandating these peacekeeping missions are often accompanied by references to the R2P (See GCR2P - www.globalr2p.org/resour ces/un-security-council-resolutions-and-presidential-statements-referencing-r2p/).

9 Though a support mechanism with capability to produce at least some useful action (see Russo, 2020). As is argued in Chapter 6, the UNSC need not be entirely relied upon for Pillar Three response.

10 See for instance the UNSC vote and meeting records in May 2014 over a draft resolution to refer the situation in Syria to the ICC (UNSC, 2014b; UNSC, 2014a).

11 The US Launched a unilateral strike against Syrian installations previously in April 2017 as a response to the reported use of chemical weapons attacks.

12 The UK is also culpable of this in Bahrain, where it has declared its concern for human rights abuses, but maintains that Bahrain is a vital ally for the UK in the Gulf Region. In April 2018, for example, Prince Andrew formally opened a new UK military base in Mina Salman (ADHRB, 2018).

13 As per a thin-cosmopolitan position, the state has a right to prioritise the interests of its own citizens at a general level, but this is morally impermissible if it results in significantly worsening the lives of outsiders to the point that their fundamental interests are threatened.

14 Such measures include the promotion of basic rights, political participation, poverty reduction, justice, and security (Bellamy and Luck 2018: pp. 117–120). These structural prevention aspects do, however, require a greater conceptual understanding of how international factors affect structural causes of atrocity violence (see Bohm and Brown, 2021).

References

Acharya, A. 2004. How Ideas Spread: Whose Norms Matter? Norm Localization and Institutional Change in Asian Regionalism. *International Organization*. 58(2), pp. 239–275.

Ainley, K. 2017. From Atrocity Crimes to Human Rights: Expanding the Focus of the Responsibility to Protect. *Global Responsibility to Protect*. 9(3), pp. 243–266.

Americans for Democracy and Human Rights in Bahrain 2018. UK Opens New Military Base in Bahrain Despite Gulf Kingdom's Human Rights Violations.

[Accessed 4 August 2019]. Available from: www.adhrb.org/2018/04/uk- opens-new-military-base-in-bahrain-despite-gulf-kingdoms-human-rights-violations/.

Amnesty International 2020a. *Military LTD: The Company Financing Human Rights Abuses in Myanmar* [Online]. [Accessed 11 September 2020]. Available from: www.amnesty.org/download/Documents/ASA1629692020ENGLISH.PDF.

Amnesty International 2020b. Myanmar: Leaked Documents Reveal Global Business Ties to Military Crimes. [Accessed 11 September 2020]. Available from: www.amnesty.org/en/latest/news/2020/09/mehl-military-links-to-global-businesses/.

Amnesty International 2022. Qatar. [Accessed 19 July 2023]. Available from: https://www.amnesty.org/en/location/middle-east-and-north-africa/qatar/report-qatar/.

Anti-Slavery International and the CORE Coalition 2020. Written submission by Anti-Slavery International and the CORE Coalition. [Accessed 9 June 2021] Available from: https://committees.parliament.uk/writtenevidence/13587/pdf/.

Axworthy, L. 2016. Resetting the Narrative on Peace and Security *In*: A. J. Bellamy and T. Dunne, eds. *The Oxford Handbook of the Responsibility to Protect.* Oxford: Oxford University Press.

Badescu, C.G. and Weiss, T.G. 2010. Misrepresenting R2P and Advancing Norms: An Alternative Spiral? *International Studies Perspectives.* **11**(4), pp. 354–374.

BBC 2013. Barack Obama Warns Syria Chemical Arms a 'Game Changer'. [Accessed 24 November 2018]. Available from: www.bbc.co.uk/news/world-middle-east-22318749.

BBC 2020. Myanmar Rohingya: World Court Orders Prevention of Genocide. [Accessed 24 January 2020]. Available from: www.bbc.co.uk/news/world-asia-51221029.

Beardsworth, R. 2011. *Cosmopolitanism and International Relations Theory.* Cambridge: Polity Press.

Beardsworth, R., Brown, G.W., and Shapcott, R. (eds.). 2019. *The State and Cosmopolitan Responsibilities.* Oxford: Oxford University Press.

Bellamy, A.J. 2006. Whither the Responsibility to Protect? Humanitarian Intervention and the 2005 World Summit. *Ethics & International Affairs.* **20**(2), pp. 143–169.

Bellamy, A.J. 2012. Mass Killing and the Politics of Legitimacy: Empire and the Ideology of Selective Extermination. *Australian Journal of Politics & History.* **58**(2), pp. 159–180.

Bellamy, A.J. 2014. *Responsibility to Protect: A Defense.* Oxford: Oxford University Press Oxford.

Bellamy, A.J. 2015. The Responsibility to Protect Turns Ten. *Ethics & International Affairs.* **29**(2), pp. 161–185.

Bellamy, A.J. 2019. *World Peace (And How We Can Achieve It).* Oxford: Oxford University Press.

Bellamy, A.J. 2022. *Syria Betrayed: Atrocities, War, and the Failure of International Diplomacy.* New York: Columbia University Press.

Bellamy, A.J. and Luck, E.C. 2018. *The Responsibility to Protect: From Promise to Practice.* Cambridge: Polity Press.

Bellamy, A.J. and Lupel, A. 2015. *Why We Fail: Obstacles to the Effective Prevention of Mass Atrocities* [Online]. New York: International Peace Institute. [Accessed 14 December 2018]. Available from: www.ipinst.org/wp-content/uploads/2015/06/IPI-E-pub-Why-We-Fail.pdf.

Bellamy, A.J. and McLoughlin, S. 2018. *Rethinking Humanitarian Intervention.* London: Palgrave Macmillan.

Bellamy, A.J. and Tacheva, B. 2019. R2P and the Emergence of Responsibilities Across Borders *In*: R. Beardsworth, G. W. Brown and R. Shapcott, eds. *The State and Cosmopolitan Responsibilities.* Oxford: Oxford University Press, pp. 15–40.

Bellamy, A.J. and Williams, P.D. 2011. The New Politics of Protection? Côte d'Ivoire, Libya and the Responsibility to Protect. *International Affairs.* **87**(4), pp. 825–850.

Bloomfield, A. 2017. Norm Complexity and Contestation: Unpacking the R2P *In*: A. Hehir and R. W. Murray, eds. *Protecting Human Rights in the 21st Century.* London: Routledge.

Bohm, A. and Brown, G.W. 2021. R2P and Prevention: The International Community and Its Role in the Determinants of Mass Atrocity. *Global Responsibility to Protect.* **13**(1), pp. 60–95.

Brown, G.W. and Bohm, A. 2016. Introducing Jus Ante Bellum as a Cosmopolitan Approach to Humanitarian Intervention. *European Journal of International Relations.* **22**(4), pp. 897–919.

Butchard, P.M. 2020. *The Responsibility to Protect and the Failures of the United Nations Security Council.* Oxford: Hart Publishing.

CAAT 2022. UK Arms to Saudi Arabia. [Accessed 29 September 2022]. Available from: https://caat.org.uk/homepage/stop-arming-saudi-arabia/uk-arms-to-saudi-arabia/.

Carayannis, T. and Fowlis, M. 2017. Lessons from African Union–United Nations Cooperation in Peace Operations in the Central African Republic. *African Security Review.* **26**(2), pp. 220–236.

Carayannis, T. and Lombard, L. 2015a. A Concluding Note on the Failure and Future of Peacebuilding in CAR *In*: T. Carayannis and L. Lombard, eds. *Making Sense of the Central African Republic: The Struggle for Democracy.* London: Zed Books, pp. 319–341.

Carayannis, T. and Lombard, L. (eds.). 2015b. *Making Sense of the Central African Republic: The Struggle for Democracy.* London: Zed Books.

Cederman, L.E., Weidmann, N.B., and Gleditsch, K.S. 2011. Horizontal Inequalities and Ethnonationalist Civil War: A Global Comparison. *American Political Science Review.* **105**(3), pp. 478–495.

CNBC 2019. China, the World's Second Largest Defense Spender, Becomes a Major Arms Exporter. [Accessed 22 April 2020]. Available from: www.cnbc.com/2019/09/27/china-a-top-defense-spender-becomes-major-arms-exporter.html.

Collins, L. 2021. The Central African Republic and the Responsibility to Protect. *ECR2P Fresh Perspectives Blog.*

Cunliffe, P. 2017. The Doctrine of the 'Responsibility to Protect' as a Practice of Political Exceptionalism. *European Journal of International Relations.* **23**(2), pp. 466–486.

Dahl-Eriksen, T. 2016. R2P and the Thin Cosmopolitan Imagination. *Fletcher F. World Aff.* **40**, pp. 123–137.

De Vries, L. and Mehler, A. 2019. The Limits of Instrumentalizing Disorder: Reassessing the Neopatrimonial Perspective in the Central African Republic. *African Affairs.* **118**(471), pp. 307–327.

Deitelhoff, N. 2019. Is the R2P Failing? The Controversy about Norm Justification and Norm Application of the Responsibility to Protect. *Global Responsibility to Protect.* **11**(2), pp. 149–171.

Deitelhoff, N. and Zimmermann, L. 2020. Things We Lost in the Fire: How Different Types of Contestation Affect the Robustness of International Norms. *International Studies Review*. 22(1), pp. 51–76.

Dunford, R. and Neu, M. 2019. The Responsibility to Protect in a World of Already Existing Intervention. *European Journal of International Relations*. 25(4), pp. 1080–1102.

Evans, G. 2008. *The Responsibility to Protect: Ending Mass Atrocity Crimes Once and for All*. Washington DC: Brookings Institution Press.

Ferguson, K. and Carver, F. 2021. *Being the Difference: A Primer for States Wishing to Prevent Atrocity Crimes in the Mid-Twenty-first Century* [Online]. [Accessed 15 December 2021]. Available from: https://img1.wsimg.com/blobby/go/131c96cc-7e6f-4c06-ae37-6550dbd85dde/Being%20the%20difference%20Final.pdf.

Finnemore, M. and Sikkink, K. 1998. International Norm Dynamics and Political Change. *International Organization*. 52(4), pp. 887–917.

Fung, C. 2019. *China and Intervention at the UN Security Council: Reconciling Status*. Oxford: Oxford University Press.

Gallagher, A. 2014. What Constitutes a 'Manifest Failing'? Ambiguous and Inconsistent Terminology and the Responsibility to Protect. *International Relations*. 28(4), pp. 428–444.

Gallagher, A. 2015. The Responsibility to Protect Ten Years on from the World Summit: A Call to Manage Expectations. *Global Responsibility to Protect*. 7(3–4), pp. 254–274.

Gallagher, A. 2022. An International Responsibility to Develop in Order to Protect? A Responsibility Too Far. *Journal of International Relations and Development*. 25(4), pp. 1–26.

Gallagher, A., Raffle, E., and Maulana, Z. 2019. Failing to Fulfil the Responsibility to Protect: The War on Drugs as Crimes Against Humanity in the Philippines. *The Pacific Review*. 33(2), pp. 247–277.

Getachew, A. 2019. The Limits of Sovereignty as Responsibility. *Constellations*. 26(2), pp. 225–240.

Gholiagha, S. and Loges, B. 2020. Telling the Story of R2P: The Emplotment of R2P in the UN Security Council's Debates on Libya *In*: C. T. Hunt and P. Orchard, eds. *Constructing the Responsibility to Protect: Contestation and Consolidation*. London: Routledge, pp. 69–88.

Glanville, L. 2016. Does R2P Matter? Interpreting the Impact of a Norm. *Cooperation and Conflict*. 51(2), pp. 184–199.

Glanville, L. 2021. *Sharing Responsibility: The History and Future of Protection from Atrocities*. Princeton, NJ: Princeton University Press.

Glanville, L. and Pattison, J. 2021. Where to Protect? Prioritization and the Responsibility to Protect. *Ethics & International Affairs*. 35(2), pp. 213–225.

Glanville, L. and Widmaier, W.W. 2020. R2P and the Benefits of Norm Ambiguity. *In*: C.T. Hunt and P. Orchard, eds. *Constructing the Responsibility to Protect: Contestation and Consolidation*. London: Routledge, pp. 50–68.

Global Centre for the Responsibility to Protect n.d. UN Security Council Resolutions and Presidential Statements Referencing R2P. [Accessed 1 January 2023]. Available from: www.globalr2p.org/resources/335.

Harff, B. 2003. No lessons Learned from the Holocaust? Assessing Risks of Genocide and Political Mass Murder since 1955. *American Political Science Review*. 97(1), pp. 57–73.

Hehir, A. 2013. The Permanence of Inconsistency: Libya, the Security Council, and the Responsibility to Protect. *International Security*. 38(1), pp. 137–159.

Hehir, A. 2017. "Utopian in the Right Sense": The Responsibility to Protect and the Logical Necessity of Reform. *Ethics & International Affairs*. 31(3), pp. 335–355.

Hehir, A. 2018. *Hollow Norms and the Responsibility to Protect*. London: Palgrave Macmillan.

Hubert, D. and Blätter, A. 2012. The Responsibility to Protect as International Crimes Prevention. *Global Responsibility to Protect*. 4(1), pp. 33–66.

Human Rights Watch 2021. Bahrain: Events of 2020. [Accessed 3 August 2021]. Available from: www.hrw.org/world-report/2021/country-chapters/bahrain.

Hunt, C.T. and Orchard, P. 2020. Introduction: Consolidation and contestation of the Responsibility to Protect. *In*: Hunt, C.T. and Orchard, P. eds. *Constructing the Responsibility to Protect: Contestation and Consolidation*. London: Routledge, pp. 1–27.

International Commission on Intervention and State Sovereignty 2001. The Responsibility to Protect: Report of the International Commission on Intervention and State Sovereignty. [Accessed 14 December 2018]. Available from: http://resp onsibilitytoprotect.org/ICISS%20Report.pdf.

Jacob, C. 2021. Institutionalizing Prevention at the UN: International Organization Reform as a Site of Norm Contestation. *Global Governance: A Review of Multilateralism and International Organizations*. 27(2), pp. 179–201.

Jarvis, S. 2022. The R2P and Atrocity Prevention: Contesting Human Rights as a Threat to International Peace and Security. *European Journal of International Security*. **First View**, pp. 1–19.

Katzenstein, P.J. 1996. Introduction: Alternative Perspectives on National Security *In*: P. J. Katzenstein, ed. *The Culture of National Security: Norms and Identity in World Politics*. New York: Columbia University Press, pp. 1–32.

Linklater, A. 2001. Citizenship, Humanity, and Cosmopolitan Harm Conventions. *International Political Science Review*. 22(3), pp. 261–277.

Mars, E.-C. 2015. Too Little, Too Late: Failing to Prevent Atrocities in the Central African Republic. *Global Centre for the Responsibility to Protect Occassional Paper Series*. 7.

McLoughlin, S. 2014. Rethinking the Structural Prevention of Mass Atrocities. *Global Responsibility to Protect*. 6(4), pp. 407–429.

McLoughlin, S. 2019. Atrocity Prevention, National Resilience, and Implementation *In*: C. Jacob and M. Mennecke, eds. *Implementing the Responsibility to Protect: A Future Agenda*. London: Routledge, pp. 141–155.

Midlarsky, M.I. 2005. *The Killing Trap: Genocide in the Twentieth Century*. Cambridge: Cambridge University Press.

Morris, J. 2013. Libya and Syria: R2P and the Spectre of the Swinging Pendulum. *International Affairs*. 89(5), pp. 1265–1283.

Mulford, F. 2022. Circumventing the Responsibility to Protect in Yemen: Rhetorical Adaptation and the United Nations Security Council. *Global Responsibility to Protect*. 14(1), pp. 75–104.

Newman, E. 2016. What Prospects for Common Humanity in a Divided World? The Scope for RtoP in a Transitional International Order. *International Politics*. 53(1), pp. 32–48.

Nishikawa, Y. 2020. The Reality of Protecting the Rohingya: An Inherent Limitation of the Responsibility to Protect. *Asian Security*. 16(1), pp. 90–106.

OCHA 2023. Central African Republic: Situation Report. [Accessed 24 February 2023]. Available from: https://reports.unocha.org/en/country/car/.

Orchard, P. 2020. Contestation, Norms and the Responsibility to Protect as a Regime. In: C. T. Hunt & P. Orchard, eds. *Constructing the Responsibility to Protect: Contestation and Consolidation*. London: Routledge, pp. 28–49.

Panke, D. and Petersohn, U. 2012. Why International Norms Disappear Sometimes. *European Journal of International Relations*. 18(4), pp. 719–742.

Paris, R. 2014. The 'Responsibility to Protect' and the Structural Problems of Preventive Humanitarian Intervention. *International Peacekeeping*. 21(5), pp. 569–603.

Pattison, J. 2015. Mapping the Responsibilities to Protect: A Typology of International Duties. *Global Responsibility to Protect*. 7(2), pp. 190–210.

Pattison, J. 2017. Guns vs Troops: The Ethics of Supplying Arms In: A. Hehir and R. W. Murray, eds. *Protecting Human Rights in the 21st Century*. London: Routledge, pp. 201–214.

Pattison, J. 2022. Beyond Imperfection: The Demands of the International Responsibility to Protect. *Global Responsibility to Protect*. 14(1), pp. 105–108.

Pedersen, M.B. 2021. The Rohingya Crisis, Myanmar, and R2P 'Black Holes'. *Global Responsibility to Protect*. 1(aop), pp. 1–30.

Perlo-Freeman, S. 2020. The ATT and War Profiteering: The Case of the UK. *Global Responsibility to Protect*. 12(2), pp. 178–201.

Pogge, T.W. 2002. *World Poverty and Human Rights*. Cambridge: Polity.

Reike, R. and Bellamy, A. 2010. The Responsibility to Protect and International Law. *Global Responsibility to Protect*. 2(3), pp. 267–286.

Reike, R., Sharma, S.K., and Welsh, J.M. 2015. Conceptualizing the Responsibility to Prevent In: S.K. Sharma and J.M. Welsh, eds. *The Responsibility to Prevent: Overcoming the Challenges of Atrocity Prevention*. Oxford: Oxford University Press, pp. 21–37.

ReliefWeb 2023. Yemen Humanitarian Response Plan 2023. [Accessed 24 February 2023]. Available from: https://reliefweb.int/report/yemen/yemen-human itarian-response-plan-2023-january-2023.

Russo, J.B. 2020. R2P in Syria and Myanmar: Norm Violation and Advancement. *Global Responsibility to Protect*. 12(2), pp. 211–233.

Serrano, M. 2015. National Focal Points for R2P: Institutionalizing the Responsibility to Prevent In: S.K. Sharma and J.M. Welsh, eds. *The Responsibility to Prevent: Overcoming the Challenges of Atrocity Prevention*. New York: Oxford University Press, pp. 83–100.

Shapcott, R. 2008. Anti-cosmopolitanism, Pluralism and the Cosmopolitan Harm Principle. *Review of International Studies*. 34(2), pp. 185–205.

Shaw, M. 2012. From Comparative to International Genocide Studies: The International Production of Genocide in 20th-century Europe. *European Journal of International Relations*. 18(4), pp. 645–668.

Stefan, C.G. 2021. The Responsibility to Protect: Locating Norm Entrepreneurship. *Ethics & International Affairs*. 35(2), pp. 197–211.

Stensrud, E.E. 2021. The Rohingya Crisis, the Democratisation Discourse, and the Absence of an Atrocity Prevention Lens. *Global Responsibility to Protect*. 13(2–3), pp. 218–243.

Strauss, E. 2015. Institutional Capacities of the United Nations to Prevent and Halt Atrocity Crimes In: S. K. Sharma and J. M. Welsh, eds. *The Responsibility to Prevent: Overcoming the Challenges of Atrocity Prevention*. Oxford: Oxford University Press, pp. 38–82.

Syria 2014. Statement by the Syrian Arab Republic at the Informal Interactive Dialogue on the Responsibility to Protect. [Accessed 19 June 2019]. Available from: www.responsibilitytoprotect.org/Syria%20(transcribed).pdf.

Tacheva, B. and Brown, G.W. 2015. Global Constitutionalism and the Responsibility to Protect. *Global Constitutionalism*. 4(3), pp. 428–467.

The World Bank 2022. *The World Bank In Central African Republic* [Online]. [Accessed 29 September 2022]. Available from: www.worldbank.org/en/country/centralafricanrepublic/overview.

UK Foreign Affairs Committee 2021. *Never Again: The UK's Responsibility to Act on Atrocities in Xinjiang and Beyond* [Online]. [Accessed 8 July 2021]. Available from: https://committees.parliament.uk/publications/6624/documents/71430/default/.

UN 2012. Responsibility to Protect: Timely and Decisive Response. Report of the Secretary-General. A/66/874–S/2012/578. [Accessed 9 August 2021]. Available from: https://undocs.org/A/66/874.

UN 2013. The Arms Trade Treaty. [Accessed 19 June 2019]. Available from: https://unoda-web.s3-accelerate.amazonaws.com/wp-content/uploads/2013/06/English7.pdf.

UN 2014a. *Framework of Analysis for Atrocity Crimes: A Tool for Prevention* [Online]. [Accessed 29 March 2019]. Available from: www.un.org/en/genocideprevention/documents/about-us/Doc.3_Framework%20of%20Analysis%20for%20Atrocity%20Crimes_EN.pdf.

UN 2014b. Fulfilling Our Collective Responsibility: International Assistance and the Responsibility to Protect. Report of the Secretary-General. A/68/947–S/2014/449. [Accessed 30 April 2019]. Available from: http://responsibilitytoprotect.org/N1446 379.pdf.

UN 2018. Responsibility to Protect: From Early Warning to Early Action. Report of the Secretary-General. A/72/884–S/2018/525. [Accessed 25 March 2019]. Available from: http://www.globalr2p.org/media/files/1808811e.pdf.

UN 2019. Responsibility to Protect: Lessons Learned for Prevention. Report of the Secretary-General. A/73/898–S/2019/463. [Accessed 8 July 2019]. Available from: https://www.un.org/ga/search/view_doc.asp?symbol=A/73/898.

UN 2020. Prioritizing Prevention and Strengthening Response: Women and the Responsibility to Protect. Report of the Secretary-General. A/74/964 – S/2020/501. [Accessed 8 September 2020]. Available from: www.un.org/en/genocideprevention/documents/2009954E.pdf.

UN 2021. *Advancing Atrocity Prevention: Work of the Office on Genocide Prevention and the Responsibility to Protect. Report of the Secretary-General*. A/75/863–S/2021/424 [Online]. [Accessed 14 June 2021]. Available from: https://undocs.org/en/A/75/863.

UN 2022. UN Peacekeeping Data. [Accessed 22 February 2023]. Available from: https://peacekeeping.un.org/en/data.

UNGA 2005. Resolution adopted by the General Assembly on 16 September 2005. A/RES/60/1. [Accessed 15 November 2018]. Available from: www.un.org/en/development/desa/population/migration/generalassembly/docs/globalcompact/A_RES_60_1.pdf.

UNGA 2009. Implementing the Responsibility to Protect Report of the Secretary-General. A/63/677. [Accessed 3 December 2018]. Available from: https://undocs.org/A/63/677.

UNHRC 2018. Report of the independent International Fact-finding Mission on Myanmar. A/HRC/39/64. [Accessed 15 November 2018]. Available from: www.ohchr.org/Documents/HRBodies/HRCouncil/FFM-Myanmar/A_HRC_39_64.pdf.

UNSC 2014a. 7180th Meeting. S/PV.7180. [Accessed 2 August 2021]. Available from: https://undocs.org/en/S/PV.7180.

UNSC 2014b. Draft Resolution. S/2014/348. [Accessed 2 August 2021]. Available from: https://undocs.org/en/S/2014/348.

UNSC 2017. Statement by the President of the Security Council. S/PRST/2017/22. [Accessed 15 November 2018]. Available from: www.securitycouncilreport.org/atf/cf/%7B65BFCF9B-6D27-4E9C-8CD3-CF6E4FF96FF9%7D/s_prst_2017_22.pdf.

UNSC 2022. Resolution 2669. S/RES/2669. [Accessed 10 January 2023]. Available from: https://documents-dds-ny.un.org/doc/UNDOC/GEN/N22/767/33/PDF/N2276733.pdf?OpenElement.

Vilmer, J.-B.J. 2018. The Responsibility Not to Veto: A Genealogy. *Global Governance*. **24**(3), pp. 331–349.

VOX 2017. President Trump Speaks After Ordering Attacks on Syria. [Accessed 24 November 2018]. Available from: www.vox.com/world/2017/4/6/15214942/trump-syria-bombing-attack.

Walzer, M. 1977. *Just and Unjust Wars*. New York: Basic Books.

Weiss, T.G. 2006. R2P after 9/11 and the World Summit. *Wis. Int'l LJ*. **24**(3), pp. 741–760.

Welsh, J.M. 2013. Norm Contestation and the Responsibility to Protect. *Global Responsibility to Protect*. **5**(4), pp. 365–396.

Welsh, J.M. 2014. Implementing the 'Responsibility to Protect': Catalyzing Debate and Building Capacity *In*: A. Betts and P. Orchard, eds. *Implementation and World Politics: How International Norms Change Practice*. Oxford: Oxford University Press, pp. 124–143.

Welsh, J.M. 2016. R2P's Next Ten Years: Deepening and Extending the Consensus *In*: A.J. Bellamy and T. Dunne, eds. *The Oxford Handbook of the Responsibility to Protect*. Oxford: Oxford University Press, pp. 984–1000.

Welsh, J.M. 2019. Norm Robustness and the Responsibility to Protect. *Journal of Global Security Studies*. **4**(1), pp. 53–72.

Wheeler, N.J. 2000. *Saving Strangers: Humanitarian Intervention in International Society*. Oxford: Oxford University Press.

Wiener, A. 2009. Enacting Meaning-in-use: Qualitative Research on Norms and International Relations. *Review of International Studies*. **35**(1), pp. 175–193.

Wiener, A. 2018. *Contestation and Constitution of Norms in Global International Relations*. Cambridge: Cambridge University Press.

Wyatt, S.J. 2019. *The Responsibility to Protect and a Cosmopolitan Approach to Human Protection*. London: Palgrave Macmillan.

4 A Transitional Cosmopolitan Approach to R2P Reform

4.1 Introduction

So far we have explored what a cosmopolitan vision for the R2P might look like (Chapter 2), and then used this standard to measure the strength of current atrocity prevention/response efforts and where these efforts fail to realise cosmopolitan standards in practice (Chapter 3). Having identified areas of weakness, the rest of this book analyses avenues for reform through which the R2P can be strengthened.

But before we can get stuck into analysing specific reform measures, it needs to be clear how reforms ought to be assessed; how we can understand their transformative potential and practicality. Hence, this chapter lays out the approach used for assessing reform measures in the subsequent chapters of the book. Conscious of the fact that the R2P operates in a world of competing sovereign prerogatives where aspirational cosmopolitan protection demands spelled out in the previous chapters are difficult to achieve, this chapter promotes an approach which has been labelled by some scholars as one of *transitional cosmopolitanism* (Glenn, 2013; Stone-Sweet and Ryan, 2018; Beardsworth, Brown, and Shapcott, 2019; Brown and Jarvis, 2019; Brown and Hobbs, 2022). Transitional cosmopolitanism calls for incremental steps in the pursuit of normative progress, working in response to practical obstacles to reform. This chapter offers the criteria of the effectiveness and feasibility of potential reforms as a means of enhancing the methodological application of the transitional cosmopolitan approach, and sets out a framework of tests used for analysing the effectiveness and feasibility of reforms examined in Chapters 5 through 7.

The chapter proceeds in four main sections. Section 4.2 spells out the basis of transitional cosmopolitanism. It argues that the transitional cosmopolitan approach is one which attempts to merge together an aspiration for normative progress with practical demands of contextualism. Section 4.3 seeks to enhance the transitional cosmopolitan approach by proposing that the criteria of effectiveness and feasibility should be central considerations when examining the potential for reform progress. Section 4.4 lays out a series of

DOI: 10.4324/9781003394105-4

tests which can be used to assess the criteria of effectiveness and feasibility, which will be applied in later chapters when examining potential reforms. Finally, Section 4.5 calls for a statist focus when considering reform, arguing that the transitional cosmopolitan approach requires that analysis of reform work among the reality of competing state interests at the international level in order to promote the feasibility of progress (versus rendering the state as arbitrary as found in some cosmopolitan accounts).

4.2 Transitional Cosmopolitanism: Aligning Normative Aspirations and Practical Demands

At first glance, the cosmopolitan demand for positive and negative duties of human protection (outlined and assessed in the previous two chapters) may be viewed as an overly ambitious goal for the R2P. Indeed, these cosmopolitan standards might be viewed as inherently too difficult to achieve in an international environment characterised by competing interests and agendas; or at the very least, too difficult to achieve at the moment given the wealth of present challenges to global order such as Russian revisionism, the crippling effects of COVID-19 and climate change, as well as the lack of appetite for interventionism among the supposed champions of human rights. In this vein, cosmopolitan theory is sometimes accused of being too abstract and non-applicable to political realities (Brown and Jarvis, 2019, p. 203). For some, there is a lack of real means to implement cosmopolitan prescriptions, and cosmopolitanism is unable to generate practical solutions to the lived-in human problems of contemporary society (Nagel, 2005; Miller, 2007; Lenard, 2010).

In response to these challenges, a transitional approach to the attainment of cosmopolitan protection ideals is adopted here. The objective of transitional cosmopolitanism is to overcome barriers to achieving cosmopolitan outcomes, and as a consequence, to contribute some transformative progression towards a more meaningful form of cosmopolitics. In doing so, the aim is to advocate cosmopolitan values as a standard to work towards, serving as a guiding ideal to address contemporary problems, while being grounded in the imperfect and limited-cosmopolitan reality of contemporary international politics.

The specific focus on the R2P taken in this book provides an application of transitional cosmopolitanism, which acts as a practical avenue for developing the approach further. However, the application of this transitional cosmopolitan thought need not be limited to the subject of mass atrocity prevention. The discussion contained in the present chapter has wider significance for debates on how to advance cosmopolitan principles in the field of politics and international studies. The theoretical lens of transitional cosmopolitanism has the potential to be applied to other important global issues such as health and disease control, migration and border policy, and environmental protection, to name but a few.

As the previous two chapters established, the particular barrier to a cosmopolitan condition addressed here is the failures of mass atrocity prevention efforts under the R2P. Cosmopolitan protection demands provide a desirable end-point to work towards, and transitional steps can provide some progress towards this, helping to enhance R2P efforts in stymying mass atrocities. It is argued here that the R2P's problems can best be overcome if mass atrocity prevention efforts are aligned with cosmopolitan demands, which requires us to facilitate the conditions at the international level through which these cosmopolitan demands can be better met. This requires analysing the potential for reform, but also acknowledging the current retreat of liberal values internationally.

Contemporary problems faced by the international community, such as those noted above, point to an unfavourable environment for the R2P. Concerns regarding the scope for positive change are of course not unique to the field of mass atrocity prevention, and apply to any attempts to advocate for positive change internationally. At least here we can take solace in the fact that international change and progress *does* occur. History is rife with examples of change and progress that would doubtlessly have been deemed idealistic prior to its occurrence. Change happens; whether it be the establishment of a system of independent sovereign states, the creation of a United Nations, or the end of the Cold War. The point here is that we ought to remain committed to the potential for change, but to also appreciate that tempered recommendations are most likely required in order to make transitional gains at difficult times.

We need to be cautious when demanding moral action and change in state behaviour. A transitional approach takes an understanding that ideals are best understood as valuable tools when they can also be meaningfully applied to the reality of lived-in situations. That promoting at least some progress through tempered reform is better than making no progress at all. And that this is better than calling for overly ambitious and unrealisable change that is likely to be outright rejected. In other words, it is possible to apply cosmopolitan demands as a normative standard for reform of the R2P to work towards. However, this simultaneously requires an acknowledgement that achieving normative progress necessitates practical judgements on reform measures to enhance their efficacy. It also recognises that change takes time, that it is not linear, or necessarily always progressive (Brown and Hobbs, 2022).

To be clear, transitional cosmopolitanism cannot provide us with the perfect end-point. However, the aim of this transitional approach is to bring us to a middle position, wherein *some* normative progress can be made towards addressing a morally problematic situation, or where the possibility of future progress can be opened up by helping to facilitate the conditions through which iterative processes of normalisation and behavioural change can occur.

Whatever transitional cosmopolitanism is exactly, it holds the following basic tenets: i) its purpose is to help foster the conditions through which we can strengthen the pursuit of human protection, but while working among the practical constraints that stand in the way of achieving ideal progress; ii) transitional cosmopolitanism accepts that imperfect normative progress still represents progress; and iii) transitional cosmopolitanism promotes the idea that tempered progress can open up the possibility of further iterative steps and normative gains.

There are a few authors among the cosmopolitan literature who can reasonably be identified as promoting a transitional approach in the application of cosmopolitan principles. Brown and Hobbs (2022) explicitly do this. They argue that cosmopolitical change takes time to achieve, with non-ideal progress towards a cosmopolitan condition still representing at least some progress, and that this can open up the potential for further iterative advancement or opportunities for a more desirable cosmopolitan end-point (see also Brown and Jarvis, 2019). Gilabert (2017), in seeking movement from the status quo to the attainment of just principles, advocates a transitional approach that combines normative ambition with considerations of feasibility, so that both naïve idealism and conservative realism can be avoided when advocating normative change.

Beardsworth et al. (2019, p. 17) highlight a common charge against cosmopolitan thought, which is that it is viewed as too idealistic and disconnected from political reality. They appreciate that states face a balancing act between duties to their own citizens and duties to wider humanity. Consequently, they argue that cosmopolitanism needs to better identify avenues of normative progress that are able to work within ongoing and evolving political dynamics (Beardsworth et al., 2019, pp. 18–23). In essence, their position is that any cosmopolitan advancement requires contemporary grounding among practical obstacles in order to be able to offer realistic pathways for progressive change. Valentini (2011, pp. 33–34) argues that when we apply cosmopolitan principles, we need to be prepared to make 'strategic compromises' regarding facts like self-interest and existing political force. Consequently, she believes a theory is made relevant by applying it to practical cases and context-sensitive judgement (Valentini, 2011, p. 35). In this way, her approach is a transitional one which seeks compromise on ideal progress when applying normative ideals to practice. This point is also emphasised by Brown and Andenas (Brown and Andenas, 2020, p. 494), who claim that 'given the tensions manifest in contemporary international relations, it could also be argued that this weaker transitional approach is needed in practice, particularly if any form of cosmopolitan advancement is to gain traction'. Likewise, Beardsworth (2011, p. 14) has advocated for a concept of 'cosmopolitan realism', which promotes the notion that 'idealism and realism must work together for effective change to be possible'. His approach is therefore one which suggests that tempered recommendations are needed for progress, and these require compromise in the present in order to promote longer term change.

Gillian Brock's (2009) work on global justice also fits with this transitional cosmopolitan school of thought. She sees the potential for cosmopolitan transition, highlighting that the basic goals of global justice are reachable and that we do have ways of pursuing them. She is also open to the potential for iterative progress, that is, the idea that some progress can be made even without universal consensus, and that over time this progress will continue as consensus increases. In making this point, she highlights the general trajectory of human progress in the past century, including in the realm of human rights protection. In a similar vein, Habermas (2010) suggests we can interpret the development of international law as a stepping-stone towards cosmopolitan constitutionalisation at the global level, with international law 'shedding its status as soft law', representing a process of constitutionalisation and a strengthened legal position of individual subjects. In this regard, he views the UN as part of this developing process, with the UN Charter's explicit links to human rights, prohibition on state violence, the relation of sovereignty to the (expanded) goals of international peace, and universal membership as a precedent for international law (Habermas, 2010, p. 278). Notably though, Habermas does not view transitional processes as linear, appreciating instead that backsliding is both possible and historically obvious. In this context, Habermas draws to attention the need to make continuous normative evaluations about contemporary circumstances, in order to identify avenues for cosmopolitan advancement, but also to minimise normative losses wherever possible. In line with Habermas, Stone-Sweet and Ryan (2018) claim there is evidence of emerging cosmopolitan legal orders at the international level, centred on the rights of individuals, obligations to fill fundamental rights, and that is backed up by judicial systems to enforce obligations. They argue that the European Convention on Human rights, supported by the European Court of Human Rights, represents evidence of constitutionalisation at the global level, which as Brown and Andenas (2020, p. 4) and others note, is an iterative and gradual mechanism, reflecting transitional progress.

With similar themes to the transitional cosmopolitan school, Daniel Bray's (2011) 'pragmatic cosmopolitan' approach also emphasises that to make progress in overcoming identified social problems, there needs to be a focus on addressing the real-world barriers to progress. Bray's approach, drawing on the pragmatist thought of Dewey and Pappas, 'recognises the role of normative theory in articulating ideals and using them to criticise present beliefs and institutions' (Pappas, 2008, p. 66). For Bray (2011, p. 18), this does not abandon the moral principles of cosmopolitanism per se, but it does 'understand them in a different way', as it applies cosmopolitan morals as a generalising guide to contextual situations in order to promote the best outcomes that can be achieved within our current political reality. This Deweyan form of pragmatism rejects the pursuit of fixed ends as a target point for reform, and instead takes as its starting point the reality of a contemporary problem; this means that 'pragmatists cannot be committed *in advance* to a specific moral stance, social policy or political program' (Bray, 2011, p. 141).

Despite pragmatism's pronounced rejection of fixed moral ends, there are actually significant overlaps between the approaches of pragmatism and transitional cosmopolitanism. First, both are inherently normative. The application of normativity and practicality is consistent with the pragmatic tradition that normative developments are desirable and possible (Cochran, 2002, p. 547; Ralph, 2018, p. 179). Hence, normative advocacy does underpin pragmatic thought, although this underpinning is more implicit than in the theory of cosmopolitanism. As Bray (2011, p. 140) notes, 'pragmatism holds deep moral and political attachments to a particular view of moral life'. While pragmatism believes that pursuing pre-laid epistemological foundations is futile (Bray, 2011, p. 143) due to the fact we cannot automatically know *how* to achieve something, as problems are always context-specific, pragmatism does appreciate a moral value in attempting to achieve change. For pragmatists, there is an underlying ontological demand for moral progress as a result of human critical capacity to desire improvement.

While the measure of what represents long-term progress is not pre-determined in pragmatic thought, there is still a normative stipulation in the desirability of *some* form of improvement. Underlying pragmatism then is an inherent normative stipulation that improvement of a situation is morally desirable. Were this not the case, then the pragmatic approach would never seek to advocate change. So on the one hand, pragmatism holds that pursuing pre-laid epistemological foundations is undesirable due to a belief that universalised end goals do not translate across all cultures, with all problems presenting their own unique challenges and obstacles that need to be overcome (Cochran, 2002, p. 527; Bray, 2011, p. 143). On the other hand, pragmatism, as a school of thought dedicated to seeking change, believes that normative progress is desirable and attainable.

Second, transitional cosmopolitanism shares with pragmatism a belief that seeking incremental change via tempered modes of progress provides a more efficacious route than simply advocating immediate and substantial transformation of existing practice. For example, nearly all of Kant's cosmopolitan theory has a pragmatist element built into it. This starts with the very fact that Perpetual Peace (Kant, 1795) was written in the style of a 17th-century treaty. It was meant to be taken as a practical document outlining key preliminary steps (not ideal final steps) towards better-lasting peace; one that is self-perpetuating, and not one that is forever without effort.[1] In this way, both transitional cosmopolitan thinking and pragmatist thinking appreciate that context-specific barriers need to be given full consideration in order to make progress.

Where pragmatism differs from the transitional cosmopolitan approach is in the former's rejection of pre-laid ontological demands. Bray's approach, for instance, rejects the universalised interpretation of moral demands offered by cosmopolitanism, instead favouring an approach that is focused on what is practically possible in a given situation. This runs counter to the transitional cosmopolitan approach adopted here, which does accept the value of pursuing, in the long-term, universalised (though not static) ideals. Pragmatism does not seek progress to work towards a long-term end-point, and this presents what is argued here as a weak point of the pragmatic approach, as it means that pragmatism provides a limited understanding of what any form of transitional approach is meant to achieve in the way of transformative potential. Again, it is possible to say that pragmatism does share with transitional cosmopolitanism some ideas about why progress is desirable. A pragmatist, for instance, would not deny that human lives matter, or that stopping mass atrocities is something to strive for. The difference is that transitional cosmopolitans are more upfront about why they want progress, and can be clearer about the goals they set. In contrast, the lack of identified end points within the pragmatist school makes it much harder to know exactly what normative progress should look like, how to measure any level of success, and how to weigh up competing proposals for reform. As a consequence, pragmatism provides less guidance in the way of understanding the transformative potential of any given reform measure. In this sense, pragmatism lacks the normative compass – that the transitional cosmopolitanism promoted here does possess – for providing clarity and pointing us in the direction of transformative progress over time.

A caveat though is that while the transitional cosmopolitan approach is explicitly normative and does not reject set end goals, there is no overarching set cosmopolitan end goal within the transitional cosmopolitan base. As such, while the transitional cosmopolitan approach seeks transformation of the global system, there is not within the school any universally agreed cosmopolitan standard advocated for all aspects of human life. This respects the fact that end goals should not be understood as eternally static, but rather should continue to be weighed and re-assessed as normative arguments develop and change. This book is focused on the issue area of mass atrocity crimes, which represent 'conscience shocking crimes' and the 'outer edge of inhumanity' (House of Commons International Development Committee, 2022, p. 7). By arguing in favour of an end-goal of consistent satisfaction of positive and negative duties to prevent mass atrocity crime (see Chapter 2), this book offers a generally more 'basic' cosmopolitan demand, which calls for duties to reduce cases of mass atrocity crime and consequently to secure the basic rights of vulnerable peoples.

By precluding clear, pre-set normative demands, the problem pragmatism encounters is the epistemic uncertainty that comes with a judgement of whether a given reform measure ought to be adopted. What the transitional cosmopolitan approach offers instead is a two-pronged normative evaluation that can better guide practice and reform efforts. First, by accepting the concept of pre-determined moral demands and an ideal end-point to *approximate*, transitional cosmopolitanism allows us to understand the normative desirability of seeking reform efforts. This is because set normative demands allow us to judge where current practice is unsatisfactory, and identify areas for potential reform. This therefore allows the transitional cosmopolitan approach to make more judgements, and more consistent judgements, *for* action.

Second, having an end goal and a normative basis to judge the value of potential reform measures means that transitional cosmopolitanism also allows us to understand whether a given reform action can be effective, or ways it might achieve some effectiveness, in terms of overcoming the problem as a matter of judging the *effect* of an action. In other words, pre-set demands provide us with some de-ontological normative commitments that a reform action must uphold. Essentially, this means that once a normative end goal has been established, we can then weigh up different paths to determine the best one for edging us closer to the ideal, and therefore what reform action is the most useful to us when seeking tempered and incremental change.

A typical pragmatist charge against the use of normative theorising – and the reason behind its more fluid commitment to normative futures – is that laying out a long-term moral ideal can result in us advocating end goals which undermine progress, fixing attention on aspirations which may turn out to be undesirable, or may actually result in damaging practice. This critique amounts to a charge that normative end goals set us on a particular path, and one which may actually undermine the very reasons for seeking reform and positive change. Gallagher (2021, pp. 4–5) summarises this pragmatist argument when he writes that '[i]t is a mistake, therefore, to approach each problematic situation with the view that there is a fixed prescription'. In the R2P context, Ralph (2018, pp. 191–194) has argued that the Western pursuit of an 'Assad-must-go' strategy in the Syria case meant that other more feasible policy lines were not pursued, and ultimately, that this prevented the members of the UNSC from cooperating to produce outcomes to alleviate the suffering in Syria.

But this pragmatist reasoning misses the real purpose of normative theorising, which is to 'envision an ethical and political project', and *crucially*, that this is 'different from a program or plan' for achieving the desired moral end-point (Gilabert, 2017, p. 116). What this observes is that normative principles (like those of cosmopolitanism) provide us with an end goal, but this does not mean that they advocate a specific policy road that must be taken in order to get there. Instead, what normative ideals give us is a sound basis to judge *which* roads to take in order to make progress. In regard to the 'Assad-must-go' argument, for example, clearly Assad's actions have undermined cosmopolitan principles, but the transitional cosmopolitan need not have automatically advocated his removal as a policy choice that had to be pursued if this came at the expense of other more appropriate policy options in this case. Gilabert's (2017, pp. 102–104) distinction between evaluative and prescriptive considerations is useful to us here; evaluative considerations being the moral desirability of the end goal, and prescriptive considerations being what course of action is best taken once practical constraints have been weighed against the normative goal. As Gilabert (2017, p. 104) argues, by engaging in *both* evaluative and prescriptive considerations, a transitional approach to justice allows us to avoid both naïve idealistic utopian thinking and conservative status quo realism by first determining morally appropriate outcomes, and second, assessing the practical means of bringing the morally desired outcome about. In other words, by adopting a transitional approach we can judge the morality of actions with feasibility constraints factored in, allowing us to identify the best possible outcomes in a given context.

Pragmatism, while rejecting naïve idealism, risks keeping us on the conservative realism path because it avoids the question of where progress ought to direct us in the long-term. This is disadvantageous as it means pragmatism can only provide us with short-term guidance, thus ignoring the longer term iterative aspect of normative progress. For instance, the fact that present factors preclude pursuing a certain measure does not mean that measure is a worthless consideration. Circumstances may change so that the measure becomes an available option further down the line, and if we have the end goal already in our sights, then that measure can readily and quickly be drawn upon. Furthermore, keeping an end goal in sight focuses us on the relevant steps needed to achieve the more desirable measure via longitudinal change over time (Gilabert, 2017, p. 118).

Calling for an R2P approach better aligned with a cosmopolitan standard thus provides a normative benchmark to work towards, and allows us to assess the transformative potential of any given reform measure. This allows us to understand the extent to which a measure can promote progress towards establishing cosmopolitan conditions.

Before moving forward, it is important to note that themes associated with a transitional cosmopolitan approach are also evident in some R2P scholarship, with authors who similarly advocate for achieving normative progress at the international level, but also caution against demanding unobtainable progress based on an unfeasibly perfect moral standard. Gallagher (2015), for instance, has called for the managing of expectations over what we can expect to achieve from a political norm such as the R2P, suggesting that normative progress is constrained by political reality. Ralph (2018) has advocated a 'pragmatic constructivist ethic' in interpreting the usefulness of the R2P by emphasising that a norm should be judged on the extent to which it helps ameliorate the problem it purportedly addresses, even if such outcomes are not reflective of an ideal standard.

These accounts can also be compared to Hehir (2017), who in advocating the need for reform at the international level to aid in the application of the R2P, simultaneously calls for reform to be 'utopian in the right sense'. Building on the work of Carr and Booth, Hehir (2017, pp. 346–347) calls for realistic means to achieve valuable ends, noting that 'prescriptions need not be immediately feasible, but also should not be hopelessly idealistic' with the aim of promoting incremental change which can have practical utility. Crucially, this is not simply to advocate principles that can be easily

realised, but that such principles should be promoting of desirable normative prescriptions that can facilitate progress towards meeting moral goals.
However, Hehir does not provide much in the way of guidance for how this
can be achieved.

While stemming from different theoretical positions, and likely each
holding a different understanding of what a 'desirable normative standard'
should look like, these scholars ultimately point to the same conclusion: the
efficacy of potential measures to help alleviate the problems they seek to
address is dependent upon *both* the extent to which they can achieve desirable normative progress, and the extent to which they are realistically achievable within politically feasible means. A critique of the R2P's failings must
help us generate reform measures which can improve current reality, but also
modes of change which may actually be achievable. If a standard is advocated
which is too demanding, and therefore cannot be achieved in practice, then
this could result in the failure to make normative progress, thus undermining
the entire purpose of reform. It is important then to ground any demands for
normative change within the current political reality faced today, and that a
transitional approach will almost certainly be required in order to promote
progress. It is also vital to note here that this demand for moral progress is
an iterative one, which does not seek to attain desirable progress all in one.
Rather, the aim is longer term, to achieve incremental steps towards progress via different avenues of reform, effecting different aspects of the R2P at
different times and in different ways.

4.3 Transitional Cosmopolitan Criteria: Effectiveness and Feasibility

To develop transitional cosmopolitanism further, it is argued here that central
to a transitional cosmopolitan approach to reform should be the twin criteria
of the *effectiveness* and *feasibility* of progress.

Regarding the first criterion, *effectiveness* is taken here as a three-pronged
concept. First, effectiveness is understood to contain a pragmatic element.
As discussed above, transitional cosmopolitanism shares with pragmatism a
belief that a given reform measure must contribute towards overcoming the
problem which is sought to be addressed. As Pattison (2018, p. 21) argues, to
satisfy a pragmatic demand requires 'effectiveness in the purported measures
which are being promoted'. If a reform cannot be determined to contribute
some progress towards overcoming an identified problem, then it is not able
to demonstrate transitional potential. Note that this aspect of effectiveness is
not an overly demanding stipulation that a given reform must have supreme
transformational power, but merely that a reform measure must be able to
contribute at least some positive change.

Second, effectiveness also refers to the ability of a reform action to help
move us in the direction of desirable normative progress. In this book, utilising
the cosmopolitan lens of the previous two chapters, effectiveness means that
we should strive to secure fundamental human rights via the application

of positive and negative duties of human protection. This is where transitional cosmopolitanism differs from a purely pragmatic or instrumentalist approach. A pragmatic solution focuses on overcoming a given problem, without reference to an ultimate end goal. As highlighted above, a lack of pre-determined moral demands provides epistemic uncertainty as to whether it is appropriate to pursue a particular reform measure. In contrast, the cosmopolitanism applied here provides clearer guidance for what progress ought to look like and therefore what reform channels to pursue.

Third, effectiveness is also measured here as the ability of a reform measure to open up avenues or opportunities through which we may be able to attain further progress in the future. Here then, effectiveness is not simply understood as a short-term criterion. Rather, effectiveness has a long-term context, and we should not dismiss a reform simply because it can only offer limited efficacy in offering a normatively acceptable solution to a problem. This third aspect of effectiveness therefore attempts to appreciate the iterative potential of a given reform measure while also recognising that opportunities breed opportunities (Glenn, 2013).

In essence, effectiveness is about whether a measure *should* be adopted. Effectiveness is therefore judged based on the extent to which a given reform measure can help promote a coherent R2P standard aligned with cosmopolitan duties to secure the fundamental rights of the vulnerable, and consequently aid in the goal to reduce cases of mass atrocity crimes.

The second criterion that can be utilised to strengthen the transitional cosmopolitan approach is that of *feasibility*. This refers to the practical viability of whether a measure *could* be attained. If a transitional approach to cosmopolitanism calls for theory to serve in guiding practical solutions, then progress must have some probability of being achievable. For progress to be made, there must be some feasibility of achieving it. If proposed measures lack practical efficacy then they do not offer the scope for progress, and therefore would fail the transitional test. Feasibility includes considerations such as the vital interests of states, whether there is evidence to suggest some underlying progress, and whether there is a potential pathway towards achieving the measure (i.e. via theory of change modelling to identify potential pathways and barriers).

While both the concepts of effectiveness and feasibility can operate on separate conceptual levels – and it can be sound theory to suggest reform measures that could theoretically be effective but lack feasibility (or vice versa) – for a transitional cosmopolitan approach to be satisfied, both effectiveness and feasibility must operate in tandem. For if reform is to satisfy the transitional view that progress is both desirable and possible, then it must also be feasible for some progress to be achievable towards it. In sum, any given reform measure has to satisfy both the criteria of effectiveness and feasibility.

Even if a reform measure could be deemed effective by the three standards identified above, if it is also deemed to be unfeasible then the measure cannot be said to possess transitional cosmopolitan potential. On the other hand, just because a reform measure is feasible does not mean that it will automatically contribute to useful progress. Indeed, if a measure is perceived to hold a great degree of political feasibility, it is likely that it does not attempt much change from the status quo. This suggests that such a measure would likely be ineffective and undesirable.

Readers will probably observe here that there is likely to be a conflict between the criteria of effectiveness and feasibility when applied to the analysis of a given reform measure. This worry is likely to concern which of the two criteria should be given priority in situations where they clash. For instance, such a clash may occur when questioning whether it is appropriate to temper the transformational power of a given reform measure to aid in making the measure more feasible. Or conversely, a clash may occur when questioning whether a reform measure should promote greater transformation of current practice at the risk of making it challenge political interests to a greater degree.

At this point it can only be said of this potential conflict that the application of the criteria is context-specific to the particular reform issue in question. That is, when analysing the effectiveness and feasibility of a given measure, the contextual factors and potential moderators must be taken into consideration (see Gilabert, 2017, p. 101). These factors will differ from case to case, and are likely to affect how much transformative power a reform measure can appropriately attempt to generate when feasibility constraints are factored in. It is therefore not possible to say exactly how a potential conflict between effectiveness and feasibility is to be resolved *a priori*.

The criteria of effectiveness and feasibility are drawn on to aid transitional cosmopolitanism as an approach aimed at generating a 'middle position' towards progress. In doing so, the aim of the criteria is to help in assessing the *practical relevance* of any given reform measure. The middle position is understood here as a compromise on ideal progress, acknowledging that there are practical constraints which make attaining the ideal considerably unlikely in the present context. The middle position therefore represents a point which, if achieved, would provide at least some incremental progress. While this is likely to be short of a normative ideal, it can still represent a useful step on the road to potential progress. The hope is that in adopting tempered reform which represents a practical middle position, such reform can help in generating future iterative processes of change which can bring us closer towards the ideal and therefore more aligned with cosmopolitan standards in the long-term.

This iterative aspect of transitional cosmopolitanism does require some further clarification. The iterative aspect means that we must also emphasise the temporality of both effectiveness and feasibility. We need to factor in both their short-term and long-term context, and the relationship between these. Both the short and long-term need to be taken into consideration when conducting an analysis of potential reforms. A short-term consideration requires analysis of the relevant contemporary political facts conducive to whether a given measure is likely to be useful now for addressing the identified problem in a normatively desirable way, and whether the reform is likely to be accepted or not in the present. Whereas consideration of the long-term requires that the analysis of a given reform measure interpret its potential to shape future attitudinal, political, and institutional changes; whether the measure has potential as an iterative mechanism for shaping future practices and redressing the identified problem through normatively acceptable means (Gilabert, 2017, p. 118).

The contextual focus of a transitional approach would seem to demand at least a degree of short-term effectiveness and feasibility in a given reform measure. An analysis that simply focuses *entirely* on the long term would appear to risk drifting into an overly optimistic standpoint or run up against conditions of epistemic uncertainty, which may prove counter to a transitional approach. Appreciating the potential for future progress and changes in attitudes in the long term cannot necessarily help us in providing solutions to problems in the present. It is necessary to factor in long-term efficacy, but this is alone not sufficient for understanding effectiveness and feasibility. So while it is important to consider the long-term aspects of effectiveness and feasibility, this should not come at the *expense* of a consideration of the short term. Indeed, while the normative commitment to cosmopolitan principles provides a longer term compass for progress, this does not stipulate how such a long-term goal should be achieved or when. In this sense, when making short-term considerations, we can pursue any number of different avenues for potential progress.

Present practicality is required to open up the potential for more long-term change and the feasibility of more desirable progress. In other words, through pursuing reforms which can have some present effectiveness, and are also feasible, it may be possible to open up the feasibility of more desirable and effective reforms further down the line – the opportunity for further opportunity (Derrida, 2001). For instance, while a cosmopolitan ideal may advocate a certain standard to be met, this ideal is likely not immediately possible. However, adopting a much more tempered version of reform – which satisfies political constraints while offering marginal scope for overcoming a problem through normatively acceptable standards – may open up the space for future iterative processes and the eventual attainment of the morally demanded standard through further reform, deliberation, or changes in practice. As such, it is taken here that to understand the transitional effectiveness and feasibility of a given reform measure for the R2P, it needs to be understood if the measure holds at least some degree of efficacy and plausibility in the present short-term context. This is necessary before we can appreciate if the measure can also have a longer term contribution by opening up the possibility of future possibility.

4.4 A Framework for Assessing the Effectiveness and Feasibility of Reform Measures

As noted, a problem with the concepts of effectiveness and feasibility is that they are difficult to judge *a priori*. We can only theorise on whether any given reform can transition us to a more cosmopolitan application of the R2P, or on whether it is actually politically possible to attain the reform measure. However, it is still possible to make theoretical interpretations of how any given reform may work in practice, and whether it may hold some plausibility of being adopted. Again, effectiveness and feasibility are for use as reflective tools to assess the practical relevance of a given reform measure. In appreciating that the end goal of a cosmopolitan application of the R2P is difficult to achieve, the method for analysing potential reforms applied here attempts to understand and overcome current hindrances to progress. What this requires is a set of tests through which we might assess the theoretical effectiveness and feasibility of any given reform measure. This can be assisted by drawing on practical cases of where a reform measure would have been relevant and using it as a theoretical exercise to explore its potential impact. Further, it is important to draw on empirical evidence of political attitudes towards potential reforms where possible, in an attempt to ground the theoretical interpretation in current reality.

When laying out a framework for interpreting effectiveness and feasibility it may first be useful to make a distinction between what is *impossible*, and what is simply *improbable*. Gilabert and Lawford-Smith's (2012) distinction between 'hard' and 'soft' constraints is helpful here. They refer to *hard constraints* as those which make progress essentially impossible because of a lack of fundamental capacity to do it (Gilabert and Lawford-Smith, 2012, p. 813). Hard constraints are those such as the laws of physics and human ability. For instance, it is completely unfeasible to claim that human beings ought to be able to fly without technological assistance. Our lack of means to grow wings and fly serves as a hard constraint on this possibility. The point here is that we cannot recommend reforms that would encounter hard constraints as they would be inherently impossible to realise. On the other hand, *soft constraints* are those which place limits on the comparative likelihood of achieving something (Gilabert and Lawford-Smith, 2012, pp. 813–814). Soft constraints are those such as political will, economic ability, institutional structures, or current knowledge. Prior to advancements in aviation, the idea that humans could fly would likely have been perceived as impossible, yet the reality was that we had simply not invented the means of technological advancement to achieve flight, and so rather the goal was improbable in a historical context, yet clearly achievable over time.

As Estlund (2014, p. 119) notes in his discussion of 'utopophobia', the low likelihood (probability) of achieving something is usually a reflection of agent's choices rather than the limits of what is actually possible. When making recommendations for international reform to strengthen the R2P, it is important to remember that the barriers faced are generally ones of choice, and so this does not make these recommendations fundamentally impossible to achieve. Further, as Gilabert and Lawford-Smith (2012, p. 814) note, soft constraints are not permanent and static barriers, and do tend to shift over time. To put it another way, what is unlikely now is unlikely to remain so forever; while recommendations may seem improbable today, they may seem less so in the future, demonstrating that they still have normative value and that we cannot declare something unfeasible simply because we cannot obtain the perfect standard in the close-present. Rather, we need to understand that incremental progress can offer the potential for iterative processes of change that can drive us in the direction of progress. This is at the heart of the transitional cosmopolitanism applied here.

This distinction between hard and soft constraints provides us with a basis for understanding feasibility. As Lawford-Smith (2014, p. 10) puts it, 'an action is infeasible if it violates hard constraints, and an action is more feasible the more that an agent is likely to succeed in doing it'. In a similar vein, Valentini (2011, pp. 33–34) argues that radical detachment from the status quo is not the same as making claims beyond the realms of human possibility. Again, to reemphasise, the view taken here is that it is not inherently unfeasible to attain reform for the R2P. Reform should only be viewed as, at worst, improbable.

Further, just because reform may seem improbable, this does not mean we should abandon pursuing it (Brown, 2009, pp. 179–180). The foundation of normative progress is the belief and desire to bring about change, and theory has a role in setting objectives and identifying the means for pursuing them (Archibugi, 2008, p. 89). As this quote from Estlund (2014, p. 133) captures:

> The great achievements in the development of human social life have typically been preceded by incredulity about their very possibility, much less their likelihood. If theoretical inquiry had limited itself to what was plausibly thought to be achievable, the achievements might never have happened.

Similarly, as Erman and Möller (2018, p. 146 – emphasis in original) argue, 'even ideals which are unattainable may guide action and motivate stakeholders ... to act in order to come *closer* to the ideal'.

However, while Estlund (2014, p. 122) rightly argues that the attainability of a theory's recommendations does not influence the *morality* of its prescriptions, a transitional cosmopolitan approach that calls for operating in practical contexts does demand compromise between the morally ideal and the practically attainable in order to promote some progress in the present. There are trade-offs to be made when applying normative principles to context-based situations (Erman and Möller, 2018, p. 127). As Estlund (2014, p. 125) himself notes, 'non-hopeless' (less improbable) theory is better able to offer recommendations to guide current practice. Further, as Gilabert and Lawford-Smith (2012, p. 819) argue, 'considerations about what is more or less feasible must be balanced against considerations about what is more or less desirable in order to identify the political options that have maximal expected normative value'.

A framework of effectiveness and feasibility can be used to demonstrate what reform actions provide the most value in being pursued, by virtue of how a given reform can promote normative progress and whether it possesses practical utility. By taking these two themes together, it is possible to promote a transitional demand for practical solutions to lived-in contexts. In doing so, the point of hope offered is that progress towards a better functioning R2P can be achieved by enhancing the avenues for a stronger cosmopolitan application of the norm.

Here, Gilabert and Lawford-Smith's (2012, p. 822) framework for assessing the feasibility of a proposed reform measure is in-part adopted for the application of transitional cosmopolitanism.[2] This process does more than merely assess feasibility, however, for it serves to determine *both* the effectiveness and feasibility of a given measure and allows one to see how the two concepts must operate together to satisfy transitional cosmopolitanism. This can therefore enhance the theoretical strength of the transitional cosmopolitan approach by developing a stronger conceptual understanding of the requirements needed to make normative progress. These tests can serve in an analysis of whether a reform measure can be deemed suitably transitionally cosmopolitan by its alignment with the criteria of effectiveness and feasibility. For any measure to achieve this status, it must pass all three of the tests discussed below, otherwise it cannot be said that it successfully meets the requirements of effectiveness and feasibility.

The first test for assessing whether a reform measure can meet a transitional cosmopolitan standard is the *test of effective progress*. This is to determine whether effective normative progress can be made through adopting the reform measure. If the reform were to fail this test then it is likely to possess no normative value, as it could not promote progress and positive change. For our present purposes, this test is about whether a reform could strengthen the R2P's application to more effectively meet the cosmopolitan duty to halt mass atrocity crime. If the measure cannot achieve this then it cannot be said to be effective. As discussed above, the transitional cosmopolitan approach applied here accepts progress through iterative steps, and so effectiveness does not necessarily require that a given reform measure be able to achieve a perfect cosmopolitan application of the R2P in the immediate present. Rather, the approach applied here accepts that some normative progress is better than none, and that even slight progress can open up the potential for future iterative steps towards cosmopolitan standards.

The second test of this framework, the *test of moral hazard*, requires assessing whether the costs of bringing about the measure would be too morally hazardous.[3] This requires us to question whether a reform measure has the potential to introduce unwanted side-effects that would undermine the likelihood of achieving desirable normative progress. If the moral costs of bringing about a reform measure are too high, then this would serve to undermine its purpose (and therefore the de-ontological normative demands of effectiveness), while likely also making it less feasible (as agents would seem less inclined to implement it). For instance, if pursuing alternatives to the UNSC for authorising action in response to R2P crises would open the door for immoral cases of intervention that would undermine the global normative acceptance of R2P, then such a reform would fail the requirement to avoid moral hazards.

The third and final test, the *test of practical potential*, is one of access: to understand if the route to the measure is practically possible. This is, in essence, an evaluation of whether there is a possibility of the measure being successfully adopted by relevant actors. This requires us to weigh up the various soft constraints that may exist, to determine the plausibility of the reform being adopted. If the soft constraints are deemed to be too barring, then the reform cannot be said to be feasible. For example, this may require an assessment of the institutional and political barriers that stymy the possibility of a reform's chance of being implemented. It may also require an examination of the actual costs of bringing about the measure, as Lawford-Smith (2014, p. 10) notes, 'If a proposal requires more than the available resources (time, effort, money, cooperation) it will be infeasible'.

At first glance there may be a tension over whether it is appropriate to give weight to one test over another. This again relates to the question highlighted above over whether it would be appropriate to sacrifice some effectiveness of a proposed reform measure in the name of promoting improved feasibility of it being adopted (or vice versa). On the one hand, such a sacrifice seems essential for finding the middle position associated with a transitional solution. On the other, if effectiveness is sacrificed to the point that this would greatly undermine the possibility of making normative progress towards a cosmopolitical standard, then we cannot accept the measure just because its feasibility is greatly enhanced. To use UNSC veto reform as an example, it would not be acceptable from a transitional cosmopolitan view to make a recommendation for veto reform that would offer no change in practice just because such a recommendation was more tenable for the UNSC's permanent members.

The upshot is that a transitional cosmopolitan approach requires all three tests to be given due consideration and that no single test can be sacrificed entirely for the benefit of another. The aim of this is to help in finding a practical balance wherein the effectiveness and feasibility of any given reform measure are both given appropriate consideration. This is necessary for achieving the 'middle position' described above that can provide for at least some desirable cosmopolitan action while offering hope for further iterative progress in the future. Ultimately, this judgement must be context-specific relating to each reform explored. Each case will be problem-dependent with various competing factors that must affect the judgement of the balance between effectiveness and feasibility (see Gilabert, 2017).

Ultimately, progress will require reform that serves as a compromise on the ideal standard, yet nevertheless would still offer a point of normative progress. This is why reform can be advocated that has practical feasibility, even if it appears well short of an ideal standard. This approach understands cosmopolitan demands not as a requirement that any single given reform *must* achieve, but as a standard to work towards incrementally, by assessing whether a given reform can promote *some* progress towards the end goal. In this sense, the intent is not for a reform measure to serve as a perfect solution that can bring the R2P immediately in line with cosmopolitan demands, but reform must at least be able to help in generating progress that *contributes towards* meeting positive and negative cosmopolitan duties to both respond to, and prevent mass atrocity crimes.

4.5 State Interests and Transitional Cosmopolitanism

To align with transitional cosmopolitan, this book operates among the constraints of state interests in an attempt to assuage opposition to potential R2P-based reform. This is essential because the actions of states are vital for meeting cosmopolitan goals (Beardsworth, Brown, and Shapcott, 2019), and subsequently, the goals set out under the R2P. By seeking tempered reform it is hoped that state interests can become more compatible with reform, serving to make progress a more tenable prospect. Recommendations for reform have to be conscious of not demanding too much from states if they are to hold practical efficacy.

To help satisfy this practical demand, it needs to be highlighted that reform should be promoted in the interests of all. This interest is most obviously for the victims of mass violence, but also can be for the states who are charged with preventing atrocity. By working within a statist orientation, the analysis here is grounded within contemporary political reality and is therefore appreciative of political barriers which stand in the way of R2P reform. In doing so, this work seeks to build on the ideas of Beardsworth, Brown, and Shapcott (2019, p. 18) that state obligations and interests can be reconciled with their duties to wider humanity, by 'locat[ing] both realistic state-based motivations for cosmopolitan change as well as existing political pathways for its actualization'.

This view holds true to the spirit of the transitional cosmopolitan idea that normative progress is possible, drawing on the observation that most states, in general, do wish to stop mass atrocity violence.[4] States may, therefore, be willing to accept international reform which serves this interest. However, it is important that such reform does not jeopardise their other interests so much as to make them opposed to reform. This follows the transitional cosmopolitan theme by appreciating that cosmopolitan goals can be contextualised and realised within conditions of state self-interest (see Brown and Hobbs, 2022). Promoting this idea is not antithetical to cosmopolitanism, and permits the idea that state motivations do not have to be primarily driven by moral concerns for human protection, so long as an intent to protect is demonstrable in immediate practice. If R2P reform that would further a cosmopolitan condition can become more tenable by attempting to satisfy state interests, then this may in turn satisfy the transitional cosmopolitan approach.

In contrast to the above line of argument, Jeremy Moses (2017) is highly sceptical about attempts to align state interests and moral goals. He has called for a 'pacifist' approach to the R2P, arguing that moving the R2P away from its coercive links would halt the abuse of moral arguments that mask self-interested pursuits that run anathema to the normative purpose of the R2P. For Moses, moral arguments only serve as an 'enabling tool' for the interests of powerful states, with the legitimation of political violence as never entirely ethical or normative (Moses, 2017, pp. 223–224). It is accepted here that the application of the R2P will always have political connotations attached, but ultimately, self-interest need not run antithetical to the moral goals of the R2P. As Beardsworth (2018, p. 401) argues, self-interest can take an enlightened quality, 'doing good for others because one is doing good for oneself'. State interest needs to be reformulated to appreciate that halting mass atrocities is something which inherently concerns and serves states, as this may serve to turn attitudes more favourably towards the issue of halting mass atrocity violence, and consequently shape attitudes in favour of international reform to achieve this goal. Situating moral argument as inherently counter to the idea of self-interest serves only to reinforce an epistemological fatalism that states can never be the champions of normative progress, a position which is rejected here.[5] As Brown and Jarvis (2019, p. 205) note, 'any improvement in the international order would necessarily have to originate from conditions existing within the current state-based system'.

For Beardsworth (2018, p. 402), a re-interpretation of self-interest can enhance the state as a responsible actor by pre-emptively addressing potential threats to the self and one's citizens. Likewise, Brown and Jarvis (2019, pp. 206–207) see the state as a base for developing political, legal, and social mechanisms that shape communal relations and citizens' sense of cosmopolitan obligation, meaning that instrumental state interests can be aligned with cosmopolitan ends. In other words, a state's interest in securing itself can provide motivations for accepting and promoting elements of a cosmopolitan condition. This can facilitate the meeting of a collective duty to halt atrocity violence, serving to address an issue that operates transnationally and cuts across the interests of multiple international actors. In this sense, both moral and political goals can be furthered simultaneously by working towards outcomes that serve both a normatively desirable goal and state self-interest (Glanville, 2021, p. 88). For instance, in the context of mass atrocities, if states wish to quell issues of international terrorism (see Englehart, 2016), refugee crises (see Secen, 2021), the illegal flow of arms across borders (see

Malam, 2014), as well as reduce expenditure on aid and peacekeeping, then they need to better act to halt or prevent the mass violence that helps perpetuate such conditions. For instance, although focused on conflict prevention and not specifically utilising an 'atrocity lens', a recent study has shown that 'a 25% increase in effectiveness of conflict prevention would result in 10 more countries at peace by 2030, 109,000 fewer fatalities over the next decade and savings of over $3.1 trillion'. A '75% improvement in prevention would result in 23 more countries at peace by 2030, resulting in 291,000 lives saved over the next decade and $9.8 trillion in savings'. While such claims are reliant on counterfactuals, they display evidence 'of both the benefits (saved lives, displacement avoided, declining peacekeeping deployments) and cost-effectiveness of prevention (recovery aid, peacekeeping expenditures)' (Pathfinders, 2020, p. 1).

The analysis here aligns with others who argue that self-interest can provide a useful avenue for the initialisation of progress towards a cosmopolitan condition (Axelsen, 2013; Brown and Jarvis, 2019; Brown and Hobbs, 2022).[6] Brown and Hobbs argue that self-interest should be utilised to overcome the 'motivational problem': a central issue with cosmopolitan theory relating to the difficulty of translating generally accepted normative standards into actual cosmopolitical practice. Brown and Hobbs argue that morally worthy outcomes should not be dismissed simply because they did not come from strictly moral motivations. Indeed, strictly moral motivations have evidently not been enough to generate the kind of political force necessary to tackle a range of global issues from climate change to global health, to mass atrocities. For Brown and Hobbs (2022, p. 80), if an outcome of self-interested motivation broadly reflects the demands of an ideal cosmopolitan position, serves as an iterative foundation for further progress, and promotes recognition of the need for moral/political responsibilities towards human needs, then self-interest can serve a positive normative purpose. Thomas Nagel's (2005, p. 147) notion that 'the path from anarchy to justice must go through injustice' similarly captures a transitional-like sentiment, acknowledging the instrumental value of self-interest towards establishing cosmopolitical-like conditions. By arguing that progress develops over time and first requires morally imperfect conditions created by competing international states, Nagel implies that there is moral value in promoting imperfect international institutions. Institutions that can, in the long-term, be re-shaped to fulfil the demands of justice.

Crucially though, it needs to be emphasised that self-interested goals can be better realised through adopting a cosmopolitan disposition. When acting on the R2P, intent to protect vulnerable peoples must be evident, otherwise outcomes conducive to protection are less likely to follow, and as a result, state interests will be undermined. If states interpret their self-interest without some cosmopolitan intent to protect, then paradoxically they will serve to undermine the very self-interest / mutual interest they seek to promote. Powerful states will always likely be able to pursue the interests they perceive for themselves, but the argument advanced here is that these interests can be realised through pursuing moral, cosmopolitan-centred goals. This is a pragmatic acknowledgement of the existence of political decision-making conflicts, but with a normative stipulation that politics *can* favour the moral goal of protection against mass atrocities once state interest is appropriately framed. Such a standpoint feeds well into the transitional cosmopolitan ethos by acknowledging that self-interest is contextual and can be utilised to serve normative progress (Caney, 2008, pp. 511–514). However, this also comes with the acknowledgement that self-interest is only to secure the initial participation into cosmopolitan pursuits, with long-term participation requiring an iterative transition or transformation towards more robust cosmopolitan and mutually consistent outcomes (Brown and Hobbs, 2022, p. 77).[7] Indeed, states should not be encouraged to act on the R2P purely for self-interested reasons, for to do this would be to neglect the existence of a moral responsibility to act (Glanville, 2021, pp. 88–89).

The cosmopolitanism applied in this book understands though that in a world made up from (often) competing sovereign entities, special ties exist that go beyond general duties owed to humanity. This accepts that states hold special responsibilities towards their own populations that go beyond general duties owed to outsiders. General positive duties apply to compatriots first, but importantly, if the needs of outsiders are clearly greater, then these can become the priority (Miller, 2010, p. 390).[8] As Pogge argues in a similar vein to Miller, special relationships can increase what we owe to some, but this does not *decrease* what we owe to others (Pogge, 2002, p. 89). This view aligns with other scholars who do not dispute the idea that special ties create special responsibilities, but who emphasise that the greater the need of the afflicted group, the stronger the duty is to act to rectify the suffering (Nickel, 2005, p. 386; Brown, 2009, pp. 188–189; Appiah, 2010, p. 674; Fabre, 2012, chap. 1).

What is fundamental to highlight here, however, is that in the case where *mass atrocity crimes* – as outlined under the R2P framework – are being committed, to adequately meet a basic cosmopolitan standard, there is a positive duty to act which ought to take precedence over general duties to the non-essential needs of co-nationals (Fabre, 2012). There may appear to be a practical flaw here, given that in order to protect the lives of others it is sometimes the lives of co-nationals that subsequently have to be risked. This may make it so that the trade-off between duties to co-nationals and foreign nationals can become too blurred to provide an adequate framework for the prioritisation of duties and may therefore serve to demand too much from states (see Edyvane and Souter, 2019).

A useful counter to this argument, in favour of the general feasibility of aligning state interests with preventing mass atrocity, lies in the 'narrow but deep' (UNGA, 2009, p. 8) approach espoused by the R2P. This approach is valuable as it has helped garner a consensus surrounding the R2P's core objectives (Pattison, 2021, p. 900).

Relating to the R2P's 'narrowness', the argument made here is that, concerning matters of mass atrocity, the problem does not rest on balancing the basic needs of domestic civilians against the basic needs of outsiders. For it is not the case that most intervening states would have to balance against protecting their own population from mass atrocity and intervening elsewhere with the aim of protecting the population of that other state (Pattison, 2022, p. 107). As noted, the R2P concerns mass crimes which are widely understood as most 'shocking to the collective conscience of humanity' (Walzer, 1977; Wheeler, 2000, p. 50; UNGA, 2004), a view underscored by the sense that mass atrocity crimes serve to undermine the basic needs and rights associated with a view of human dignity.

There does appear to be (at least at a rhetorical level) near-universal agreement on the value of international human rights, and the notion that there are international responsibilities to secure them. This is reflected in the numerous human rights treaties and norms that exist at the international level, including the R2P itself. It therefore seems intuitive to suggest that there is genuine agreement on the need to work towards curbing mass atrocity crimes, which shows that the goal is not inherently unfeasible. It is also worth noting that the most powerful states within the international community are the ones charged with the strongest residual responsibility to take *direct* action[9] where states are 'manifestly failing' in their R2P (UNGA, 2005, para. 139) by virtue of their capability. For states such as these, their populations do not find themselves at high risk of incurring mass atrocities. As such, for states that have a consideration of whether to intervene economically or militarily, the trade-off they must make is not between balancing the fundamental needs of its own population against that of another, but rather, between risking economic advantages or military personnel and pursuing the basic needs of mass civilian lives in the target state.[10] It was argued in Chapter 2 that such a trade-off is acceptable to any cosmopolitan understanding of human worth, including both conceptions that permit the prioritisation of insider's needs and those that do not. If there is a positive duty to intervene to halt mass suffering then the intervening parties *prima facie* have a duty to incur some costs upon themselves as a consequence. These costs, however, seem plausibly acceptable by states as they do not attempt to demand too much of them, satisfying the requirement of feasibility.

The second counter argument to the above contestation and in favour of the feasibility of cosmopolitan-based reform for mass atrocity prevention efforts relates to the R2P's 'depth'. This can be seen in the R2P's preventive focus. As highlighted in Chapter 3, the R2P is understood to constitute a much broader doctrine than the mobilisation of reactive military force, for it holds a relationship with deeper preventive efforts to alleviate more indirect harms. In this connection to the deeper, preventive aspects of the R2P, contention is significantly lessened (though far from entirely absent; see Jarvis, 2022, p. 25). Therefore, if appropriately framed, preventive efforts for avoiding mass harms should theoretically be able to demand greater action from states. As argued previously, preventive methods need to incorporate a more explicit consideration of negative duties to not harm outsiders in order to have greater efficacy. These are potentially more demanding than positive duties of assistance but are not wholly unfeasible in what they would task from states (Bohm and Brown, 2021).

The R2P also speaks to a depth of tools for fulfilling a duty to react to mass atrocities. It is important to emphasise that action under Pillar Three of the R2P incorporates acts aside from military force, including measures under Chapters VI, VII, and VIII of the UN Charter; these include measures such as peaceful settlement, diplomatic shaming, targeted sanctions, and referral to the International Criminal Court (UN, 2012). While such measures obviously do still carry contention, particularly for those states who perceive any coercive threat as a prelude to forcible military action, they are clearly not as contentious as military action itself, and therefore have greater feasibility. This is particularly the case if they can be successfully separated from a connection to military force (see Akbarzadeh and Saba, 2019). This argument suggests that there are practical ways to act on the positive duty to react to mass atrocities that are less likely to contravene the interests of states than military force. The possible depth of response under the R2P enhances its feasibility of being applied by states.

The argument here is not to downplay the feasibility constraints that stand in the way of R2P progress. As noted in the book's introduction, the R2P faces a number of contemporary challenges that make reform progress difficult. The point here is simply that in order to promote progress, and to remain committed to the potential for progress, there is a need to work within a conception of state interests via tempered reform proposals. Cosmopolitan justice can be promoted by incremental reform, which is feasible, not overly demanding, but still promoting of normative progress towards an R2P that better serves the goal of reducing mass atrocities. To frame Gallagher's (2015, p. 273) perspective on the need to rein in expectations of what the R2P can deliver, and apply it to this context, to ultimately promote a 'reasonable expectation that there will be less mass violence, rather than none, in a post-R2P world'.

4.6 Conclusion

This chapter has laid out the theoretical approach used for assessing reform measures examined in the following chapters. The cosmopolitan demand to halt mass-scale egregious suffering, may, on the face, seem to be making too great a demand of states operating in a heavily politicised international context. If viewed through a doctrinal realist lens, this would almost certainly be the case.

But to simply dismiss such demands as overly idealistic and of no value is too fatalistic. Halting mass atrocities is a normative demand which ought to be aspired to for a host of legitimate reasons. Such normative demands should never be dismissed if we, as a species, are serious about overcoming the issue of mass atrocity violence. However, while the importance of making normative demands should never be underplayed, it is also acknowledged here the value of not attempting to demand too much change too quickly, and instead viewing the issue through a transitional lens. As such, while normative prescriptions ought to set a standard to work towards which would represent an improvement on current reality, it is important to appreciate that to realise normative progress, incremental steps are likely of greater efficacy. To miss this point is to demand too much from actors, which may serve to achieve little in the way of progress.

Taking these points into consideration, this chapter has argued in favour of adopting a transitional cosmopolitan approach to R2P reform. In doing so, it promotes incremental progress towards a cosmopolitan condition by operating among the context of practical obstacles to progress. This calls for reform measures which can serve the criteria of effectiveness and feasibility. To help promote the successful application of these criteria, it has been argued that working within a statist conception of international relations, and attempting to align state self-interest with the goals of reform, can help satisfy this transitional cosmopolitan ethos. The second half of the book now shifts into applying this transitional cosmopolitan approach to the matter of R2P reform.

Notes

1 I am grateful to Garrett W. Brown for this example.
2 The first part of this framework is to determine the desirability of reaching the end goal. As this normative element of the analysis has already been covered in Chapter 2 and Chapter 3, it is excluded from the framework here.
3 There is a debate within the R2P literature regarding the issue of whether the R2P is itself a morally hazardous norm. The argument that the R2P is itself a moral hazard follows the line that military intervention *causes* genocidal violence that would not otherwise occur (Kuperman, 2009b, p. 33; 2009a, p. 282), and prolongs conflicts by incentivising armed groups to continue the use of violence rather than seek peaceful settlement as they believe international intervention will occur in their favour (Crawford, 2005, pp. 182–183; Kuperman, 2009a). However, Bellamy and Williams (2012) have effectively debunked these claims, arguing that these accounts oversimplify the R2P by equating the norm with military intervention, and also that moral hazard theory places too much emphasis on the single variable of expectation of third-party intervention, ignoring the wide range of causal factors involved in instances of mass atrocity.
4 This is evident in numerous human rights developments which have occurred since the UN was established in 1945. This point suggests that promotion of human rights internationally has (as one consideration) become part of (many) state's national interests.
5 This view does not ignore the fact that often states are often a cause of insecurity themselves (Jones, 1995). However, the view offered here merely promotes the

idea that states *can* be vehicles for cosmopolitan goals if these goals can be aligned with their self-interest.

6 It must be noted here that self-interest cannot be relied on interminately; self-interest 'is best understood as simply one important transitional component among others that can potentially motivate a nascent cosmopolitical condition' (Brown and Hobbs, 2022, p. 75). The long-term sustainability of the R2P will also rely on further iterative acceptance of moral responsibility.

7 Even if such longer-term participation in achieving cosmopolitan outcomes is not possible, any initial progress made towards meeting a cosmopolitan condition by utilising self-interest as a motivator is better than no progress at all.

8 This is not simply a basic utilitarian argument of prioritising the higher number, but rather is highly contextual and dependent upon the specific circumstance in question. Here the discussion is about mass atrocity crimes, which represent an egregious level of suffering, imposing a duty to halt them which takes precedence over general duties to co-nationals.

9 All states have a responsibility to contribute, however they can, to the alleviation of mass violence. However, the number of states with the capability to undertake a direct military intervention is confined to a very select number who possess the capability to do so. For example, those who possess the requisite air and sea lift capacity.

10 Of course, this is an oversimplification since these states must also balance against wider responsibilities to international peace and security. Further, the intervening states have to be sure that an intervention can satisfy Just War requirements of reasonable chance of success, which should include *both* short-term and long-term aims of peace (see Pattison, 2019).

References

Akbarzadeh, S. and Saba, A. 2019. UN Paralysis Over Syria: The Responsibility to Protect or Regime Change? *International Politics.* 56(4), pp. 536–550.

Appiah, K.A. 2010. Morality: Aid, Harm, and Obligation. *Boston University Law Review.* 90(2), pp. 661–696.

Archibugi, D. 2008. *The Global Commonwealth of Citizens: Toward Cosmopolitan Democracy.* Princeton, NJ: Princeton University Press.

Axelsen, D.V. 2013. The State Made Me Do It: How Anti-cosmopolitanism is Created by the State. *Journal of Political Philosophy.* 21(4), pp. 451–472.

Beardsworth, R. 2011. *Cosmopolitanism and International Relations Theory.* Cambridge: Polity Press.

Beardsworth, R. 2018. Our Political Moment: Political Responsibility and Leadership in a Globalized, Fragmented Age. *International Relations.* 32(4), pp. 391–409.

Beardsworth, R., Brown, G.W., and Shapcott, R. (eds.). 2019. *The State and Cosmopolitan Responsibilities.* Oxford: Oxford University Press.

Bellamy, A.J. and Williams, P.D. 2012. On the Limits of Moral Hazard: The 'Responsibility to Protect', Armed Conflict and Mass Atrocities. *European Journal of International Relations.* 18(3), pp. 539–571.

Bohm, A. and Brown, G.W. 2021. R2P and Prevention: The International Community and Its Role in the Determinants of Mass Atrocity. *Global Responsibility to Protect.* 13(1), pp. 60–95.

Bray, D. 2011. *Pragmatic Cosmopolitanism: Representation and leadership in Transitional Democracy*. London: Palgrave Macmillan.

Brock, G. 2009. *Global Justice: A Cosmopolitan Account*. Oxford: Oxford University Press.

Brown, G.W. 2009. *Grounding Cosmopolitanism: From Kant to the Idea of a Cosmopolitan Constitution*. Edinburgh: Edinburgh University Press.

Brown, G.W. and Andenas, M. 2020. The European Convention of Human Rights as a Kantian Cosmopolitan Legal Order. *Global Constitutionalism*. 9(3), pp. 490–505.

Brown, G.W. and Hobbs, J. 2022. Self-interest, Transitional Cosmopolitanism and the Motivational Problem. *Journal of International Political Theory*. 19(1), pp. 1–23.

Brown, G.W. and Jarvis, S. 2019. Motivating Cosmopolitanism and the Responsibility for the Health of Others *In*: *The State and Cosmopolitan Responsibilities*. Oxford University Press Oxford, pp. 203–223.

Caney, S. 2008. Global Distributive Justice and the State. *Political Studies*. 56(3), pp. 487–518.

Cochran, M. 2002. Deweyan Pragmatism and Post-positivist Social Science in IR. *Millennium*. 31(3), pp. 525–548.

Crawford, T.W. 2005. Moral Hazard, Intervention and Internal War: A Conceptual Analysis. *Ethnopolitics*. 4(2), pp. 175–193.

Derrida, J. 2001. *On Cosmopolitanism and Forgiveness*. London: Routledge.

Edyvane, D. and Souter, J. 2019. Good International Citizenship and Cosmopolitan Responsibilities to Protect: Balancing Responsibilities and Dirty Hands *In*: R. Beardsworth, G.W. Brown and R. Shapcott, eds. *The State and Cosmopolitan Responsibilities*. Oxford: Oxford University Press, pp. 41–60.

Englehart, N.A. 2016. Non-state Armed Groups as a Threat to Global Security: What Threat, Whose Security? *Journal of Global Security Studies*. 1(2), pp. 171–183.

Erman, E. and Möller, N. 2018. *The Practical Turn in Political Theory*. Edinburgh: Edinburgh University Press.

Estlund, D. 2014. Utopophobia. *Philosophy & Public Affairs*. 42(2), pp. 113–134.

Fabre, C. 2012. *Cosmopolitan War*. Oxford: Oxford University Press.

Gallagher, A. 2015. The Responsibility to Protect Ten Years on from the World Summit: A Call to Manage Expectations. *Global Responsibility to Protect*. 7(3–4), pp. 254–274.

Gallagher, A. 2021. To Name and Shame or Not, and If So, How? A Pragmatic Analysis of Naming and Shaming the Chinese Government over Mass Atrocity Crimes against the Uyghurs and Other Muslim Minorities in Xinjiang. *Journal of Global Security Studies*. 6(4), pp. 1–16.

Gilabert, P. 2017. Justice and Feasibility *In*: M. Weber and K. Vallier, eds. *Political Utopias: Contemporary Debates*. Oxford: Oxford University Press, pp. 95–126.

Gilabert, P. and Lawford-Smith, H. 2012. Political Feasibility: A Conceptual Exploration. *Political Studies*. 60(4), pp. 809–825.

Glanville, L. 2021. *Sharing Responsibility: The History and Future of Protection from Atrocities*. Princeton, NJ: Princeton University Press.

Glenn, H.P. 2013. *The Cosmopolitan State*. Oxford: Oxford University Press.

Habermas, J. 2010. A Political Constitution for the Pluralist World Society? *In*: G. W. Brown and D. Held, eds. *The Cosmopolitanism Reader*. London: Polity.

Hehir, A. 2017. 'Utopian in the Right Sense': The Responsibility to Protect and the Logical Necessity of Reform. *Ethics & International Affairs*. 31(3), pp. 335–355.

House of Commons International Development Committee 2022. *From Srebrenica to a Safer Tomorrow: Preventing Future Mass Atrocities Around the World* [Online]. House of Commons. [Accessed 17 October 2022]. Available from: https://committ ees.parliament.uk/publications/30270/documents/175201/default/.

Jarvis, S. 2022. The R2P and Atrocity Prevention: Contesting Human Rights as a Threat to International Peace and Security. *European Journal of International Security.* 8(2), pp. 243–261.

Jones, R.W. 1995. 'Message in a Bottle'? Theory and Praxis in Critical Security Studies. *Contemporary Security Policy.* 16(3).

Kant, I. 1795. Perpetual Peace: A Philosophical Sketch. Translated by Smith, M. Campbell. 1917 (3rd edition). London: George Allen & Unwin Ltd.

Kuperman, A.J. 2009a. Darfur: Strategic Victimhood Strikes Again? *Genocide Studies and Prevention.* 4(3), pp. 281–303.

Kuperman, A.J. 2009b. Rethinking the Responsibility to Protect. *Whitehead J. Dipl. & Int'l Rel.* 10, p. 33.

Lawford-Smith, H. 2014. Cosmopolitan Global Justice: Brock v. the Feasibility Sceptic. *Global Justice: Theory, Practice, Rhetoric.* 4, pp. 1–12.

Lenard, P.T. 2010. Motivating Cosmopolitanism? A Skeptical View. *Journal of Moral Philosophy.* 7(3), pp. 346–371.

Malam, B. 2014. Small Arms and Light Weapons Proliferation and its Implication for West African Regional Security. *International Journal of Humanities and Social Science.* 4(8), pp. 260–269.

Miller, D. 2007. *National Responsibility and Global Justice.* Oxford: Oxford University Press.

Miller, D. 2010. Cosmopolitanism *In*: G.W. Brown and D. Held, eds. *The Cosmopolitanism Reader.* Cambridge: Polity Press.

Moses, J. 2017. The Limits of R2P and the Case for Pacifism *In*: A. Hehir and R. W. Murray, eds. *Protecting Human Rights in the 21st Century.* London: Routledge, pp. 215–230.

Nagel, T. 2005. The Problem of Global Justice. *Philosophy & Public Affairs.* 33(2), pp. 113–147.

Nickel, J.W. 2005. Poverty and Rights. *The Philosophical Quarterly.* 55(220), pp. 385–402.

Pappas, G.F. 2008. *John Dewey's Ethics: Democracy as Experience.* BloomingtonN: Indiana University Press.

Pathfinders for Peaceful, Just and Inclusive Societies 2020. *Forecasting the Dividends of Conflict Prevention from 2020–2030.* New York: Center on International Cooperation. [Accessed 27 July 2020]. Available from: https://www.sdg16.plus/.

Pattison, J. 2018. *The Alternatives to War: From Sanctions to Nonviolence.* Oxford: Oxford University Press.

Pattison, J. 2019. The Ethics of Foreign Policy: A Framework. *SAIS Review of International Affairs.* 39(1), pp. 21–35.

Pattison, J. 2021. The International Responsibility to Protect in a Post-Liberal Order. *International Studies Quarterly.* 65(4), pp. 891–904.

Pattison, J. 2022. Beyond Imperfection: The Demands of the International Responsibility to Protect. *Global Responsibility to Protect.* 14(1), pp. 105–108.

Pogge, T.W. 2002. Cosmopolitanism: A Defence. *Critical Review of International Social and Political Philosophy.* 5(3), pp. 86–91.

Ralph, J. 2018. What Should Be Done? Pragmatic Constructivist Ethics and the Responsibility to Protect. *International Organization.* 72(1), pp. 173–203.

Secen, S. 2021. Explaining the Politics of Security: Syrian Refugees in Turkey and Lebanon. *Journal of Global Security Studies.* 6(3).

Stone-Sweet, A. and Ryan, C. 2018. *A Cosmopolitan Legal Order: Kant, Constitutional Justice, and the European Convention on Human Rights.* Oxford: Oxford University Press.

UN 2012. Responsibility to Protect: Timely and Decisive Response. Report of the Secretary-General. A/66/874–S/2012/578. [Accessed 9 August 2021]. Available from: https://undocs.org/A/66/874.

UNGA 2004. A More Secure World: Our Shared Responsibility. Report of the High-level Panel on Threats, Challenges and Change. A/59/565. [Accessed 6 May 2019]. Available from: www.un.org/ruleoflaw/files/gaA.59.565_En.pdf.

UNGA 2005. Resolution adopted by the General Assembly on 16 September 2005. A/RES/60/1. [Accessed 15 November 2018]. Available from: http://www.un.org/en/development/desa/population/migration/generalassembly/docs/globalcompact/A_RES_60_1.pdf.

UNGA 2009. Implementing the Responsibility to Protect Report of the Secretary-General. A/63/677. [Accessed 3 December 2018]. Available from: https://undocs.org/A/63/677.

Valentini, L. 2011. *Justice in a Globalized World: A Normative Framework.* Oxford: Oxford University Press.

Walzer, M. 1977. *Just and Unjust Wars.* New York: Basic Books.

Wheeler, N.J. 2000. *Saving Strangers: Humanitarian Intervention in International Society.* Oxford: Oxford University Press.

5 Ending UN Security Council Paralysis
Responsible Veto Restraint

5.1 Introduction

Having spelled out a cosmopolitan vision for the R2P (Chapter 2), assessed the current state of the norm by using this standard (Chapter 3), and then espoused a framework for assessing how reform mechanisms can provide transitional progress towards this cosmopolitan vision (Chapter 4); this chapter now begins the exploration of reform measures for strengthening the Responsibility to Protect. It examines what is perhaps the most significant institutional barrier to the R2P's implementation: the 'veto' power held by the UNSC's five permanent members (P5).[1]

The responsibility to respond to mass atrocity crimes under Pillar Three of the R2P lies predominantly in the hands of the UNSC (UN, 2005b, para. 139), meaning that the R2P and the veto power are bounded in a tricky and often conflicting relationship. The veto has remained largely unchanged since 1945,[2] meaning that the P5 members still possess the power to block the UNSC from passing any legally binding resolution, including resolutions pertaining to the R2P and mass atrocity crimes. This reduces the likelihood that the UNSC will successfully pass resolutions (Lättilä and Ylönen, 2019, p. 166) and creates the potential for deadlock and barriers to action on atrocities. Wheeler (2005), Weiss (2006), and Bellamy (2006) all predicted shortly after the adoption of the R2P in 2005 that the failure to accept a form of veto restraint would undermine the implementation of the R2P in practice. This prediction came true. The most pertinent example of this is the Syria crisis, over which, at the time of writing, 17 draft resolutions have been vetoed in the UNSC. However, while Syria is the clearest case of where the veto has impinged on the UNSC's response to mass atrocity, unfortunately it is far from the sole example.[3]

Hehir (2018, p. 120) argues that even though the veto exists for a good reason (more below), it has inhibited the UNSC's response to human rights violations. Similarly, Bellamy and Luck (2018, p. 100) claim that P5 disagreements often lead to UNSC ineffectiveness, while Coen (2015, p. 1051) notes that P5 members effectively get to choose which cases of atrocity crime warrant a response. Welsh (2019, p. 63) asserts that while the

DOI: 10.4324/9781003394105-5

R2P's three pillars are meant to be taken as equal, there has been evidence of pillar sequencing and preferentialism, with Pillar Three being favoured the least by the international community. This contestation and distancing from Pillar Three is intrinsically tied to the use of the veto power, as veto use can effectively stall Pillar Three, undermining the international responsibility to respond to atrocity crimes. A restricted use of the veto is necessary as a moral counterweight against great power domination in the UNSC (Archibugi, 2008, pp. 162–164). If the UNSC continues to be sought as the main means for atrocity response, then avenues of veto reform must be explored.

This chapter applies transitional cosmopolitanism to make a new and improved proposal for veto restraint. In doing so, its aim is to promote incremental progress towards desirable UNSC voting behaviour. Building on the suggestions of the Accountability, Coherency and Transparency (ACT) Group's Code of Conduct, and the France-Mexico initiative for veto restraint, the chapter calls for a 'Responsible Veto Restraint' (RVR) proposal. As a transitional and politically grounded recommendation, RVR can help to promote an application of the R2P better aligned with cosmopolitan responsibilities to curb mass atrocity crime.

RVR differs from previous veto restraint proposals in several key aspects. The RVR proposal provides that coercive measures such as sanctions, criminal prosecutorial mechanisms, and non-consensual military force should not apply to veto restraint. RVR also calls for the removal of subjective get-out clauses for the P5, and includes a more stringent trigger system for when veto restraint should become active. It is argued that by adopting these aspects, RVR can be a more effective and feasible measure for veto restraint than the ACT Code or France-Mexico initiative. As a recommendation grounded in practical reality, that attempts to not (too greatly) undermine the UNSC's mandate to international peace, or the P5's interests, RVR can help in passing non-coercive and potentially useful R2P action in the UNSC. This may include, but is not limited to, rhetorical condemnations of actors, humanitarian access for life-saving aid, and counter-narratives to combat atrocity violence. In the short term, this could mean helping in passing immediate action that helps ameliorate mass atrocity crises. In the longer term, RVR can help in establishing the conditions in which it is possible to make iterative behavioural progress towards satisfying the goal of cosmopolitan human protection. Regarding veto restraint, this means contributing to normative practice wherein it is understood that veto use needs to be precluded over cases of mass atrocity, or at least where certain conditions are satisfied, that veto use ought to be precluded over particular types of UNSC draft resolution. RVR offers a potential avenue for addressing the problem of weak UNSC response to atrocity crimes.

The chapter includes four key sections. Section 5.2 examines the veto reform movement to date, while outlining some important feasibility constraints that must be taken into consideration when examining the issue of veto reform. Section 5.3 analyses the ACT Code of Conduct and the

France-Mexico initiative as the two most significant veto restraint proposals made to date. This section determines that both the ACT Code and France-Mexico initiative fail to meet the transitional cosmopolitan criteria of effectiveness and feasibility due to the fact they contain get-out-clauses for the P5, have potential to undermine the UNSC's responsibility to maintaining international peace and security, and are politically undesirable due to their relationship with the use of coercive force. Section 5.4 seeks to build on these proposals, offering nuanced changes to produce the RVR proposal. It is argued that RVR is more strongly aligned with the transitional cosmopolitan approach, offering a more effective and feasible avenue for veto reform progress. Finally, section 5.5 examines the case of Syria, serving as an example to demonstrate the potential transitional cosmopolitan value of the RVR proposal.

5.2 Veto Reform: An Avenue for Progress?

Veto reform is deemed by some as an impossible task. As one scholar noted in an article on UNSC reform, 'recognising the seemingly insurmountable obstacles to genuine reform of the veto, this issue is not given any real attention' (Wilson, 2018, p. 8). Given the less than favourable attitude of certain P5 members towards veto reform this is perhaps understandable. Yet to deem veto reform impossible is to neglect a vital area for UNSC improvement and a transitional avenue for the advancement of the R2P. The obstacles to implementing veto restraint are 'soft constraints' (political and institutional), which do not make reform inherently impossible (Gilabert and Lawford-Smith, 2012). This means that it may be possible to make progress in the area of veto reform, but this of course requires tempering expectations over what we can achieve in the present.

There have been previous recommendations aimed at overcoming the veto problem. In 1950, the 'Uniting for Peace' (UfP) resolution (UNGA, 1950) was adopted by the UNGA. This mechanism is effectively a declaration that in cases of veto misuse, the matter can be referred to, or taken up by, the UNGA to be dealt with. UfP and the powers of the UNGA is the focus of Chapter 6, where there is a thoroughgoing examination of the UNGA as an alternative means for responding to mass atrocities in the wake of UNSC failure.

More recently, the Responsibility Not to Veto (RN2V) movement has called on the P5 to refrain from veto use over cases of mass atrocities where a UNSC majority would otherwise be possible and the P5's vital interests are not at stake (Blätter and Williams, 2011, p. 303). The 2001 ICISS R2P report put forward this recommendation to prevent veto use in the case of 'a significant humanitarian crisis' (ICISS, 2001, p. 51). The recommendation was also taken up by UN Secretary-General Kofi Annan's 2004 High level Panel, which recommended to curtail veto use in 'cases of genocide and large-scale human rights abuses' (UNGA, 2004, p. 68). Neither the ICISS nor High Level Panel's recommendations made it into the internationally accepted version of the R2P in 2005. The recommendations of the RN2V movement were though taken up by the 'Small Five' group of Switzerland, Lichtenstein, Costa Rica, Jordan, and Singapore. On three occasions they sought to put forward a resolution to the General Assembly (2006, 2011, and 2012). However, diplomatic manoeuvring by the P5 ensured that the draft proposals were withdrawn before they were put to any vote (Morris and Wheeler, 2016, p. 233). Importantly though, the proposals were well received and subsequently led to the formation of the ACT Group's 'Code of Conduct'. As of June 2022, the ACT Code has the support of 121 UN member states (plus two observers) – well over half the UN's membership (GCR2P, 2022). Near simultaneously with the development of the ACT Group's Code of Conduct has been the development of the 'France-Mexico initiative' for veto restraint, which, as of July 2022, also garners widespread support from 104 states (plus two observers) (GCR2P, 2022).

It should also be briefly noted here that Lichtenstein, in March 2022, put forward a 'veto initiative' proposal which was adopted by the UNGA under resolution 76/262 in April 2022 (UNGA, 2022). This mechanism means that the UNGA will now routinely convene whenever a veto is cast in the UNSC, enabling the vetoing member to publicly defend its veto, the UNGA to discuss whether the veto use was legitimate, and for the UNGA to *potentially* take action in response (UNA-UK, 2022). Despite being named the 'veto initiative', this proposal is actually most relevant to the powers of the UNGA rather than the UNSC P5's veto power itself. As such, this proposal is given due consideration in Chapter 6 and is not discussed in the present chapter.

Given the nature of power politics, reforming the veto power is very difficult and some preliminary feasibility constraints are worth clarifying here. First, veto reform challenges the vital interests of the P5 who have instrumental reasons to preserve their veto power (Morris and Wheeler, 2016). The veto ensures that the P5 members hold a permanent position of authority within the international community, and enables them to further their own causes by blocking any UNSC action that they perceive as threatening their interests. It is therefore highly improbable that any of the P5 members would agree to forfeit their veto rights entirely. The idea of *abolishing* the veto power would be met by too strong opposition from the P5 and is therefore politically untenable as a suggestion. Consequently, this line of argument is not pursued here.

A second constraint is that the veto is a necessary tool for the management function of the P5 states in their responsibility for maintaining international peace and security. The veto is not just a means to realise national interests of the states that granted themselves veto rights, but exists to prevent great power conflict by guaranteeing the participation of the great powers in the UN system (Morris and Wheeler, 2016, p. 229). In this regard, it is worth remembering that without the veto power, the US and Soviet Union would not have signed up as member states in 1945 (Kennedy, 2007, p. 28).

In 1945, the desire for P5 unanimity was based solely on questions of the use of force in the name of collective security and the prevention interstate war (Trahan, 2020, pp. 74–75). However, the UNSC's function has evolved since then, and the Council is now also expected to act to prevent civilians from suffering mass atrocities as a matter of its vital function (Bellamy and Tacheva, 2019). Consequently, the legitimacy of the veto gets called into question where it obstructs UNSC response to mass atrocity (Blätter and Williams, 2011). Morris (2015) refers to this dilemma as the 'dual responsibility' of the P5. As Morris (2015, p. 400) argues, the growth in solidaristic values through norms such as the R2P conflicts with the UNSC's traditional obligations to peace and security, meaning that meeting both these special responsibilities is immensely difficult in practice. For instance, authorising military action vis-à-vis the R2P can disrupt a region and undermine the UNSC's traditional responsibility to international stability.[4] To overcome the problem of conflicting UNSC responsibilities, veto reform must help in facilitating action that contributes towards the UNSC's human protection obligations under the R2P, but simultaneously does not undermine its ability to maintain international stability.

Linking on from this, a third constraint to think about when considering veto reform is that abolishing the veto may pave way for actions which are not aligned with the underlying normative logic of the R2P. Without a check on the application of military force, for instance, states may too easily be able to authorise interventions that could potentially undermine human protection (Adediran, 2018, p. 478). This may stifle the ability for exploring other measures that may be more appropriate for alleviating suffering in a case of mass atrocities (see Pattison, 2018). This point further supports the argument that the veto should not be abolished entirely.

A final constraint to note here is that any *formal* amendment to the veto under the UN Charter is politically unfeasible. Article 108 of the Charter refers to the consensus required by the P5 in adopting any Charter amendment (UN, 1945). A formal commitment to limiting their veto power would therefore be a legally binding decision that the P5 would be unable to easily reverse. Intuitively, this seems as though it would carry considerably less chance of being accepted than an informal and non-binding amendment. Webb (2014, p. 481) even goes as far to say that 'it would probably be easier to dissolve the UN than to amend the veto power under the Charter'. It therefore seems that we need to focus on pursuing only non-formal amendments, at least in the short term.

While in current circumstances UNSC veto reform is politically difficult, if achieved, a form of tempered veto restraint can help serve the cosmopolitan end of human protection, and consequently, the goals of the R2P. Veto restraint offers a potential avenue for normative progress towards addressing the problem of atrocity crimes. Yet, reform suggestions must be pragmatic and politically aware, accounting for the realities of feasibility constraints.

5.3 Evaluating the ACT Code and France-Mexico Initiative

5.3.1 *Test of Effective Progress*

This section evaluates the ACT Code and France-Mexico initiative as the two most prominent veto restraint recommendations to date.[5] Should these measures appear satisfactory to the transitional cosmopolitan approach then this would suggest that they possess effectiveness and feasibility and should therefore continue to be promoted as the strongest recommendations for veto restraint. However, should they fail to satisfy the transitional cosmopolitan approach, it would seem that an alternative veto restraint measure needs to be promoted if progress is to be made. The first test to apply is the test of effective progress, to determine if the ACT Code and France-Mexico initiative can help in addressing the veto problem.

Launched in July 2015, the ACT Code calls on UN member states to 'pledge to support timely and decisive action by the Security Council aimed at preventing or ending the commission of genocide, crimes against humanity or war crimes'. The Code calls on all UNSC members to refrain from voting against 'credible' draft resolutions pertaining to the crimes listed (ACT Group, 2015). This acts as something of a 'get out clause' for the P5, as it allows veto use if the (vague notion) of 'credible' is not met. The Code also calls for an explanation by a P5 member of why it has exercised its veto right. The trigger for applying the ACT Code is flexible, as it only refers to the 'facts on the ground' of an atrocity case (ACT Group, 2015).

The France-Mexico initiative has its roots in French policy circles as far back as November 1999, but it was French foreign affairs minister, Laurent Fabius, that in September 2012 articulated a call for P5 veto restraint over 'situations of serious humanitarian crises when their vital interests are not in play' (quoted in Vilmer, 2018, p. 335). In an October 2013 joint New York Times and Le Monde article, minister Fabius (2013) spelled out additional specifics of the French proposal, namely that it should include a procedural trigger for 50 UNGA members to call upon the UN Secretary-General to determine if an issue is one of mass atrocity crime, and if deemed so, then the P5 would be required to suspend their right to veto over the issue. Like the ACT Code, the French proposal also includes a get out clause here for the P5; this time, for veto use to remain in cases where 'vital interests' of the veto-wielding powers are at stake. In September 2015, France and Mexico jointly launched a 'Political statement on the suspension of the veto in case of mass atrocities' which proposes 'a collective and voluntary agreement among the permanent members of the Security Council to the effect that the permanent members would refrain from using the veto in case of mass atrocities' (France and Mexico, 2015). This 2015 declaration is vaguer than the earlier formulation, as it leaves out specificities of a procedural trigger or a 'vital interests' clause that were previously articulated. However, it is the present author's understanding that these specifics remain a part of non-public negotiations between the P5 regarding the French proposal. In the literature, the specific procedural trigger and vital interests clause are also understood to be part of the France-Mexico initiative (see Morris and Wheeler, 2016; Adediran, 2018; Vilmer, 2018; Luck, 2019). For these reasons, the present chapter does analyse the technicalities of the procedural trigger and vital interests clause.

The ACT Code and France-Mexico initiative have some merit from the transitional cosmopolitan perspective. While differences exist between both recommendations, both are ultimately aimed at restraining veto use in cases of R2P concern. In this vein, both are theoretically aligned with a cosmopolitan demand to see international action in response to all instances of mass atrocity.

However, the proposals of the ACT Code and the France-Mexico initiative are far from perfect, and their chance of being adopted by all P5 states remains unlikely. It is for this reason that this chapter argues that we need to temper these reform initiatives under an RVR proposal.

A major issue with the ACT Code and France-Mexico initiative is the vagueness of the terms 'credible' and 'vital interests' employed by the respective proposals. First, as Vilmer (2018, p. 339) argues, 'credibility' is highly subjective, 'what is credible to a state that supports a resolution is not credible to a state that does not'. In practice then, were the ACT Code adopted, current disagreements on draft resolutions between UNSC members would remain, and veto use would likely follow where disagreements exist. Second, as Morris and Wheeler (2016, p. 237) argue, the differences inherent in the P5's interpretation of 'vital interests' could make implementing veto restraint very difficult in practice. This suggests that the France-Mexico initiative would also run afoul in practice. Adediran (2018, p. 474) sums up the 'credible' and 'vital interests' issue well when he writes:

> in many such cases the state casting the veto could simply claim a "vital national interest"… or claim that the draft resolution was not "credible" … allowing it to continue obstructing timely action.

The ACT Code and France-Mexico initiative therefore fail the first part of the transitional cosmopolitan test applied here as the measures would likely lack practical efficacy. The criteria of credibility and vital interests would reinforce the status quo of a deadlocked UNSC. It should be noted that these criteria are intended to make the proposals more politically feasible, by providing P5 members with reassurance that they can still safeguard their interests. However, since this would seem to come entirely at the expense of the effectiveness of the proposals, it would appear untenable for the normative progress required by a transitional cosmopolitan approach.

5.3.2 *Test of Moral Hazard*

Moving on to the second test of this book's transitional cosmopolitan framework, regarding the question of whether the ACT Code and France-Mexico initiative would introduce undesirable moral hazards that may weaken their scope for providing effective and feasible reform suggestions; here the ACT Code and France-Mexico initiative may appear to some as falling afoul of similar arguments against abolishing the veto entirely (see section 5.2).

It is notable that with both the ACT Code and the France-Mexico initiative there is (beyond the vague notion of 'credibility' in the ACT Code) no stipulation over what measures should or should not be supported in the name of preventing mass atrocities. In other words, neither mechanism suggests that peaceful or non-peaceful measures are preferable, and therefore they don't offer much of any guidance to states in the UNSC for deliberating over what types of draft resolution they should support in the name of atrocity prevention. In doing so, these proposals for veto restraint might effectively suggest that any draft resolution concerning a situation of mass atrocity cannot legitimately be vetoed by a P5 member.

For Vilmer (2018, p. 343), this is problematic as it means that these proposals would introduce a risk of passing resolutions that are 'too strong', and that this would therefore potentially do more harm than good. This is most relevant to the problem of potentially too readily authorising military interventions before peaceful or different forms of coercive measures were fully explored (Levine, 2011). Another way of framing this argument is that if the P5 members of the UNSC were unable to legitimately utilise their veto power to prevent the passage of harmful action in the name of atrocity prevention, then this might actually result in the violation of cosmopolitan commitments to uphold fundamental human rights by the passage of measures that would not only lack efficacy in addressing mass atrocity, but actually contribute to its perpetuation.

These claims carry significance, even if they are not *entirely* warranting of concern. In a similar sort of vein, Adediran (2018, p. 478) argues that veto restraint 'advocates for the commitment of states to a specific course of action'. This logic is questionable though since veto restraint wouldn't itself lead to an advocation for any particular course of action. It must also be remembered that veto restraint does not equate to the cessation of democratic deliberation in the UNSC. Any given draft resolution would still require the support for at least 9/15 members, providing some safeguard against the passage of undesirable action. Nonetheless, Adediran is still right to caution against overzealously promoting military action which veto restraint could *potentially* assist if non-forceful measures are not given due consideration. As noted, over-zealousness in promoting military action could undermine both the R2P, as well as the UNSC's function in maintaining international peace and security. It is also worth adding here that the current triggering systems for veto restraint in place in the ACT Code and France-Mexico initiative may also exacerbate this potential moral hazard, by enabling veto restraint too readily. As noted, the ACT Code does not have a clear triggering mechanism, which means that there is a lack of clarity for determining when it should rightfully be applied. The France-Mexico initiative meanwhile requires only 50 states to bring a matter to the attention of the Secretary-General for them to determine whether veto restraint ought to apply; this is arguably too small a number, and could pave way for over-zealousness in applying veto restraint.

The ACT Code and France-Mexico initiative may then also seem to fail on the second transitional cosmopolitan test. The potential moral hazard, exacerbated by their triggering mechanisms, of undermining the veto's original normative purpose by removing one of the safeguards in place for promoting international peace and security – as well as the potential to undermine the normative underpinning of the R2P in its goal to protect populations from mass atrocities – would serve to undermine their effectiveness for working towards an R2P standard that fulfils cosmopolitan protection values. This fact also weakens the feasibility of these reform measures actually being adopted. What this further suggests is that these two veto restraint proposals are likely untenable from the transitional cosmopolitan position and are therefore in need of further refinement.

5.3.3 Test of Practical Potential

Third and finally, to assess the transitional cosmopolitan strength of the ACT Code and France-Mexico initiative, we must assess if the feasibility constraints in the way of adopting these measures are too barring.

A strength of the ACT Code and France-Mexico initiative is that both represent informal methods for reforming UNSC practice. The lack of Charter amendment required would seem to offer better promise for their acceptance, as their adoption would not necessitate the more rigorous requirements for formal Charter reform, which, as noted (section 5.2), presents a feasibility problem in terms of the finality and irreversibility of reform.

In contrast to this claim, however, Adediran (2018, p. 476) argues that 'a Code of Conduct, just like Article 108, requires the acquiescence of all permanent members … [and therefore] it is not immediately clear how it considerably differs from the cumbersome demands of the Charter regarding Council reform'. While it is true that even an informal restraint measure would still require the support of all P5 states, this does not make such a recommendation worthless. For one, voluntary restraint offers a more transitional route because it wouldn't force the P5 into a long-term binding commitment. Rather, it would give an opportunity to see how voluntary restraint operates in practice with the knowledge that should it serve to grossly undermine their interests or the function of the UNSC, it would be possible to revert back to the previously accepted application of the veto. It is hoped that voluntary restraint could help to socialise the P5 towards more appropriate behaviour, suitably aligned with R2P values (Schaefer, 2016, p. 76). Informal veto restraint could act as an iterative mechanism, helping in generating a norm that veto restraint should be expected over situations of mass atrocity, and as a result, help to slowly change practice over time. Furthermore, as Gifkins (2021, p. 18) has highlighted, the most promising UNSC reform avenues are informal changes to practice, given the nature of how informal practices do 'change over time'. This further highlights the compatibility between transitional cosmopolitan thinking and informal reform avenues, as it emphasises the temporal and fluctuating nature of feasibility barriers.

The support that both the ACT Code and France-Mexico initiative have garnered in a short life-span is also promising, reflecting the fact that veto restraint 'is not an idle hope' (Bellamy, 2019, p. 187). In the 2021 Formal Interactive Dialogue on the R2P, 59 member states and the European Union spoke on behalf of 88 countries. Of these, 29 different actors explicitly spoke out in support of veto restraint efforts. These speakers included a diverse range of significant global actors, including the European Union, Qatar, South Korea, and Turkey. What this demonstrates is the substantial global support that veto reform proposals enjoy among the international community. That these states utilise the platform of the UNGA's R2P debates to formally express this position is significant, and it shows that the issue of veto reform is not likely to go away until significant progress is made. This is reflected in the fact that nearly 50 per cent of actors that delivered a statement at the 2021 formal R2P debate spoke in support of veto restraint; a substantial figure which suggests that veto reform is an issue which will carry through to future formal annual debates as well.

This widespread advocacy for veto restraint does seem to be putting increased pressure on the P5 members. Indeed, as Adediran (2018, p. 472) notes, the reaction by members of the P5 to prevent the 'S5' from tabling of their RN2V proposal in 2012 shows that the matter is a real concern for the P5 states. The P5 understand that veto restraint is a prominent issue for UN members and one which they cannot ignore. For Luck (2019, p. 86), veto restraint measures 'have generated renewed interest in prevention, protection, and R2P; have forced members of the Council to reflect (at least a bit) on their Charter responsibilities'. The emergence of both the France-Mexico initiative and the ACT Code of Conduct highlights UN member states' dissatisfaction with UNSC practice over cases involving mass atrocity crime (Wenaweser and Alavi, 2020, pp. 67–68). The fact that these initiatives can be directly linked to the R2P is important then, for it shows that there is appetite among the members of the international community for a stronger R2P approach in combatting mass atrocity, and one that is therefore better aligned with cosmopolitan protection standards.

Nonetheless, despite these noteworthy points of political progress, the primary feasibility constraint operating with regard to the ultimate acceptance and functionality of the ACT Code and France-Mexico initiative is of course the political will of the P5 states themselves. This is because it is they that actually hold the veto power and therefore the ability to action the proposals. Notably though, this point does not apply to all of the P5 members. One of these measures comes from France, which is itself a P5 member, while the UK is also a signatory to the ACT Code. The UK has also previously stated that '[w]e cannot envisage the circumstances in which the United Kingdom would use its veto to block an appropriate response to a mass atrocity' (UK, 2014).

Morris and Wheeler (2016, p. 236) have doubted the importance of France and the UK's support for veto restraint, arguing that it is effectively meaningless without support of all five permanent members. Vilmer (2018, p. 340) suggests that despite its rhetorical support for constraint, the UK remains sceptical that it may be open to abuse. Adediran (2018, p. 472) also argues that France and the UK's support for veto restraint is perhaps simply a tacit acknowledgement of their own diminishing power in international politics. This suggests that their support may be an attempt to maintain their own legitimacy as 'great powers' and members of the P5, rather than as a result of their normative commitment to veto reform. However, it does seem important that veto reform has some support among P5 members. If all were opposed to restraint, this would make it seem even less feasible. Further, when supplemented with additional pressure from a wider group of UN members and civil society groups, support of some P5 states may help grow a stronger consensus in favour of reform, which other permanent members of the Council may struggle to ignore in the face of mounting political costs. Indeed, if veto restraint proposals garnered the support of the near-entire UN membership and the remaining permanent members ignored such calls, the UNSC's legitimacy would be greatly called into question as the medium through which to manage international security.

What is particularly problematic for the feasibility of these restraint measures though is the position held by the US, Russia, and China. All three have thus far rejected calls for (directly) restraining their right to veto.[6] The US has noted that it 'remain[s] opposed to any expansion or alteration of the veto' (UNGA, 2016), despite its repeated calls for decisive action in the face of mass human rights violations. This is also despite its condemnation of Russian and Chinese 'blanket' veto use over Syria (The Guardian, 2015). This contradiction is most obviously explained by the US's desire to protect Israel, over which the US has regularly exercised its veto power. Further, while the US is a member of the R2P Group of Friends, which consistently affirms its support for veto restraint initiatives (UNGA, 2021a, p. 5), the US's own position cannot necessarily be inferred from its membership of this grouping. What is more telling is the fact that the US chooses the avoid referencing the veto power during UNGA debates on R2P, which reflects its unease at the veto restraint movement, even if this sits in contradiction with its consistent statements of support for the R2P and condemnation of actors that violate the norm. In the political aftermath of Russia's invasion of Ukraine in February 2022, the US has seemingly been more open to calls for veto restraint. On 8 September 2022, the United States UN Ambassador, Linda Thomas-Greenfield, announced that 'the United States will subscribe to six clear principles for responsible behaviour for Security Council Members', the third of which noted that the US 'will refrain from the use of the veto except in rare, extraordinary situations' (United States Mission to the United Nations, 2022). Optimists may read this as another P5 member signing up to veto restraint, yet those more sceptical might view it simply as a vague and rhetorical commitment that will mean little in situations where US national interests are at stake. Further, it cannot be ignored that the US is still yet to sign up to either the ACT Code or France-Mexico initiative.

China has emphasised that the UNSC should be the one to lead the direction of UNSC reform (UNSC, 2018a) and remains unconvinced by calls for veto restraint. This seems particularly problematic, for as Morris (2016, p. 211) notes of China, 'given its predicted material trajectory over coming decades, its stance is likely to be the most significant among those who have traditionally cast doubt on the veracity of intervention'. The Russian position notes that 'any steps to improve working methods must be taken only by the Security Council itself' (UNSC, 2018a). As Vilmer (2018, p. 349) notes of Russia, the veto power remains one of its few attributes of international power. It is therefore no surprise that it opposes reform to the veto power, while seeking to ensure that decisions surrounding the use of force remain in the sole remit of the UNSC (Orchard and Rae, 2020, pp. 176–177). Further, both Russia and China have seen their traditional opposition to interventionism reinforced in the wake of the Libyan intervention (Garwood-Gowers, 2013, pp. 27–32), which would seem to entrench their desire to leave the veto power unaltered. For instance, at the 2021 UNGA Formal Debate on R2P, China stated 'some countries have been broadening their interpretation of the concept, even distorting and abusing it, and making extensive efforts to hype it up' (UNGA, 2021b, p. 22), while Russia was even more emphatic in its use of language, claiming that the consequences of the R2P have been 'illegal armed intervention, regime change, the destruction of statehood and economic collapse' (UNGA, 2021c, p. 5).

The connection between veto restraint and the increased possibility of military force exercised under R2P Pillar Three remains a problem for veto reform, making it unlikely that either state would accept these two restraint proposals while this connection remains. The reticence of the US, Russia, and China towards veto restraint – and in particular the connection veto restraint holds to increasing the likelihood of military measures – suggests that the political obstacles to the ACT Code and the France-Mexico initiative are too demanding to make them feasible recommendations.

By failing the three tests, the ACT Code and the France-Mexico initiative fall short of satisfying the transitional cosmopolitan criteria of effectiveness and feasibility. However, in contrast to some scholars such as Adediran (2018), the fatalistic interpretation of this problem must be rejected if we are to follow the transitional cosmopolitan line that it is possible to make some incremental progress towards desirable veto practice.

5.4 Reforming the Reform Proposals: Responsible Veto Restraint

In this section an alternative veto restraint proposal is offered which seeks to build on the ACT Code and France-Mexico initiative. It proposes a recommendation for Responsible Veto Restraint (RVR) which seeks to better align the veto restraint movement with the transitional cosmopolitan approach and subsequently offer a more effective and feasible avenue for veto reform. The section begins by outlining the core elements of the RVR proposal, before then assessing these recommendations via the three transitional cosmopolitan tests.

First, to clarify, both the ACT Code and France-Mexico initiative relate directly to the R2P in the context of generating stronger responses to cases of mass atrocity crimes. This theme is also central to RVR as a transitional cosmopolitan reform measure. RVR is a recommendation for the P5 to display restraint in using their veto powers, and it is aimed at enabling the UNSC to pass resolutions for action in all relevant cases of mass atrocity, preventing draft resolutions from being scuppered by a single member. Notably, this means that RVR adopts the France-Mexico initiative's focus on the veto power of the P5 members, and rejects the ACT Code's focus on the whole of the UNSC membership.

Second, the RVR recommendation adopts an altered (and improved) trigger system to that of the France-Mexico initiative. RVR would require a hybrid UNGA / UN Secretary-General system for being triggered; a two-thirds majority vote of the UNGA would recommend that the Secretary-General determine whether a matter was likely a case of genuine R2P concern with relevance to mass atrocity prevention. If the Secretary-General were to determine that this was indeed the case, then RVR would come into action, and the P5 would be expected to avoid utilising their veto right.

Third, RVR does not include any subjective get-out clause for the P5, such as the 'credibility' of a given draft resolution (ACT Code) or infringement on the 'vital interests' of the P5 members (France-Mexico initiative). This is with the aim of preventing a continuation of the status quo that subjective get-out clauses for veto restraint could enable.

Finally, and where RVR perhaps differs most considerably from previous veto restraint recommendations, the RVR mechanism would not apply to UNSC votes on the application of coercive measures such as sanctions, criminal prosecutorial mechanisms (including ICC referrals), or the authorisation of coercive military force without host-state consent. RVR would apply to any Pillar Two action, as well as Pillar Three action which precludes coercive mechanisms. This means that RVR would apply to actions such as condemnatory statements, including determinations that atrocity situations warrant threats to international peace and security; the establishment of consent-based peacekeeping missions; the provision of humanitarian aid; and the establishment of fact-finding and / or monitoring teams to assess the on-ground facts of an atrocity crisis.

5.4.1 *Test of Effective Progress*

Let us now assess the value of these recommendations. First, RVR can help to facilitate UNSC action in response to mass atrocities. Excluding sanctions, criminal prosecutorial mechanisms, and coercive military measures from RVR should, in theory, help to assuage fears that veto restraint would be open to abuse. This would hopefully make it more likely that the P5 members would employ veto restraint in votes over non-coercive measures short of the use of non-consensual force. Precluding coercive mechanisms would make redundant any argument that said measures could have a directly destabilising effect on the target state, or that veto restraint would automatically lead to such measures. It should therefore prevent a P5 member from being able to cloud self-interested veto use within the reasoning of preserving regional stability or maintaining international peace. As Morris (2016, p. 209) has similarly argued when suggesting a removal of coercive elements from R2P more generally,[7] it can 'deprive those who cite such fears as a cloak for ulterior reasons for wanting to prevent intervention of a means of rationalising and justifying their stance'.

Pattison's (2018) analysis on the alternatives to war helps to highlight the theoretical value of RVR. Pattison (2018, p. 222) argues that the use of coercive military force should always be the 'presumed last resort' in response to atrocity crimes. He argues that alternatives to war can always make at least some contribution towards protecting fundamental human rights, without the unwanted side-effects that military actions bring. RVR is compatible with this approach as it can help to promote measures such as declaratory statements and condemnations of violence to delegitimise actors and demonstrate the international community's willingness to act on the situation; humanitarian access to provide vital resources and life-saving aid to those in need; fact-finding missions and/or monitoring teams to bring greater accountability and knowledge of crises; mediation efforts to help in brokering peace; as well as providing counter-narratives to atrocity violence to promote the norm that atrocity crimes are unacceptable. While these measures are far from guaranteed to end cases of mass atrocities, they can at least promote action that helps ameliorate suffering and represents an attempt to fulfil cosmopolitan protection demands.

For example, rhetorical condemnation of actors responsible for mass crimes can sometimes have efficacy by raising the political costs of breaching a norm's rules (Bellamy and Luck, 2018, pp. 39; 47; Gallagher, 2021, p. 5). Condemnations also promote norms of human protection and reject impunity for mass crimes, potentially influencing the potential for future transgressions elsewhere (Pattison, 2018, pp. 92–98). It could also be added to this that condemnation can serve as ample warning to transgressors that future, more robust action, may be considered should they not quickly cease their actions. RVR would make it easier to adopt such measures, without imposing a looming spectre that they are merely the 'thin-end of the wedge' before coercive military intervention. Further, it is important to highlight that nothing in the proposals here calls for the entire removal of consideration for the use of sanctions, criminal prosecution, or coercive military force as part of the R2P. The use of these measures in mass atrocity situations would (and should) remain available to the UNSC on a case-by-case basis as part of the R2P toolkit.

Some might argue that only applying veto restraint to measures short of sanctions, criminal prosecution, and coercive military force would make RVR too weak. Ultimately, however, tempering the mechanism's scope is a necessary step to make veto restraint more tenable. The desired outcome being to avoid *complete* UNSC deadlock over major atrocity crises of the future, and as a consequence serve as an effective incremental step towards a more consistent application of the R2P that aligns with the cosmopolitan demands. Furthermore, were the P5 to accept veto restraint in this form, it would at least send a powerful message that the UNSC is devoted to fulfilling its R2P, and would be an acknowledgement of the need to limit veto usage. This may provide the potential for longer term and incremental progress towards achieving consistent veto restraint by acting as an iterative mechanism through which the P5 become socialised into a new practice of veto use. In this sense, RVR attempts to push practice in a favourable direction over time. The hope is that through the gradual socialisation of P5 members into a practice of veto restraint, more robust measures will become more feasible as trust is built between P5 members that veto restraint does not equate to automatically authorising the use of coercive military force or regime change. While opposition to military force may remain unmoved, RVR can still aid in pushing practice towards other robust measures short of coercive military force over time. The point is that excluding these measures now is necessary to offer the tentative, first transitional steps towards progress in the long term, and that in doing so, at least some positive progress can be offered immediately. Perhaps in the long term, sanctions and criminal prosecution could be dropped as part of RVR, or from a potential formal Charter amendment to the veto power. But for now, they are necessarily excluded from RVR as a means of enabling short-term and feasible progress.

Second, due to its specificity, including a clear and specified trigger system for when RVR becomes active, means that the mechanism is more aligned with the transitional cosmopolitan demand for effective progress than a vaguer notion such as 'facts on the ground' in the ACT Code. This is because a trigger system is less open to interpretation and political manoeuvring. However, as noted above, the trigger system in place in the France-Mexico initiative is troublesome. Hence, an altered triggering system is called for in the RVR proposal. The trigger system recommended here (two-thirds UNGA majority vote followed by UN Secretary-General affirmation) would allow the UNGA to act quickly in calling on the Secretary-General to determine whether a case is reflective of R2P concern; whether there are likely atrocities occurring; or whether there is clear potential for atrocities to occur. This would enable the UN system to act in accordance with its responsibility to provide timely and decisive R2P response, ensuring that the UNSC cannot be obstructed by a single vote when it comes to matters short of coercive response.

Third, removing the notions of 'credible' and 'vital interests' as subjective get-out clauses for the P5 also attempts to make the recommendation here more effective. The vital interests concept is too open to abuse as self-interest often accounts for the underlying reason as to why the veto is exercised in the first place (Security Council Report, 2015, p. 5). Further, and perhaps more importantly, the self-interest of the UNSC members should be subservient to their management of international security and promotion of fundamental human rights. Including a vital interest clause would seem to undermine the cosmopolitan normative aspect of veto reform too heavily, weakening the claim that the UNSC members have a responsibility to act under the R2P. Similarly, including a clause for the 'credibility' of resolutions would open the door for abuse of the concept by P5 members wishing to preserve their self-interests. Removing these clauses seeks to make the proposal more aligned with the transitional cosmopolitan call for effective progress by attempting to make P5 members more accountable to their mandate under the R2P. The recommendation here removes subjective get-out clauses for the P5 that could be interpreted by the P5 to instrumentally further self-interest. One may riposte here that removing these clauses undermines the feasibility of the RVR proposal too greatly. However, since the measure promoted here calls for the separation of veto restraint from coercive mechanisms, the clauses of 'credible' resolutions or 'vital interests' shouldn't be necessary for P5 members to feel like their interests are guarded, as separation from coercive mechanisms should go a long way towards assuaging fears that veto restraint could be abused.

5.4.2 *Test of Moral Hazard*

More than simply easing P5 tensions, separating sanctions, criminal prosecution mechanisms, and coercive military measures from veto restraint also serves to ease the tension discussed above regarding the UNSC's dual responsibility. RVR would not bind the P5 over morally hazardous resolutions that threaten international peace and security through the potentially destabilising effect of those measures. In this regard, the veto would stay true to its original normative purpose as RVR would not undermine the UNSC as the medium for managing international peace and security. RVR would in fact strengthen this function by helping to ameliorate the tension between its competing responsibilities, enabling the UNSC to meet its responsibility to protecting fundamental human rights via the R2P, but without threatening the destabilisation of international peace and security as an unwanted side effect.

In particular, precluding coercive military measures from the RVR recommendation makes it more cautious than previous veto restraint proposals, as it would make the UNSC unlikely to consider the use of coercive military force as a first resort. As the potential for veto would remain over such a proposal, the UNSC would seem forced to discuss the alternatives to coercive military measures as a first resort. Here it is again worth drawing on

Pattison's analysis. Pattison (2018, pp. 215–216) argues that war is known to cause unwanted death and destruction, often involves *doing harm,* and there is also uncertainty about its potential effectiveness in any given situation. Precluding coercive military measures should enhance RVR as an effective mechanism by avoiding the moral hazards associated with war that may undermine normative progress. Further, this helps contribute to the RVR's feasibility as it should help assuage fears that RVR could lead to damaging side-effects.

Second, the trigger system proposed in the RVR recommendation also seeks to align the measure with the transitional cosmopolitan approach by addressing a potential moral hazard. Increasing the number of states required for raising the issue with the Secretary-General to a two-thirds majority of UN members makes the process more democratic than the France-Mexico initiative trigger system, while also helping to alleviate the potential for abuse by states attempting to overzealously advocate cases as necessitating veto restraint. Requiring only a small number of states to raise a case may lead to an overabundance of cases being brought forward for Secretary-General action that may actually undermine attention to other cases which are more genuine manifest R2P failings. In contrast, by having a more stringent trigger system, the recommendation made here allows for a more cautious trigger system, much less prone to abuse. Further, requiring a two-thirds majority vote in the UNGA also aligns the RVR mechanism with the UNGA's working methods, by acknowledging that '[d]ecisions of the General Assembly on important questions shall be made by a two-thirds majority of the members present and voting', which includes 'recommendations with respect to the maintenance of international peace and security' (UN, 1945, art. 18(2)). This should help address any concern that RVR goes beyond the constitutional bounds of the UN Charter.

Third, by applying only to the P5 members, another point RVR addresses is the potential for abuse if states are compelled to accept any resolution pertaining to an R2P issue. Adediran (2018, p. 477) argues that adopting a code of conduct for veto use would undermine the contribution of the UNSC's non-permanent members as their votes would become pre-determined. This would seem the case were the ACT Code's focus on the whole UNSC membership adopted, as the Code would compel all UNSC members to vote in favour of a given resolution. However, this argument doesn't apply to the France-Mexico initiative, which only calls on the P5 states to suspend their veto power, rather than all UNSC members to avoid voting against a resolution. By adopting this aspect of the France-Mexico initiative, RVR can also allay the tension highlighted by Adediran, promoting a form of veto reform that would still require a draft resolution to obtain a favourable vote of 9 from 15 UNSC members.

What must be emphasised here is that the purpose of veto restraint is not to create scenarios where *any* R2P-based action is automatically accepted, but to improve the deliberation process of the UNSC when voting on a resolution.

By making it so that a draft resolution could no longer be scuppered by one member, the UNSC's voting process would be made significantly more democratic and able to promote action which the majority of the UNSC deems to be appropriate, rather than granting excessive power in the hands of five states. This would prevent a draft resolution being blocked by any one state, but would also remove fears that the UNSC would be bound to accept any given draft resolution relevant to R2P and mass atrocities. This should serve to alleviate fears of potential abuse. It should also be noted here that the P5 members could still continue to voice their dissent towards a draft resolution by abstention from voting, as has become customary practice where they have not wished to exercise a formal veto.

5.4.3 *Test of Practical Potential*

RVR attempts to avoid greatly undermining the vital interests of the P5 states. The P5's veto power and its relationship with the authorisation of the use of force is intrinsically tied to the problem of competing interests at the UNSC. By precluding the use of military measures as a given, RVR would serve what Vilmer (2018, p. 342) refers to as 'responding to the risk of abuse' of veto restraint. Separating sanctions, criminal prosecution mechanisms, and coercive military force from veto restraint can allow the P5 members to feel that their interests are less threatened. For example, where a P5 member has strong ties to a particular state or regime, such as Russia to Assad in Syria, or the US to Israel, it would be of assurance to these states that they could still prevent the passage of coercive actions that might be perceived as greatly threatening their interests.

It is also worth noting that the three P5 members who remain unconvinced by calls for veto restraint (the US, Russia, and China) are the same three P5 members that have not ratified the Rome Statute of the ICC. Excluding ICC referrals, as a form of criminal prosecutorial mechanism, from measures which require P5 veto restraint would help enhance the feasibility of RVR by avoiding a politically controversial area; one which has been linked to both military force and regime change (see Saba and Akbarzadeh, 2020). Further, the reservations of states such as Russia and China regarding military measures are arguably not entirely instrumental as they hold a normative belief that the use of force can rarely serve a positive humanitarian purpose (Paris, 2014; Allison, 2017; Foot, 2020). Separating military measures from a veto restraint initiative could assuage the fears of certain P5 members that suspending their veto right will inevitably lead to the application of potentially destabilising military measures. It is argued here that including a clause for 'measures short of sanctions and coercive military force' is vital if the P5 – who are inherently split over the normative value in applying the use of forceful measures for humanitarian purposes – are ever to be united over veto restraint for R2P matters. In doing so, it is tentatively hoped that by easing the tensions between the P5 and their attitudes to coercive action under R2P

Pillar Three, RVR could help begin to repair the relationship between P5 members and consequently promote a consistent demand to produce at least some form of international response to all mass atrocity cases.

Second, adopting the RVR recommendation can be in the interests of the P5 members themselves. The UNSC is dependent on maintaining its own legitimacy in the international community (Hurd, 2007). Where the UNSC fails to live up to its responsibilities under the R2P, its own authority comes into question.[8] If the P5 are seen to be in favour of progress towards UNSC reform, this may help to strengthen the acceptance of their authority from the wider UN membership. Linked to this, veto restraint should be viewed as a way to strengthen the veto power and not to undermine it. As Vilmer (2018, p. 343) notes, 'repeated vetoes like in the case of Syria undermine the authority and eventually the centrality of the Security Council, restricting the veto gives it its full international effectiveness'. If the veto is to remain a meaningful tool of international management, then it requires acceptance by UN members. Reform may help to strengthen this acceptance, meaning that veto reform is likely in the long-term interests of the P5. Further, adopting the RVR proposal and improving the potential for action to stymy mass atrocities can actually serve the direct interests of the P5 as well. This can satisfy any normative interest they hold in preventing and responding to mass atrocity crimes, but also their more instrumental interests such as stymying refugee flows and the growth of international terrorism which are directly linked to outbreaks of mass violence (World Bank Group, 2018). Further, successfully curbing atrocities is likely to bring economic advantages in the long term by lowering the amount of international aid required in conflict-ridden states, peacekeeping, and intervention expenditures, while also promoting long-term sustainability in target countries and reducing the necessity for future interventions (see Pathfinders, 2020).

It cannot be conclusively determined if the measures recommended here could successfully overcome the reservations of the three remaining P5 members currently opposed to veto reform, and the above arguments are not at all meant to downplay the very significant political obstacles standing in the way of achieving full P5 support. The measures could have an impact in the longer term though. For instance, they could help to assuage fears in certain sections of the international community – particularly non-P5 BRICS states and other medium powers – who have been troubled by the application of military force too readily in Libya, but who are supportive of the tenets of the R2P more generally. By doing so, the reform measures proposed here should theoretically be able to garner wider support, which, as noted, would enhance the pressure on the US, Russia, and China to adopt veto restraint. The generally favourable attitude of the US towards the R2P, and China's desire to be perceived as a responsible world leader (Foot, 2016, p. 938), offers potential openings for this political pressure to reap some (limited) success. For instance, Odgaard (2020) has argued that China's policy of 'coexistence' with liberal internationalist principles has meant that China is on occasion willing to compromise on its non-interventionist preference. Others, such as Fung (2019), Foot (2020), and Teitt (2020), claim that China is not an outright R2P rejectionist state; although notably, China's support for the concept is rooted in a particular statist, and limited-interventionist position that likely does not align with calls for veto restraint over matters of R2P response emergency (see Fung, 2019, pp. 135–141). Nevertheless, China's rise as a world power and desire to be perceived as a responsible leader (Breslin, 2013, p. 1274; Vilmer, 2018, p. 349) perhaps offers hope that it may one day accept some tempered form of veto restraint.[9]

Moreover, by only applying to non-coercive measures, RVR would undermine arguments made by veto-casting members that international action over an atrocity case is a prelude to authorising coercive military force. As noted above, this would prevent P5 members from being able to cloak self-interest in the name of normative reasoning, such as for preserving regional stability. With the safeguard against sanctions and coercive military force offered by RVR, if P5 members continued to veto proposed non-military measures then international pressure would mount as it would be clear that vetoes were being cast simply to further the self-interest of the veto-casting members. This pressure would raise the political costs of vetoing. As Bellamy (2019, p. 186) notes, 'with sustained pressure, vetoes could be made so politically expensive that the permanent members would consider employing them only when absolutely necessary'. Whether desire to avoid this pressure would be enough to actively change P5 attitudes remains to be seen, and we can therefore only speculate as to whether this proposal can feasibly overcome soft constraints in the way of reform.[10] Overall though, the tempered nature of the RVR recommendation would seem better placed to satisfy the transitional cosmopolitan test for overcoming soft constraints in the way of progress. Therefore, RVR offers a more feasible avenue for progress than the ACT Code or the France-Mexico initiative.

The RVR recommendation better satisfies the transitional cosmopolitan tests for effectiveness and feasibility than the ACT Code and France-Mexico initiative. In doing so, RVR attempts to help in establishing the middle position for promoting progress, providing a recommendation which can help us achieve a more consistent implementation of the R2P. RVR attempts to satisfy the transitional cosmopolitan approach by aligning the currently diverging positions of the P5 members vis-à-vis veto restraint, reducing the tensions between the UNSC's dual responsibility, and promoting at least some R2P action that can contribute to R2P's application as a cosmopolitan responsibility.

5.5 Syria and the Necessity of Responsible Veto Restraint

We can identify an example of where the veto has been exercised over a mass atrocity case and use this as a hypothetical to explore the transitional cosmopolitan value of the RVR proposal. As noted in the chapter's introduction, there are numerous cases of where a veto has scuppered a UNSC resolution pertaining to a human protection issue (Bellamy, 2019, p. 186). However, the most pertinent of these examples comes from the crisis in Syria, where 17 UNSC draft resolutions have been vetoed to date. The Syrian case is reflective of a clear R2P crisis, wherein the international community has often failed to live up to its responsibility to protect. Most recently, vetoes have been cast on resolutions regarding the delivery of life-saving humanitarian aid. Back-to-back vetoes occurred on 7 and 10 July 2020, with Russia and China vetoing draft resolutions which sought to extend for six months the delivery of humanitarian aid into Syria through the Bab al-Salam and Bab al-Hawa crossings in Turkey (UN, 2020). Sherine Tadros, Amnesty International's Head of UN Office, described the vetoes as 'despicable and dangerous', since for many Syrians, humanitarian aid is 'the difference between having food to eat and starving' (Amnesty International, 2020). On 8 July 2022, Russia, alone this time, vetoed a draft resolution which sought to extend the delivery of aid through the border crossing at Bab al-Hawa – now the sole access point for aid into Syria – for six months, with an optional further six months beyond this. On 12 July 2022, the members of the UNSC did reach a compromise to extend aid through the crossing for six months, but the fact that one member of the Council was able to obstruct the original resolution demonstrates the egregiousness of how the veto can prevent the passage of even non-coercive and vital mechanisms like aid. It is for draft resolutions such as these that veto restraint is clearly morally necessitated and where the RVR mechanism could readily be applied.

However, the example in this section focuses on the earlier part of the Syria crisis in 2011–12, specifically, on the first two UNSC draft resolutions that were put forward and subsequently vetoed by Russia and China. The contrast between these two draft proposals provides useful insight into the transitional cosmopolitan value of RVR. The case demonstrates that were RVR in place at the early part of the Syrian crisis, it would have been possible to pass R2P action in the UNSC that may have helped ameliorate the situation and allowed the UNSC to meet its responsibilities.

On 4 October 2011, the UNSC put to vote its first draft resolution for the Syrian crisis (UNSC, 2011b). The draft received the requisite nine votes in favour, with four abstentions. However, vetoes were cast by Russia and China, preventing the resolution from being adopted. The draft declared that there had been 'continued grave and systematic human rights violations and the use of force against civilians by the Syrian authorities' (UNSC, 2011b). The draft also called for access for humanitarian work and human rights monitors. Importantly though, it also stated that the Council 'would consider its options, including *measures under Article 41* of the Charter' (UNSC, 2011b, emphasis added), referring to the option of applying sanctions against Assad under the UNSC's Chapter VII remit.

A second draft resolution over the Syria case was put forward on 4 February 2012 (UNSC, 2012). This time, 13 members voted in favour of the draft. Again though, Russia and China cast vetoes. This draft called for 'an immediate end to all violence' in addition to the granting of humanitarian access (UNSC, 2012). Again, it still sought to directly condemn the Syrian authorities. However, the draft also reaffirmed the sovereignty and territorial integrity of Syria, while *specifically* ruling out Article 42 measures (use of force). There was also no mention made of Article 41 or potential sanctions. Notably though, the draft resolution did declare that the Council '[f]ully supports ... the League of Arab States' 22 January 2012 decision to facilitate a Syrian-led political transition' (UNSC, 2012, para. 7), which could be interpreted as a call for Syrian regime change. The draft, though, did not explicitly call for Assad's removal. Regardless of whether this clause actually equated to an implied call for the removal of Assad, it offered an easy way for Russia and China to justify their vetoes (Ralph and Gifkins, 2017). This likely demonstrates that the potential success of RVR would also be dependent on careful 'penholding' and wording Council draft resolutions to avoid heavily contentious demands, or possibly even a further stipulation in the RVR proposal that it should not apply to calls for 'political transition' or other similarly worded clauses.

Nevertheless, it is argued here that the use of the veto on this second draft resolution was again a failure to meet the UNSC's responsibilities under the R2P. Crimes against humanity and war crimes were committed in Syria in this period, a fact confirmed at the time by the UN High Commissioner for Human Rights (Nanda, 2013, p. 15). Yet the Council failed to respond, with the vetoes leaving it effectively paralysed (Weiss, 2014, p. 13). Additionally, it could also be claimed that failed action over Syria was a failure of the Council's responsibility to maintain international peace and security, as the inability to halt the conflict also helped foster the growth of terrorist groups, such as the so-called 'Islamic State of Iraq and the Levant', causing further regional disruption, as well as severely undermining fundamental human rights.

However, one might contend that the use of the veto over the Syrian case is reflective of the exact reason why the veto exists in the first place. Russia perceives the stability of the Assad-led Syrian regime as one of its own vital interests, and so a threat to this from another powerful state risks raising international tensions. When we examine the public arguments made by Russia and China for their vetoes, their veto use over the first draft resolution may actually seem consistent with the purpose of the veto. The first draft referred to the use of sanctions – albeit only an acknowledgement that they would be considered – which can be viewed in the wider context of the P3's desire to see regime change in Syria (Ralph, 2018). This made Russia and China's rhetorical concerns arguably well-founded, even if the drafts themselves were not aimed at regime change. As such, while the threat of sanctions remained on the table with the first draft, the Chinese and Russian argument was, if nothing else, consistent. Even though veto use contravened the UNSC's responsibility under the R2P – and the resolution had been so toned down from earlier drafts to the point that 'almost everything' in it reflected political compromise (Bellamy, 2022b, p. 39) – a tension between this and the Council's responsibility to international peace was evident.

Yet the same cannot be said for the second draft resolution. The second draft explicitly ruled out coercive measures and would have provided beneficial R2P action, such as humanitarian access and rhetorical condemnation of the Assad regime's actions. As noted above, these actions can help in protecting fundamental human rights, while also contributing to the normative drive of the R2P that atrocity crimes will not go unpunished (Pattison, 2018). This would have contributed to the UNSC meeting its responsibility under the R2P. Further, the second draft resolution had been so toned down from the first that there was little to suggest a conflict between the UNSC's dual responsibility. The exercise of the veto over the second draft was therefore a clear failure to meet the UNSC's cosmopolitan responsibility under the R2P, and cannot be excused by the argument of a tension between its dual responsibility. It must therefore be concluded that the use of the veto over the second draft was irresponsible.

The vetoes harmed the normative development of the R2P. This led to scholars such as Nuruzzaman declaring the norm's 'death' (Nuruzzaman, 2013), while others, such as Zifcack, saw the Syrian situation as a reality check on the use of coercive force under the R2P (Zifcack, 2012). In truth, the situation really only highlighted something already known: the disagreement over how to apply R2P Pillar Three in practice. As Hehir has written, the Syria case highlights that the P5 will 'treat each case put before the Security Council on a case-by-case basis following evaluation of their respective interests' (Hehir, 2013, p. 150). The Syria case highlights this continued problem. It shows that separating sanctions and the coercive use of force from UNSC resolutions is essential to realising R2P action in the future where there is substantive disagreement regarding the use of force and a conflict between the Council's special responsibilities is evident, or where major P5 interests are at stake. While the tenets of the R2P are generally accepted, including by all P5 members, this is not enough to overcome such conflicts of interest where the threat of military action exists.

In regard to the effect that RVR could have had; as the first draft resolution over Syria related to the potential for sanctions under article 41, RVR would not have applied. As noted, Russia and China had been very fervent in their opposition to the potential use of sanctions against the Assad regime, perceiving them as a prelude to military force. However, the second draft explicitly ruled out the use of force and made no mention of potential sanctions. Were RVR honoured then, the second draft resolution would have been passed. Russia and China may have still claimed that the motive of Assad's removal was driving the draft, however, as RVR would have been active, they would be obliged to avoid voting against the draft. As RVR would preserve their power to prevent the use of coercive measures further down the line, it is possible that they would have honoured a commitment to RVR. One might observe that despite its cautious wording, Russia and China did still veto the second draft resolution anyway. But the guarantee provided by RVR that the veto power would be maintained over any future consideration of sanctions or coercive military force, combined with the potential political costs of foregoing their RVR commitment, *may* have been enough to influence Russia and China to avoid veto use. What this example demonstrates is that RVR can create the space for at least some action in response to mass atrocities in cases where P5 interests clash. This is likely to be action well short of what would be the ideal UNSC response, but this is still better than the complete failure to produce any action. In opening up the space for action, RVR could help in the norm building of the R2P, helping to alter UNSC behaviour over time as an understanding of the need to avoid veto use over less robust R2P actions is generated. Again, this is consistent with the transitional cosmopolitan approach which calls for incremental normative progress while operating among practical constraints.

Had a resolution of condemnation and humanitarian access been passed in the early days of The crisis, this would have helped in passing useful action to fulfil the UNSC's cosmopolitan responsibilities. As Gareth Evans (2013, p. 19) has argued:

> the case for a condemnatory statement was overwhelming and had that been supplemented by the kind of measures that were initially applied in Libya … Assad would certainly have been given cause for pause.

Had RVR been in place, the Council would have been in a better place to meet its responsibility to act on the Syrian crisis, serving to quell claims of its illegitimacy, while also contributing to the normative development of the R2P, and more importantly, could have paved way for the stemming of violence in Syria. Action fostered by RVR may itself not be particularly robust, but it can nevertheless help in ameliorating R2P crises. In the Syria case, had the UNSC been able to pass early action, then Assad's sense of impunity may have been reduced, potentially causing him to scale back his campaign of force and helping to stymy the conflict before it spilled into all-out civil war. The second vetoed UNSC draft resolution was particularly emboldening for Assad, as it signalled a clear message that the UNSC was unable to foster any kind of significant collective response to events in Syria. Violence in the month immediately following the February 2012 vetoed resolution was the highest it had reached at any point so far in the conflict (Bellamy, 2022b, p. 56).

We should also remember that the use of diplomatic pressure can have a meaningful effect. This is highlighted by the later example of the pressure applied against Assad following his use of chemical weapons attacks (Weiss, 2014, p. 17). This particular diplomatic response backed Assad into a corner where he was forced to comply, showing that when the international community makes a concerted effort to apply diplomatic pressure, this can reap success. At the very least, the second draft resolution would have permitted humanitarian access early on during the crisis which would have actively worked to save lives and helped meet the UNSC's responsibility under the R2P. Such steps would have represented an attempt to meet the demands of human protection. This would have satisfied the transitional cosmopolitan demand for at least some action in response to a clear manifest failing of R2P Pillar One, acknowledging that while over the Syria case the ideal cosmopolitan line was not possible, it can still be possible to work among practical constraints in order to promote some normatively desirable progress. Furthermore, as noted, RVR does not in any way close down the potential for more robust R2P action. This further supports the notion that RVR can help in establishing the middle position associated with transitional cosmopolitanism, where some positive action is possible in the present, and the potential for further action also remains possible. RVR would merely serve to make less controversial R2P action a stronger possibility.

Less optimistically, it may simply be the case that due to the deep complexities of the Syria case, including the instrumental ties between Russia and Assad, Russia and China would have vetoed the draft resolution anyway. Perhaps it is just simply too much to expect that a P5 member will ever forego its instrumental interests to promote R2P action. A more optimistic caveat, however, could be that mass atrocity crises of the future may not be quite so morally and politically complex as the Syria case (Glanville, 2021, pp. 147–149). So long as there are not significant instrumental interests at stake, and rather only more normative opposition to the use of force more generally, RVR can still help to promote at least some R2P-based action in response to the crises of the future. For instance, where a P5 member is sceptical of the interests of other Council members, and only has minor interests at stake itself, it would seem fair to suggest that they would be conducive to at least accepting action short of sanctions, criminal prosecutorial mechanisms, and coercive military force. Over time, as trust is rebuilt between the P5, they may even become conducive to accepting more robust action, so long as they have the assurance provided by RVR that veto restraint in the face of R2P breaches does not equate to automatically authorising the use of coercive military force. RVR can help in rebuilding the relationship between P5 members which has been so heavily tarnished by the events in Libya and Syria. If honoured by Russia and China, it can show the P3 members that it is possible to act through the Council on R2P matters. And if the P3 members operate through the Council and avoid unilateral action, they can show Russia and China that they can be trusted to honour the purpose of the Council. Without RVR or some other form of veto restraint measure, the UNSC seems destined to fail to meet its responsibilities under the R2P for any future mass atrocity crisis where competing P5 interests are at stake.

5.6 Conclusion

This chapter has argued for the adoption of an informal RVR measure. This nuanced approach to altering recent ACT Code and France-Mexico initiative proposals presents an avenue for veto reform that is transitional, appreciative of the purpose of the veto, and, in theory, able to help in overcoming UNSC inaction over contentious mass atrocity cases. While practical constraints – mainly the opposition of some of the veto-wielding states themselves – make veto reform immensely difficult, the transitional cosmopolitan approach demands that these constraints not be interpreted fatalistically. It may be possible to achieve a degree of veto restraint that can aid in the application of the R2P in meeting cosmopolitan protection demands. However, the transitional cosmopolitan line requires that if we are to achieve this, we must temper expectations over what reform can help us achieve in the present, while fostering the avenues through which further progress can be made. RVR, in satisfying the requirements of the transitional cosmopolitan tests for effectiveness and feasibility of reform, attempts to help in establishing this transitional middle position. RVR is not intended as an ideal solution to the veto problem, but at the very least its adoption could signal the potential for progress and act as a positive step in the direction of a cosmopolitan approach to human protection.

The hard truth is that imposing veto restraint remains extremely difficult with the attitudes of some P5 members remaining far less than favourable. Perhaps the case is that striking a transitional cosmopolitan balance for veto reform is too difficult: in attempting to make reform more feasible we perhaps only undermine its potential effectiveness and vice versa. Finding the balance between the two is immensely challenging, but not something that should be given up on. While even a mild proposal like the one offered here has issues – such as whether it would be effective in practice, and whether it could actually be tenable to the P5 – it attempts to strike a balance between the concerns of P5 members and the cosmopolitan goals of the R2P. The success of veto reform will rest on continued campaigning in the UN, wider advocacy groups, and in particular on the attitudes of the P5 members themselves.

A functioning UNSC is desirable for an effective R2P, and it may be too premature to declare the UNSC unfit for realising the R2P, yet if the Council continues to fail to provide meaningful action in the face of mass atrocities, and it becomes apparent that reforming the Council is not possible, then the international community will be forced to consider alternatives for implementing R2P action under Pillar Three. The following chapter turns to one such alternative: the Uniting for Peace mechanism and the powers of the UNGA.

Notes

1 While the UN Charter does not directly refer to a veto power as such, it is implicitly found in the text of Chapter V, Article 27, where it states that decisions of the

Security Council require 'the concurring votes of the permanent members' (UN, 1945). In other words, if any of the P5 members vote against a draft, it cannot be passed as a legally binding resolution.

2 During the Council's consideration of the Spanish question in 1946, it was determined that the abstention of a permanent member (in that case, the USSR) did not violate the stipulation of 'concurring votes' under Article 27(3).

3 See for instance the Russian veto over the resolution to mark the 20th anniversary of the Srebrenica massacre (UNSC, 2015); US vetoes of Israel-Palestine issues (UNSC, 2006a; UNSC, 2006b; UNSC, 2011a; UNSC, 2018c); the Russian veto over the Yemeni-Saudi crisis (UNSC, 2018b); the Chinese-Russian veto over Venezuela (UNSC, 2019); and cases such as Myanmar (Rohingya abuses) and North Korea that failed to make it onto the UNSC's formal agenda for fear of veto (the so-called 'hidden veto').

4 This is an idea that came to the fore with the 2011 intervention in Libya and the subsequent disruption through the region and to the state itself (see Kuperman, 2015).

5 See Vilmer (2018) for a detailed genealogy of both the ACT Code and France-Mexico initiative's development.

6 The US did, interestingly, co-sponsor Lichtenstein's 'veto initiative' in April 2022, with this initiative meaning that any vetoed resolution in the UNSC will now trigger a meeting of the UNGA. Notably though, the US still doesn't support any direct alteration to the veto, or support any direct restraint mechanism.

7 Morris' view on removing R2P's coercive elements entirely is not supported here, as a transitional cosmopolitan would maintain that in order to identify and efficacious middle position, it must be possible to make some progress towards the normative end goal. Some form of coercion such as rhetorical condemnation is likely necessary for meeting the UNSC's R2P. Morris does suggest that the UNSC would maintain its right to exercise force outside the R2P framework, however, this would seem to weaken the doctrine as a whole by undermining the responsibility to react (see Bellamy, 2022a).

8 This has been especially evident in recent action taken by the UNGA (see Chapter 6). For instance, in the wake of Russia's invasion of Ukraine and the subsequent adoption of Lichtenstein's 'veto initiative' by the UNGA.

9 Ongoing events in Xinjiang province do, however, suggest that China will remain unreceptive to calls for veto restraint at least for the foreseeable future.

10 As a side but related note, the present author also supports Trahan's (2022, p. 132) recommendation for the UNGA to call on the ICJ to deliver an advisory opinion on the legality of veto use surrounding cases of mass atrocity, as this would be another way of significantly ramping up political pressure on the P5 to avoid veto use. It is interesting that Trahan believes that raising the possibility of a UNGA request for an ICJ advisory opinion may help pressure the P5 into adopting voluntary veto restraint mechanisms (such as proposed here), as this would be less costly to the P5 than an ICJ ruling on the veto's illegality in cases of atrocity.

References

Accountability, Coherence and Transparency Group 2015. Explanatory Note on a Code of Conduct regarding Security Council action against genocide, crimes against humanity or war crimes. [Accessed 18 May 2018]. Available from: http://responsibilitytoprotect.org/ENG%20FINAL%20ACT%20code%20of%20conduct.pdf.

Adediran, B. 2018. Reforming the Security Council through a Code of Conduct: A Sisyphean Task? *Ethics & International Affairs.* **32**(4), pp. 463–482.

Allison, R. 2017. Russia and the Post-2014 International Legal Order: Revisionism and Realpolitik. *International Affairs.* **93**(3), pp. 519–543.

Amnesty International 2020. UN: Russia and China launch despicable veto of lifesaving aid for millions of civilians in Syria. [Accessed 10 August 2020]. Available from: https://www.amnesty.org/en/latest/news/2020/07/un-russia-and-china-lau nch-despicable-veto-of-lifesaving-aid-for-millions-of-civilians-in-syria/.

Archibugi, D. 2008. *The Global Commonwealth of Citizens: Toward Cosmopolitan Democracy.* Princeton, NJ: Princeton University Press.

Bellamy, A.J. 2006. Whither the Responsibility to Protect? Humanitarian intervention and the 2005 World Summit. *Ethics & International Affairs.* **20**(2), pp. 143–169.

Bellamy, A.J. 2019. *World Peace (And How We Can Achieve It).* Oxford: Oxford University Press.

Bellamy, A.J. 2022a. R2P and the Use of Force. *Global Responsibility to Protect.* **14**(3), pp. 277–280.

Bellamy, A.J. 2022b. *Syria Betrayed: Atrocities, War, and the Failure of International Diplomacy.* New York: Columbia University Press.

Bellamy, A.J. and Luck, E.C. 2018. *The Responsibility to Protect: From Promise to Practice.* Cambridge: Polity Press.

Bellamy, A.J. and Tacheva, B. 2019. R2P and the Emergence of Responsibilities Across Borders *In*: R. Beardsworth, G. W. Brown and R. Shapcott, eds. *The State and Cosmopolitan Responsibilities.* Oxford: Oxford University Press, pp. 15–40.

Blätter, A. and Williams, P.D. 2011. The Responsibility Not to Veto. *Global Responsibility to Protect.* **3**(3), pp. 301–322.

Breslin, S. 2013. China and the South: Objectives, Actors and Interactions. *Development and Change.* **44**(6), pp. 1273–1294.

Coen, A. 2015. R2P, Global Governance, and the Syrian Refugee Crisis. *The International Journal of Human Rights.* **19**(8), pp. 1044–1058.

Evans, G. 2014. The Consequences of Non-Intervention in Syria: Does the Responsibility to Protect Have a Future? *In*: R.W. Murray and A. McKay, eds. *Into the Eleventh Hour: R2P, Syria and Humanitarianism in Crisis.* Bristol: E-International Relations, pp. 18–25.

Fabius, L. 2013. A Call for Self-Restraint at the UN *New York Times.* [Online]. [Accessed 2 January 2023]. Available from: www.nytimes.com/2013/10/04/opin ion/a-call-for-self-restraint-at-the-un.html.

Foot, R. 2016. The State, Development, and Humanitarianism: China's Shaping of the Trajectory of R2P *In*: A.J. Bellamy and T. Dunne, eds. *The Oxford Handbook of the Responsibility to Protect.* Oxford: Oxford University Press, pp. 932–947.

Foot, R. 2020. *China, the UN, and Human Protection: Beliefs, Power, Image.* Oxford: Oxford University Press.

France and Mexico 2015. Political statement on the suspension of the veto in case of mass atrocities. [Accessed 21 June 2019]. Available from: www.globalr2p.org/ resources/political-declaration-on-suspension-of-veto-powers-in-cases-of-mass-atr ocities/.

Fung, C. 2019. *China and Intervention at the UN Security Council: Reconciling Status.* Oxford: Oxford University Press.

Gallagher, A. 2021. To Name and Shame or Not, and If So, How? A Pragmatic Analysis of Naming and Shaming the Chinese Government over Mass Atrocity

Crimes against the Uyghurs and Other Muslim Minorities in Xinjiang. *Journal of Global Security Studies*. 6(4), pp. 1–16.

Garwood-Gowers, A. 2013. The BRICS and the Responsibility to Protect: Lessons from the Libyan and Syrian Crises. *In*: V. Sancin and D. Masa, eds. *Responsibility to Protect in Theory and Practice*. Ljubljana: GV Zalozba, pp. 291–315.

GCR2P 2022. Political Declaration on Suspension of Veto Powers in Cases of Mass Atrocities. [Accessed 14 June 2022]. Available from: www.globalr2p.org/resources/political-declaration-on-suspension-of-veto-powers-in-cases-of-mass-atrocities/.

Gifkins, J. 2021. Beyond the Veto: Roles in UN Security Council Decision-making. *Global Governance: A Review of Multilateralism and International Organizations*. 27(1), pp. 1–24.

Gilabert, P. and Lawford-Smith, H. 2012. Political Feasibility: A Conceptual Exploration. *Political Studies*. 60(4), pp. 809–825.

Glanville, L. 2021. *Sharing Responsibility: The History and Future of Protection from Atrocities*. Princeton, NJ: Princeton University Press.

Global Centre for the Responsibility to Protect 2019. *List of Signatories to the ACT Code of Conduct* [Online]. [Accessed 12 September 2021]. Available from: www.globalr2p.org/resources/list-of-signatories-to-the-act-code-of-conduct/.

Hehir, A. 2013. The Permanence of Inconsistency: Libya, the Security Council, and the Responsibility to Protect. *International Security*. 38(1), pp. 137–159.

Hehir, A. 2018. *Hollow Norms and the Responsibility to Protect*. London: Palgrave Macmillan.

Hurd, I. 2007. *After Anarchy: Legitimacy and Power in the United Nations Security Council*. Princeton, NJ: Princeton University Press.

International Commission on Intervention and State Sovereignty 2001. The Responsibility to Protect: Report of the International Commission on Intervention and State Sovereignty. [Accessed 14 December 2018]. Available from: http://responsibilitytoprotect.org/ICISS%20Report.pdf.

Kennedy, P. 2007. *The Parliament of Man: The United Nations and the Quest for World Government*. London: Penguin Books.

Kuperman, A.J. 2015. Obama's Libya Debacle: How a Well-Meaning Intervention Ended in Failure. *Foreign Affairs*. 94, pp. 66–78.

Lättilä, V. and Ylönen, A. 2019. United Nations Security Council Reform Revisited: A Proposal. *Diplomacy & Statecraft*. 30(1), pp. 164–186.

Levine, D.H. 2011. Some Concerns About 'The Responsibility Not to Veto'. *Global Responsibility to Protect*. 3, pp. 323–345.

Luck, E.C. 2019. Could a United Nations Code of Conduct Help Curb Atrocities? A Response to Bolarinwa Adediran. *Ethics & International Affairs*. 33(1), pp. 79–87.

Morris, J. 2015. The Responsibility to Protect and the Great Powers: The Tensions of Dual Responsibility. *Global Responsibility to Protect*. 7(3–4), pp. 398–421.

Morris, J. 2016. The Responsibility to Protect and the Use of Force: Remaking the Procrustean bed? *Cooperation and Conflict*. 51(2), pp. 200–215.

Morris, J. and Wheeler, N.J. 2016. The Responsibility Not to Veto *In*: A.J Bellamy and T. Dunne, eds. *The Oxford Handbook of the Responsibility to Protect*. Oxford: Oxford University Press, pp. 227–248.

Nanda, V.P. 2013. The Future Under International Law of the Responsibility to Protect After Libya and Syria. *Michigan State International Law Review*. 21(1), pp. 1–42.

Nuruzzaman, M. 2013. The 'Responsibility to Protect' Doctrine: Revived in Libya, Buried in Syria. *Insight Turkey.* **15**(2), pp. 57–66.

Odgaard, L. 2020. Responsibility to Protect Goes to China: An Interpretivist Analysis of How China's Coexistence Policy Made it a Responsibility to Protect Insider. *Journal of International Political Theory.* **16**(2), pp. 231–248.

Orchard, P. and Rae, H. 2020. Russia and the R2P: Norm Entrepreneur, Anti-preneur, or Violator? *In:* C.T. Hunt and P. Orchard, eds. *Constructing the Responsibility to Protect: Contestation and Consolidation.* London: Routledge, pp. 168–186.

Paris, R. 2014. The 'Responsibility to Protect' and the Structural Problems of Preventive Humanitarian Intervention. *International Peacekeeping.* **21**(5), pp. 569–603.

Pathfinders for Peaceful, Just and Inclusive Societies 2020. *Forecasting the Dividends of Conflict Prevention from 2020–2030.* New York: Center on International Cooperation. [Accessed 27 July 2020]. Available from: www.sdg16.plus/.

Pattison, J. 2018. *The Alternatives to War: From Sanctions to Nonviolence.* Oxford: Oxford University Press.

Ralph, J. 2018. What Should Be Done? Pragmatic Constructivist Ethics and the Responsibility to Protect. *International Organization.* **72**(1), pp. 173–203.

Ralph, J. and Gifkins, J. 2017. The Purpose of United Nations Security Council Practice: Contesting Competence Claims in the Normative Context Created by the Responsibility to Protect. *European Journal of International Relations.* **23**(3), pp. 630–653.

Saba, A. and Akbarzadeh, S. 2020. The ICC and R2P: Complementary or Contradictory? *International Peacekeeping.* **28**(1), pp. 84–109.

Schaefer, K. 2016. *Reforming the United Nations Security Council Feasibility or Utopia?* Montreal: McGill University.

Security Council Report 2015. *The Veto.* [Accessed 12 April 2022]. Available from: www.securitycouncilreport.org/research-reports/the-veto.php.

Teitt, S. 2020. Resistance and Accommodation in China's Approach Toward R2P *In:* C.T. Hunt and P. Orchard, eds. *Constructing the Responsibility to Protect: Contestation and Consolidation.* London: Routledge, pp. 149–167.

The Guardian 2015. Russian vetoes are putting UN Security Council's legitimacy at risk, says US. [Accessed 21 July 2018]. Available from: www.theguardian.com/world/2015/sep/23/russian-vetoes-putting-un-security-council-legitimacy-at-risk-says-us.

Trahan, J. 2020. Questioning Unlimited Veto Use in the Face of Atrocity Crimes. *Case Western Reserve Journal of International Law.* **52**, pp. 73–100.

Trahan, J. 2022. Why the Veto Power Is Not Unlimited: A Response to Critiques of, and Questions About, Existing Legal Limits to the Veto Power in the Face of Atrocity Crimes. *Case Western Reserve Journal of International Law.* **54**(1), pp. 109–140.

UN 1945. Charter of the United Nations. [Accessed 5 June 2018]. Available from: www.un.org/en/charter-united-nations/.

UN 2020. In Two Separate Votes, Security Council Fails to Adopt Resolutions Extending Cross-Border Mechanism for Humanitarian Aid Delivery into Syria. [Accessed 10 August 2020]. Available from: www.un.org/press/en/2020/sc14246.doc.htm.

UNA-UK 2022. Security Council veto use: the UK should champion action for accountability. [Accessed 6 April 2022]. Available from: https://una.org.uk/news/security-council-veto-use-uk-should-champion-action-accountability.

UNGA 1950. Uniting for Peace. A/RES/377(V). [Accessed 22 July 2018]. Available from: http://www.un.org/en/sc/repertoire/otherdocs/GAres377A(v).pdf.

UNGA 2004. A More Secure World: Our Shared Responsibility. Report of the High-level Panel on Threats, Challenges and Change. A/59/565. [Accessed 6 May 2019]. Available from: https://www.un.org/ruleoflaw/files/gaA.59.565_En.pdf.

UNGA 2005. Resolution adopted by the General Assembly on 16 September 2005. A/RES/60/1. [Accessed 15 November 2018]. Available from: http://www.un.org/en/development/desa/population/migration/generalassembly/docs/globalcompact/A_RES_60_1.pdf.

UNGA 2016. 42nd Plenary Meeting. Question of equitable representation on and increase in the membership of the Security Council and other matters related to the Security Council. A/71/PV.42. [Accessed 20 June 2019]. Available from: https://undocs.org/pdf?symbol=en/A/71/PV.42.

UNGA 2021a. 64th plenary meeting. The Responsibility to Protect and the prevention of genocide, war crimes, ethnic cleansing and crimes against humanity. A/75/PV.64. [Accessed 8 September 2022]. Available from: https://documents-dds-ny.un.org/doc/UNDOC/GEN/N21/121/10/PDF/N2112110.pdf?OpenElement.

UNGA 2021b. 65th plenary meeting. The Responsibility to Protect and the prevention of genocide, war crimes, ethnic cleansing and crimes against humanity. A/75/PV.65. [Accessed 8 September 2022]. Available from: https://documents-dds-ny.un.org/doc/UNDOC/GEN/N21/121/16/PDF/N2112116.pdf?OpenElement.

UNGA 2021c. 66th plenary meeting. The Responsibility to Protect and the prevention of genocide, war crimes, ethnic cleansing and crimes against humanity. A/75/PV.66. [Accessed 8 September 2022]. Available from: https://documents-dds-ny.un.org/doc/UNDOC/GEN/N21/122/25/PDF/N2112225.pdf?OpenElement.

UNGA 2022. 69th plenary meeting. Strengthening of the United Nations system. A/76/PV.69. [Accessed 23 September 2022]. Available from: https://documents-dds-ny.un.org/doc/UNDOC/GEN/N22/330/25/PDF/N2233025.pdf?OpenElement.

United Kingdom 2014. Security Council reform: The UK supports new permanent seats for Brazil, Germany, India and Japan, alongside permanent African representation. [Accessed 17 July 2018]. Available from: https://www.gov.uk/government/speeches/security-council-reform-the-uk-supports-new-permanent-seats-for-brazil-germany-india-and-japan-alongside-permanent-african-representation.

United States Mission to the United Nations 2022. Remarks by Ambassador Linda Thomas-Greenfield on the Future of the United Nations. [Accessed 16 March 2023]. Available from: https://usun.usmission.gov/remarks-by-ambassador-linda-thomas-greenfield-on-the-future-of-the-united-nations/.

UNSC 2006a. Draft Resolution. S/2006/508. [Accessed 19 July 2018]. Available from: www.securitycouncilreport.org/un-documents/document/IP%20S2006508.php.

UNSC 2006b. Draft Resolution. S/2006/878. [Accessed 19 July 2018]. Available from: www.securitycouncilreport.org/un-documents/document/ME%20consultations%20S2006878.php.

UNSC 2011a. Draft Resolution. S/2011/24. [Accessed 19 July 2018]. Available from: www.securitycouncilreport.org/un-documents/document/ME%20consultations%20S2006878.php.

UNSC 2011b. Draft Resolution. S/2011/612. [Accessed 31 July 2018]. Available from: www.securitycouncilreport.org/un-documents/document/syria-s2011-612.php.

UNSC 2012. Draft Resolution. S/2012/77. [Accessed 1 August 2018]. Available from: https://www.securitycouncilreport.org/un-documents/document/syria-s 2012-77.php.

UNSC 2015. Draft Resolution. S/2015/508. [Accessed 16 July 2018]. Available from: www.securitycouncilreport.org/atf/cf/%7b65BFCF9B-6D27-4E9C-8CD3-CF6E4FF96FF9%7d/s_2015_508.pdf.

UNSC 2018a. 8175th Meeting. S/PV.8175. [Accessed 20 July 2018]. Available from: www.securitycouncilreport.org/atf/cf/%7b65BFCF9B-6D27-4E9C-8CD3-CF6E4FF96FF9%7d/s_pv_8175.pdf.

UNSC 2018b. Draft Resolution. S/2018/156. [Accessed 20 August 2018]. Available from: www.securitycouncilreport.org/un-documents/document/s2018156.php.

UNSC 2018c. Draft Resolution. S/2018/516. [Accessed 17 July 2018]. Available from: https://www.securitycouncilreport.org/un-documents/document/s2018516.php.

UNSC 2019. Draft Resolution. S/2019/186. [Accessed 21 June 2019]. Available from: www.un.org/en/ga/search/view_doc.asp?symbol=S/2019/186.

Vilmer, J.-B.J. 2018. The Responsibility Not to Veto: A Genealogy. *Global Governance*. **24**(3), pp. 331–349.

Webb, P. 2014. Deadlock of Restraint? The Security Council Veto and the Use of Force in Syria. *Journal of Conflict & Security Law*. **19**(3), pp. 471–488.

Weiss, T.G. 2006. R2P after 9/11 and the World Summit. *Wisconsin International Law Journal*. **24**(3), pp. 741–760.

Weiss, T.G. 2014. Military Humanitarianism: Syria Hasn't Killed It. *Washington Quarterly*. **37**(1), pp. 7–20.

Welsh, J.M. 2019. Norm Robustness and the Responsibility to Protect. *Journal of Global Security Studies*. **4**(1), pp. 53–72.

Wenaweser, C. and Alavi, S. 2020. Innovating to Restrain the Use of the Veto in the United Nations Security Council. *Case Western Reserve Journal of International Law*. **52**, pp. 65–72.

Wheeler, N.J. 2005. A Victory for Common Humanity: The Responsibility to Protect after the 2005 World Summit. *Journal of International Law & International Relations*. **2**(1), pp. 95–105.

Wilson, G. 2018. Enhancing Diversity and Representation Within the United Nations Security Council: The Dilemmas of Reform. *International Politics*. **56**(4), pp. 495-513.

World Bank Group 2018. Pathways for Peace: Inclusive Approaches to Preventing Violent Conflict.

Zifcack, S. 2012. The Responsibility to Protect After Libya and Syria. *Melbourne Journal of International Law*. **13**, pp. 59–93.

6 Overcoming the Authority Dilemma

Uniting for Peace Through the UN General Assembly

6.1 Introduction

The previous chapter looked at reforming the veto power of the UNSC's P5 members as a means of overcoming a central difficulty with implementing R2P enforcement action; that the UNSC is the preponderant body for R2P response under the version of R2P that was agreed by states in 2005 (UNGA, 2005, para. 139), but the P5 are able to veto any form of UNSC resolution pertaining to an R2P-relevant situation. However, as that chapter reflected, reforming UNSC veto practice is difficult, and unlikely to overcome institutional problems of Pillar Three implementation alone.

Failures to act on mass atrocity have presented something of an 'authority dilemma' in international relations (Gallagher, 2013, pp. 111–115), as the authority of the UNSC as the sole legitimate body for authorising international intervention has come into question following its failures in Rwanda, Srebrenica, and more recently with standout failures in Syria, Myanmar, and Ukraine. At times, states have sought channels beyond the UN for acting on atrocity prevention, as they did in Kosovo in 1999 through an (illegal) NATO-led intervention, and as they did when conducting a military response to Assad's use of chemical weapons in Syria in 2017 and 2018. It is interesting that the International Independent Commission on Kosovo (2000, p. 4) found the intervention to be 'illegal but legitimate', suggesting that actions with morally desirable outcomes are permitted even if they violate the international legal agreement that only the UN has the authority to legitimise the use of military force. However, the Commission also noted later in the report (2000, p. 174) that the Kosovo instance ought not to serve as a precedent for future action, as this would undermine the centrality of the UNSC and its primary role in maintaining international peace and security.

R2P does not address a fundamental problem of responding to human protection crises effectively because it relies predominantly on an untouched UNSC for its Pillar Three implementation (Hehir, 2012, p. 216). While the ICISS report (2001, p. 49) did acknowledge the UNSC's failings and sought channels for implementing R2P response action in the event of UNSC failure, it still sought to keep the Council as the preponderant body for questions

DOI: 10.4324/9781003394105-6

over when intervention is appropriate. However, even more troublingly, the version of R2P accepted in 2005 fails to even acknowledge that implementing atrocity prevention through the UNSC is problematic. As Gallagher (2013, pp. 134–135) notes, the WSOD paragraphs read 'as though there is nothing wrong in upholding the existing UNSC system … a consensus was forged regarding Plan A: the UNSC should act as the overseer of force, but problematically, there appears to be no Plan B to address the deadlocked Security Council'. This leaves entirely unaddressed the question of how the international community should proceed when the UNSC is left, for whatever reason, unable to discharge its R2P,[1] and whether other means may legitimately be utilised for R2P enforcement (Buchanan and Keohane, 2011, p. 42). Where the UNSC will not act, R2P Pillar Three can be left stalled, with vital response lacking, and the cosmopolitan responsibility to act on crises of human protection left wanting.

Much has been written on how to improve the function of the UN system by focusing on the UNSC itself (including the veto debate discussed in Chapter 5), while scholars such as Walzer (1995), Fabre (2012, chap. 5), and Erskine (2019) have argued that there is a duty to intervene which sometimes necessitates military action that entirely circumvents UN authority. This chapter prefers a middle-ground between this 'UNSC or no UN response' dichotomy.

The powers of the UNGA have been largely overlooked within the R2P literature to date.[2] This is quite remarkable given the potential that UNGA action has for strengthening response to mass atrocity. This chapter argues that the powers of the UNGA offer a mostly effective and feasible avenue through which the international community can respond to atrocity situations in line with R2P Pillar Three. The R2P supports a collective security system with the UN at its heart (Ramsden, 2016, p. 276), and while utilising the UNGA's powers may challenge the centrality of the UNSC as the primary body for implementing Pillar Three, the use of the UNGA's powers would keep R2P response aligned with a legal and UN-centred collective international response that permits the UNGA to recommend a host of potential measures, including peaceful, coercive, and military means, that may be useful in addressing mass atrocity situations (Barber, 2021).

This chapter makes a novel contribution, however, by arguing that the powers of the UNGA can best overcome the R2P's authority dilemma if a new 'Uniting for Peace' (UfP) mechanism is passed by the UNGA, which makes some tweaks to both its language and procedure in order to further enhance the measure's effectiveness and feasibility. The chapter recommends a nuanced alteration to UfP's trigger procedure in order to reduce friction between the UNSC and UNGA. It recommends that the UNSC be placed as the principle body for triggering UfP, except for in circumstances where the Council is not actively exercising its Charter responsibilities. To this end, it proposes some clear criteria for determining when the UNGA can rightly step in.

Examples of crises which have failed to receive *any* formal UNSC vote have included some of the most extreme and protracted instances of atrocity crimes in recent years, for instance, the Rohingya crisis in Myanmar, the persecution of Uyghur Muslims in Xinjiang province, and ethnic violence committed in Ethiopia since November 2020.[3] Placing the UNSC as the primary body for triggering UfP except for matters that have witnessed Council paralysis would maintain the UNSC's preponderance over matters of international peace and security, but not to the extent that this prevents the UNGA from rightfully acting on its secondary responsibility under the UN Charter.

The chapter also calls for the removal of the 'lack of P5 unanimity clause' in UfP; to emphasise that UfP is a response to UNSC failure and one that can rightfully be triggered in instances where there is no explicit indication of a lack of P5 unanimity. Finally, to enhance UfP's feasibility, the chapter also recommends that UfP language be altered to place less emphasis on the use of military force, and instead emphasise that there is a wealth of international responses available to the UNGA.

The chapter is structured as follows. Section 6.2 provides an overview of two political developments in the UNGA which are especially pertinent to debates surrounding the use of the UNGA's powers to respond to mass atrocity situations under the UN Charter: the UfP mechanism and the recent adoption of Lichtenstein's 'veto initiative' proposal. Section 6.3 delves into a transitional cosmopolitan analysis of the powers of the UNGA, arguing that while the UNGA provides a mostly effective and feasible avenue for discharging R2P, there are some issues here, in particular relating to the potential circumvention of UNSC primacy. Section 6.4 provides a recommendation for a revised UfP mechanism that seeks to ensure UNSC primacy in its triggering procedure, while still allowing the UNGA to fulfil its secondary responsibility. Here some alterations to UfP language are also offered in attempt to enhance the measure's feasibility. This section argues that these alterations to UfP can better align the mechanism with the transitional cosmopolitan approach, providing an effective and feasible means for discharging the R2P in the event of UNSC impasse.

6.2 Developments in the UN General Assembly

6.2.1 *The Uniting for Peace Mechanism*

UNGA Resolution 377(V), containing the UfP mechanism, was passed on 3 November 1950 as an attempt to galvanise the UNGA into acting on its Charter-based powers. The resolution noted that the UN organisation, as a whole, possesses a collective responsibility for the maintenance of international peace and security, and that where the UNSC fails in discharging its primary responsibility to this end, the UN's duty does not simply end there (UNGA, 1950, p. 10). Section A of the UfP resolution itself contained five provisions (Parts A-E), however, most of the provisions here, with the exception of Part A, were left dormant in the years following the resolution's passage (See Petersen, 1959). It is therefore Part A which is the focus of this chapter. Part A(1) of section A of Resolution 377(V) states that the UNGA:

> Resolves that if the Security Council, because of lack of unanimity of the permanent members, fails to exercise its primary responsibility for the maintenance of international peace and security in any case where there appears to be a threat to the peace, breach of the peace, or act of aggression, the General Assembly shall consider the matter immediately with a view to making appropriate recommendations to Members for collective measures, including in the case of a breach of the peace or act of aggression the use of armed force when necessary, to maintain or restore international peace and security.

Although UfP did expand the political capital of the UNGA's smaller states (Mamlyuk, 2014, pp. 131–132), the proposal had been put forward because it served US and Western interests (in Korea especially). This was the case because, prior to the process of decolonisation, the overwhelming majority of UN member states were Western, or allied with Western states and the US. On the passage of UfP in November 1950, there were 36 UN member states. This made the UNGA considerably more predictable in its voting behaviour than it is today with its 193 members. As Bourantonis and Magliveras (2002, p. 65) note, '[a]t the time, the Assembly remained a Western-controlled organ in which the Soviet Union and its satellites were relatively isolated and from which there was no escape through the veto'. UfP was therefore part of a US-led agenda to increase the prominence of the UNGA in light of UNSC ineffectiveness, supported, albeit reluctantly, by Britain and France (Zaum, 2008, pp. 157–158).

Currently, UfP can be triggered by either UNSC referral via a procedural vote under Article 27(1) of the Charter (not subject to P5 veto rights), or by the UNGA itself through a two-thirds voting majority of member states. The passage of Resolution 377(V) was an affirmation by the UNGA that the body possesses a secondary responsibility for the maintenance of international peace and security, and holds the power to recommend measures to this end, including its ability to authorise the use of force if necessary.

To date there have been 13 instances[4] of where the UfP mechanism has been triggered: eight times by the UNSC, and five times by the UNGA (Security Council Report, 2013; UN, 2022). This has included cases as varied as: a means to establish a UN peacekeeping mission over the situation in Suez 1956 (UNGA, 1956a); to condemn Soviet military aggression against Hungary in 1956 (UNGA, 1956b); to condemn Israeli policies following US vetoes surrounding Israeli actions in occupied Palestinian territories (UNGA, 1967; UNGA, 1980—1982; UNGA, 1982; UNGA, 1997—2006); and calls for sanctions against South Africa in response to its occupation of Namibia

(UNGA, 1981). The most recent invocation of UfP came in February-March 2022 in response to Russia's invasion of Ukraine, when the UNSC referred the matter to the UNGA following the Russian veto of a draft resolution which sought to condemn Russian aggression.

6.2.2 *Lichtenstein's 'Veto Initiative'*

As Gowan (2022) recently noted in response to Russia's February 2022 invasion of Ukraine and the damage this may present to the UNSC's ability to cooperate and address issues of international peace and security; states will likely need to invest in the parts of the UN system which can help mitigate conflicts without UNSC mandates. This is a call which states themselves appear to appreciate. Gaston (2022) writes on the Ukraine fallout that '[t]he war in Ukraine has unleashed terrible destruction and suffering, but it has also galvanized a level of energy, attention and political will that could lead to new pathways for sustaining peace'.

This political will is perhaps none-more-so evident than in Lichtenstein's recent 'veto initiative' proposal. The veto initiative is a slightly misleading name, as really the mechanism relates most to invoking the powers of the UNGA to act in response to UNSC failure than it does to amending the veto power itself. The mechanism was sponsored by 83 member states, which notably included the US, Britain, and France as three permanent members of the UNSC. Adopted by the UNGA in resolution 76/262 on 28 April 2022, without a vote, this mechanism means that a meeting of the UNGA will now automatically be convened within ten days of a draft resolution having been vetoed in the UNSC (UNA-UK, 2022). Further, in accordance with Article 24(3) of the Charter, the UNSC will be invited prior to the convening of the UNGA to submit a special report on the use of the veto; the P5 member/s which cast the veto will also be given priority speaking to explain their use of the veto to the UN's wider membership (Wenaweser and Alavi, 2020, pp. 70–71).

The veto initiative is quite a remarkable development. Russia's illegal and abhorrent full-scale invasion of Ukraine – and the unity which was fostered between UN member states in response – led to more progress being made in addressing veto abuse in a matter of weeks than had been made in all the years since R2P's adoption in 2005, and arguably since the adoption of UfP in 1950. Again, while the veto initiative does not attempt to reform the veto power itself, meaning that debates discussed in Chapter 5 remain very relevant to the discussion on R2P's successful implementation, the veto initiative still provides a novel mechanism through which the UNGA can do something in response to the UNSC's failure to discharge its responsibilities. The mechanism is also reflective of an increasing call for greater UNSC accountability in the implementation of the R2P (Hunt, 2020, p. 105). In this case, regarding the selectivity and non-implementation of the concept in situations where it should clearly apply.

It is, at the time of writing, too early to know how the veto initiative will play out in the UN's practice of responding to mass atrocity situations moving forward. Nevertheless, the veto initiative does still raise some issues which are relevant to utilising the powers of the UNGA, including the question of at what trigger point the UNGA should rightfully step in to respond to the UNSC's failure, as well as the related issue of the potential circumvention of UNSC authority. These points of contention are explored below.

While Lichtenstein's veto initiative represents a generally positive evolution in UN practice and normative direction, it is argued in this chapter that rather than rely on the mechanism as providing a permanent solution to R2P's authority dilemma, transitional cosmopolitan progress would be better served by the UNGA passing a revised version of the UfP mechanism; one which allows the Assembly to discharge its R2P responsibilities in an effective way, without overstepping its responsibilities under the UN Charter.

6.3 Are the Powers of the General Assembly a Solution to R2P's Authority Dilemma?

6.3.1 Test of Effective Progress

The powers of the UNGA, channelled through the UfP mechanism, may offer an effective and feasible avenue to help overcome the 'authority dilemma' (Gallagher, 2013, pp. 111–115) that comes with a UNSC-centric vision for the R2P. The UNGA has means for responding to situations containing what Gowan (2021, p. 6) has referred to as 'profound divisions' among UNSC members. Such situations are those in which clashes of interest between UNSC members, with particular reference to the P5 and their power of veto, mean that the UNSC is unlikely to deliver a resolution with aim to address a crisis. Ukraine is a prime example of this given that the state in breach of international law (Russia) is itself a P5 member. In such circumstances, the UNGA can act effectively to promote UN action in situations where the UNSC is obstructed and unable to deliver an appropriate response itself.

The UNGA holds the power under the UN Charter to seize the mantle of responsibility from the UNSC in this way. Article 24(1) of the Charter confers on the UNSC the primary responsibility for the management of international peace and security (UN, 1945), but this primary responsibility is meant to be understood as the UNSC acting on behalf of the wider UN membership (Wenaweser and Alavi, 2020, p. 69). It also does not denote that the UNSC holds an *exclusive* responsibility to international peace and security.

First, Article 1(1) of the Charter notes that a core purpose and principle of the UN organisation as a whole is to 'maintain international peace and security, and to that end: to take effective collective measures for the prevention and removal of threats to the peace'. This does not stipulate that it is only the UNSC that holds a responsibility in this vein, but rather infers that this is a general responsibility that rests on the shoulders of all UN actors. Second, it has been explicitly acknowledged that the UNGA holds a secondary responsibility for the maintenance of international peace and security. The ICJ affirmed this in its advisory opinion for the *Certain Expenses of the United Nations* case, noting 'the Court found that under Article 24 the responsibility of the Security Council in the matter was "primary", not exclusive. The Charter made it abundantly clear that the General Assembly was also to be concerned with international peace and security' (ICJ, 1962, p. 61).

The UNGA's powers in the context of its secondary responsibility are laid out in Chapter IV of the Charter. Article 10 (UN, 1945) states that:

> The General Assembly may discuss any questions or any matters within the scope of the present Charter or relating to the powers and functions of any organs provided for in the present Charter, and, except as provided in Article 12, may make recommendations to the Members of the United Nations or to the Security Council or to both on any such questions or matters.

Specifically relating to the UNGA's powers vis-à-vis international peace and security, Article 11(2) (UN, 1945) states that:

> The General Assembly may discuss any questions relating to the maintenance of international peace and security ... and ... may make recommendations with regard to any such questions to the state or states concerned or to the Security Council or to both. Any such question on which action is necessary shall be referred to the Security Council by the General Assembly either before or after discussion.

Various scholars have argued that UN Charter provisions give the UNGA a degree of overlap in function with the UNSC, highlighting that is it consistent with the Charter that the UNSC can be substituted in order to appropriately respond to any threat to international peace (Andrassy, 1956, pp. 564, 574; Barber, 2019b, p. 102; Nanda, 2020, p. 137). The UNGA has ample scope to respond assertively to crises of international peace and security, which can include humanitarian emergencies, and therefore, those crises relevant to R2P (Krasno and Das, 2008, p. 182). It is these Charter-based powers which permit the UNGA to recommend – though not enforce (Henderson, 2014, pp. 506–507; Higgins et al., 2017, p. 977) – the use of coercive and non-coercive measures. This can include recommendations for the use of military force if necessary (Richardson, 2014, p. 140; White, 2015, p. 305),[5] but also, among other things: recommendations for the adoption of sanctions; measures in the name of preventive diplomacy; fact-finding commissions of inquiry; and requests for advisory opinions from the ICJ (Barber, 2021).

This has profound implications for the R2P and its current authority dilemma. UN-centred Pillar Three response need not be solely dependent on the UNSC, and where the Council fails, the UNGA has the authority to step in and make a host of potential recommendations. Such recommendations may not be enough to end cases of atrocity crimes, but they can nonetheless promote effective responses (see Pattison, 2018); for instance, via accountability for violations, the alleviation of suffering through the provision of aid and humanitarian access, and signal to victims and international actors that R2P matters, and that victims will not be left to their fate.

A key question which remains, however, is what actually constitutes a UNSC failure for which the UNGA should rightly step in? Veto use to prevent a UNSC response to mass atrocities may present such a failure. Carswell (2013, p. 472) has argued that, as per the 'good faith' principle under Article 2(2) of the Charter, the P5 members do not possess a right to veto resolutions at will, and that the UNGA's UfP mechanism can rightfully be triggered in instances of veto abuse. Indeed, where the veto has been exercised, this a reflection of a 'lack of unanimity' between the P5 members, which is a requisite for the UfP mechanism to become applicable in accordance with its current wording (Reicher, 1981, p. 11).

The Syria case is a clear example of where protracted veto use meant that the UfP mechanism could have rightfully been triggered (Udoh, 2015; Melling and Dennett, 2017; Nahlawi, 2019). Nahlawi (2019, pp. 124–126) argues that Russian and Chinese vetoes were politically motivated and exercised in bad faith, with the fact that UN members consistently decried the use of the veto power on the Syria issue as evidence that the international community considered the repeated use of the veto indicative of the UNSC's failure to discharge its primary responsibility. Subsequently, she argues that the UNGA should have stepped in to take forceful action in accordance with its secondary responsibility: 'UNGA recommendations in this sense could have assumed the form of public condemnation; the imposition of sanctions, an asset freeze and an arms embargo; or a call to sever diplomatic ties with Syria' (Nahlawi, 2019, p. 131). Similarly, with particular reference to the use of chemical weapons by the Syrian regime and subsequent (illegal) military response by the US, Britain and France in 2017 and 2018, Barber (2019b, p. 108) argues that multiple vetoes cast over the Syria case reflect a clear instance of UNSC failure for which UfP response could rightfully have been called upon. Invocation of UfP over the Syria case certainly could not have made the situation any worse than it already was, and may have offered a useful avenue for the UN to take more meaningful and robust action.

However, veto use should not be taken as an essential requisite for the UNGA to step in. It is not the case that a draft resolution must be vetoed in order for a 'lack of unanimity' between the P5 members to have prevented the UNSC from adequately discharging its responsibilities. Barber (2019a, p. 577), in reference to Myanmar and atrocities committed against the Rohingya, claims that a lack of P5 unanimity is evidenced in UNSC debate statements and conflicting positions between the P5 members – with Russia and China contesting calls for accountability and favouring an approach which maintains the sovereign prerogatives of the Myanmar government.

For her, this, combined with lack of any formal UNSC action, is reflective of Council failure, and provides scope for action to be taken by the UNGA, including, for instance, the establishment of an international criminal tribunal to prosecute those actors responsible for atrocities in Myanmar (Barber, 2019a, pp. 579–581). Likewise, Khan and Ahmed (2020, p. 125) argue that the Myanmar issue has not successfully breached the vital interests of the P5 to lead to effective UNSC action. Accordingly, they argue that the UNGA can step in and act on its own responsibilities, noting that '[a]ll that is required is the political leadership in the UNGA to practice and exercise its competence proactively' (Khan and Ahmed, 2020, p. 134).

Were only instances of veto use able to be deemed as UNSC failures, then this would prevent the UNGA from acting on cases like Myanmar where, despite atrocities committed against the Rohingya, no formal UNSC resolution was put to vote. Additionally, atrocities committed by the Tatmadaw following the military coup in February 2021 (WBFO, 2021) produced, to say the least, a sluggish response from the UNSC, with the Council taking 22 months to pass its first formal resolution over the crisis (UNSC, 2022). This was the case despite the fact that the UN's Special Rapporteur for Myanmar highlighted as early as March 2021 that the Myanmar military 'is now likely engaging in crimes against humanity, including the acts of murder, enforced disappearance, persecution, torture, and imprisonment in violation of fundamental rules of international law' (OHCHR, 2021). Pedersen (2021) has argued that international R2P-based response to events in Myanmar is severely limited given the country's lack of receptiveness to international pressure, as well as the protection it receives from regional allies such as China. Yet, Pedersen fails to account for other forms of international response that may allow the international community to discharge its R2P and help to influence events. Diplomatic shaming may not have much effect on stubborn rulers with genocidal intent, yet there is still a necessity to cut funding to the Tatmadaw wherever possible; to limit the supply of arms flowing into the country; and it is also important, at the very least for the strength of anti-atrocity and anti-impunity norms, that international justice is directed against perpetrators.

Given the glacial pace of UNSC action, the situation in Myanmar would appear to have provided (and as of early 2023 likely still does provide) a prime opportunity for the application of UfP action by the UNGA. An approach which only permits the activation of UfP in response to an explicit demonstration of a lack of P5 unanimity via a vetoed draft resolution would run against the spirit and purpose of the UfP mechanism. Notably, this is a concern which also applies to Lichtenstein's 'veto initiative', as its activation depends on the UNSC putting a resolution to vote. Situations in which the UNSC fails to even put a resolution to veto cannot therefore adequately be addressed by the 'veto initiative', and instead would justify a more proactive response from the UNGA via the invocation of its Charter powers through the UfP mechanism.

UNSC failure can be demonstrated by the Council's failure to even take a matter of atrocity crime to a formal resolution vote. It is for this reason that one of the recommendations offered below is to remove the 'lack of unanimity of the permanent members' clause from the UfP mechanism, as this would make clear that UfP and the powers of the Assembly can rightfully be triggered without a P5 veto.

Beyond the issue of whether a veto is essential in order to display Council failure and permit the application of UfP, there are other potential points of concern for the effective use of the UNGA's powers that should be addressed here. First, Article 11(2) of the UN Charter states that any 'question on which action is necessary shall be referred to the Security Council by the General Assembly either before or after discussion' (UN, 1945). *Prima facie*, this may seem as though the UNGA is not permitted to make recommendations without prior or subsequent UNSC approval. However, it has been argued that 'action' in this context refers exclusively to binding enforcement action (Hailbronner and Klein, 2002, pp. 264–265; Nahlawi, 2019, p. 118), which is only in the remit of the UNSC to authorise, given that the UNGA is simply empowered to make *recommendations* in the name of international peace and security. The ICJ affirmed in its advisory opinion on the *Certain Expenses* case that Article 11(2) has no application where necessary action is not enforcement (which UNGA recommendations are not) (ICJ, 1962). Hence, it is not the case that Article 11(2) requires the UNGA to refer all situations back to the UNSC, and the Assembly is, therefore, free to make recommendations as its members decide. Though, it is perhaps worth noting that when invoking UfP, the UNGA has sought to affirm the primary role of the UNSC and for the need for effective Council engagement with the situation (Miluna, 2014, p. 122).

There is a potentially more significant obstacle to the UNGA's powers that presents itself from Article 12(1) of the Charter, which declares that '[w]hile the Security Council is exercising in respect of any dispute or situation the functions assigned to it in the present Charter, the General Assembly shall not make any recommendation with regard to that dispute or situation unless the Security Council so requests'. This may suggest that recommendations under UfP are precluded if the matter currently exists on the UNSC's formal agenda. However, this is not so much of an obstacle (in terms of the applicability of UfP) as it may initially appear. The UNSC is able to discharge itself of any matter on its agenda by a 9/15 procedural vote as per Article 27(2). A vote to refer a matter to the UNGA via the UfP mechanism is not subject to the veto power of the P5 (Andrassy, 1956, p. 577; Ramsden, 2016, p. 298; Barber, 2021, p. 16), meaning that the UfP mechanism can be triggered by the UNSC when the matter lies on its own agenda without fear that this could be blocked by a single P5 state.

Regarding the question of whether the UNGA can make recommendations over matters which the UNSC has not referred, it has been argued elsewhere that UN practice has evolved over time so that the UNGA does act on cases concurrently with the UNSC (White, 2015, p. 303). The ICJ noted in its advisory opinion on the *Construction of a Wall* case that Article 12(1) provision is no longer an absolute bar on the UNGA's ability to offer recommendations on a case for which the UNSC is actively seized. Here, the ICJ (2004, p. 149) noted that 'there has been an increasing tendency over time for the General Assembly and the Security Council to deal in parallel with the same matter concerning the maintenance of international peace and security'. Furthermore, the ICJ (2004, p. 17) also drew on the interpretation of the Legal Counsel of the UN that the words 'is exercising the functions' contained within Article 12(1) refer only to whether the UNSC 'is exercising the functions at this moment'. These points may suggest that the Article 12(1) provision is no longer something to be concerned with (Barber, 2022, p. 102).

Though, as is argued below, the Article 12(1) provision does pose issues relevant to the circumvention of UNSC primacy over matters of international peace and security (Carswell, 2013, p. 472) which may present a moral hazard or weaken the feasibility of applying UfP in practice. It should nonetheless be emphasised that the provision in Article 12(1) only applies when the UNSC is formally discussing a matter. Hence, if the UNSC fails to act on a case at all, then the UNGA can assume responsibility, and Article 12(1) would have no bearing.

The UNGA holds a secondary responsibility over matters of international peace and security and has the authority to make recommendations (including the authorisation for coercive measures) in the name of upholding international peace and security which would overlap with its duties under R2P. UfP can offer an effective mechanism for overcoming the R2P's authority dilemma, providing a means for the international community to meet its cosmopolitan responsibilities by taking collective Pillar Three action in the wake of UNSC failure.

While acting through the UN in this way can bring a collective and unified response to atrocity situations, it must be noted that the invocation of UfP would not automatically lead to more, or to effective, R2P action (Ramsden, 2016, p. 303). UfP recommendations still require a two-thirds voting majority of UNGA members, which will not be a given in any case. Arguments presented by Russia and China for their use of their veto power may hold sway among large sections of the international community, or states may simply not possess the political will to call for concerted action in cases of mass atrocities. Nonetheless, as argued further below, the UNGA has demonstrated that it is willing to act on its responsibilities in instances of UNSC paralysis. Furthermore, an attempt at invoking UfP over situations concerning mass atrocities would send a message that the UN is actively committed to upholding its R2P commitments, and send a powerful signal to the victims of atrocity that their plight is not being ignored.

6.3.2 *Test of Moral Hazard*

One of the more contentious elements of the UfP mechanism is that it permits the UNGA to call a session and make recommendations at its own discretion, regardless of whether a matter is currently on the formal agenda of the UNSC. While it was noted above that the ICJ's opinion, and state practice, has shown that the UN's two principle organs have increasingly addressed cases simultaneously – and therefore that Article 12(1) is not a barring constraint in terms of UfP's practical effectiveness – there does nonetheless appear to be a problem relating to the circumvention of UNSC primacy in the realm of international peace and security if the UNGA makes recommendations when the UNSC is technically still seized of a matter, with the item existing on its formal agenda.

What this suggests is that there may be a moral hazard in utilising the UNGA's powers; the possibility of introducing an unwanted side-effect that undermines the possibility of achieving desirable transitional and normative progress. What should be remembered here is that the UN system is built around the UNSC as the primary organ for maintaining international peace and security by the management of the P5 in particular (Gallagher, 2013, p. 102). If UNSC primacy is circumvented, then this may destabilise UN order. Now, while the UNGA's legal power under the Charter may well be readable in such a way that they grant the authority for the Assembly to act in this way, this still presents a point of *political* contention that may, at worst, seriously damage the relationship between the UN's two principle organs, or at the very least, undermine the feasibility of whether states are willing to utilise the measure for fear that doing so may damage their own relationship with the P5 states.

Determining UNSC failure, and hence where the UNGA can rightfully step in, is not a straightforward task. While veto use may reflect UNSC failure, this does not mean that it automatically equates to failure. This may be a problem for the recent 'veto initiative' proposal adopted by the UNGA, as the initiative essentially ignites the UNGA's powers in response to any veto use. The problem with convening a meeting of the UNGA every time that a draft resolution is vetoed in the UNSC is that it seems to overstep the UNGA's constitutional powers by effectively (though not literally) calling for an invocation of Uniting for Peace every time that the veto is exercised. What this would do in effect is therefore automatically allow the UNGA to question whether a single veto use amounts to a failure of the UNSC's responsibility, before the UNSC has had an opportunity to make this determination itself. As was discussed in Chapter 5, the veto power exists for a good reason as it is a tool for managing international peace and security by preventing tensions between the great powers rising to dangerous levels (Morris and Wheeler, 2016). Therefore, even when the veto has been exercised, it is difficult to determine if the UNSC is actually failing to exercise its responsibilities when the Council has at least *attempted* to pass a resolution on a matter, given that veto use may itself be a responsible action if it is to prevent the passage of a damaging resolution. Hence, while the veto initiative represents an attempt to more closely scrutinise the work of the UNSC and hold it to account, it seems questionable whether it is an appropriate solution, given this potential overstepping of UNSC primacy.

Ramsden (2016, pp. 301–302) claims that UNSC failure should be judged on whether there is risk of significant human rights abuse as a result of Council inaction. However, he himself notes that finding evidence of veto abuse is likely to prove elusive given that 'most negative votes are, at least ostensibly, connected to the Council's broad purposes' (Ramsden, 2016, p. 300). Barber (2019a, p. 569) has argued that UNSC failure can be demonstrated by whether veto use has violated Article 2(2)'s provision of the good faith principle, or Article 24(2) which states that the UNSC must act in accordance with the Purposes and Principles of the United Nations.[6] However, again, such determinations would not be straightforward ones to make given that a P5 member will likely always justify the exercise of its veto rights by reference to its Charter-based responsibilities for maintaining international peace.[7] Furthermore, Woolsey (1951, p. 132) poses the question of whether UfP recommendations would be permissible even when the UNSC has taken action on a case, but action which has been limited and/or ineffective. Again, this raises the problem of whether in acting while the UNSC is still formally seized of a matter, the UNGA may simply be overstepping its authority as only a secondary duty bearer of a responsibility towards maintaining international peace and security. Carswell (2013, p. 472), for instance, argues of the UfP mechanism that, due to the UNGA's ability to bring matters currently on the UNSC's agenda onto its own, 'the original resolution gives the General Assembly a role that effectively usurps the primacy of the Security Council … and thereby contradicts articles 12 and 24'.

The upshot of this is that it is inappropriate for the UNGA to determine when UfP can rightfully be triggered if the UNSC has recently attempted to pass a resolution over the issue. Therefore, the determination of where a matter can be passed from the agenda of the UNSC to that of the UNGA is something which, ideally, the UNSC should make itself. There is a general consensus in the literature that UNSC referral to the UNGA is the best way to utilise the mechanism in a way which does not damage the relationship between the two organs. Ramsden (2016, p. 298) argues that so long as UfP is triggered by the UNSC, harmony can be maintained between the UNSC and UNGA, as 'to do so respects the language of Article 12 of the UN Charter in that the Council's request would constitute a certification that it is no longer "exercising" its functions on a particular situation'. Similarly, Melling and Dennett (2017, p. 300) argue that the UNSC should be responsible for triggering UfP, noting that 'a principal objection to the use of [UfP] is that it upsets the "delicate balance of powers" between the General Assembly and the Security Council under articles 11(2), 12 and 24'. As a consequence they argue that UfP should be re-envisaged as a mechanism of the UNSC, through which it can refer cases to the UNGA to take action where a majority of UNSC members determine a P5 member's veto use to be illegitimate in accordance with its legal and moral responsibilities (Melling and Dennett, 2017, pp. 300–303). Likewise, Carswell (2013, pp. 472, 479) believes that leaving the UNSC as the body to determine when matters can be passed to the UNGA ensures the primacy of the body while preventing the UNGA from overstepping its powers. Barber (2019b, p. 107) also favours UNSC referral over the UNGA commencing sessions itself, claiming that UNSC referral can ensure Council primacy and allay concerns about the UNGA unconstitutionally usurping the UNSC's power.

However, as is discussed below, the view of the present author is that while UNSC referral is ideal, it would be inappropriate to place *sole* triggering power for UfP with the UNSC itself, as this may preclude the UNGA from acting in cases of total UNSC paralysis. In attempting to ameliorate the tension between UfP action and the circumvention of UNSC primacy for matters which it is actively exercising its responsibilities, the recommendation for altering the UfP mechanism offered later in this chapter argues that when a UNSC resolution has been voted on within the previous 30 days, the Council should be the one to trigger UfP.

Another potential moral hazard presented by invoking the UNGA's powers relates to whether this would result in the passage of damaging action that would actually undermine the international community's R2P.[8] Melling and Dennett (2017, p. 304), for instance, have claimed that there is a fear among some UN members that negating the effect of the veto by resorting to UfP action may lead to over-use of damaging military responses, and that circumventing the veto may raise tensions between P5 members, especially if UfP recommendations concern the legitimation of military action. It would be impermissible to the transitional cosmopolitan approach if the application of the UNGA's powers greatly threatened the passage of damaging action, or action that posed a significant escalation in great power tensions. Indeed, this is one of the reasons as to why one of the recommendations offered below is to alter UfP language to place less emphasis on the use of military force.

However, what is important to remember is that such a determination requires a two-thirds majority of UN members, meaning that there is an institutional safeguard in place against undesirable action. Chapter 5 (section 5.3) noted a concern relevant to existing veto restraint proposals is that they may lead to an over-application of military response. This concern is, however, significantly less applicable to action taken through the UNGA, since votes of the Assembly can be participated in by the entirety of states in the international community. Hence, there would be a much stronger deliberative safeguard in the UNGA (with its 193 members) against undesirable action than there would be in a UNSC compelled to observe veto restraint (with its 15 members).

The UNGA, unlike the UNSC, is a universal body within which all member states are given an equal chance to represent their views, and where action cannot be obstructed by one single member. As those such as Andrassy (1956, p. 571), Krasno and Das (2008, p. 191), and Nahlawi (2019, p. 120) note, this means that UNGA decisions carry a high degree of moral legitimacy, and are largely representative of the will of the international community. This means that an intervention (broadly conceived) with the backing of the UNGA would 'clearly have powerful moral and political support' (ICISS, 2001, p. 48).

6.3.3 *Test of Practical Potential*

The UfP mechanism has never been explicitly invoked to promote a UNGA response in the name of the R2P.[9] However, this is indicative of the general historical reticence about deploying the mechanism, and not exclusive to the R2P. Webb (2014, p. 486), for instance, wrote that 'the increased use of the General Assembly as a counter-weight [to UNSC deadlock] is highly unlikely'. Zaum (2008, p. 166) similarly claimed that, given the divide between the G77 and Western states, there is a belief among the Western powers that due to the expanded membership of the UNGA, the body is unreliable in terms of its voting behaviour. Zaum (2008, p. 166) further stressed that there is no guarantee that states can achieve their desired outcomes if they seek to utilise UfP, highlighting the example of the USSR, which, following its failed draft resolution in the UNSC in 1967, found that it was successfully able to invoke UfP in order to get the UNGA to discuss Israel-Palestine crisis. However, its subsequent attempt at passing a resolution to call out Israel as an aggressor state was rejected by the UNGA. During the Kosovo crisis in 1999, Canada briefly considered invoking UfP in order to attain legality and legitimate UN backing for a NATO-led intervention, however, in the end it decided not to due to fears that the non-aligned movement had residual support for Yugoslavia, and that this might have led to a rejection of any attempt at passing a UNGA resolution under UfP (Independent International Commission on Kosovo, 2000, p. 174; Heinbecker, 2004, p. 543; White, 2015, p. 312). Wheeler (2000, p. 158) claims that NATO 'did not go down the Uniting for Peace road because they could not guarantee securing the two-thirds [UNGA] majority to pass a resolution recommending military action'.

Johnson (2014, p. 114) is correct when he asserts that the UNSC's P5 would prefer to keep preponderance over decision making, particularly regarding the use of force, within the UNSC itself. According to him, the US and its allies did not attempt to gain UNGA approval for the Kosovo intervention due to a desire to avoid a 'slippery slope' scenario where the UNGA would end up taking decisions on the use of military force too regularly, leaving the UNSC effectively side-lined. Indeed, the UfP resolution's specific emphasis on the use of military force may be problematic in the sense that it seems to emphasise the use of force before the use of other measures that may be more efficacious in addressing an atrocity crimes situation (see

Pattison, 2018). The 1950 version of UfP was a response to political realities surrounding the Korean War and was indeed focused as a mechanism through which to allow the UNGA to recommend military enforcement action. However, today, large sections of the international community are considerably wary regarding the use of force (Morris, 2016), and this is one reason for unease towards UfP (Johnson, 2014; Melling and Dennett, 2017). In this way, the resolution's language may simply need updating in order to better reflect the political reality that the use of force is highly contentious, and that recommendations for non-military measures are likely to have a greater chance of acceptance by member states.

The political barrier of P5 unwillingness to trigger UfP may be problematic in the sense that there is limited chance for UNSC-UfP referral, but this fact does not affect whether the UNGA would be likely to recommend measures via UfP to be taken up by UN members. Zaum's (2008, p. 166) concerns are misplaced when he argues that a split between Western and G77 states would prevent the passage of UfP recommendations. It should be noted that Zaum's argument predates some significant UNGA developments pertaining to the R2P. Indeed, as Welsh (2021, p. 239) notes, the recommendation of ICISS in 2001 that the UNGA be utilised in instances of UNSC deadlock 'might have appeared overly optimistic in their expectations of the General Assembly' at the time. It is clear that in more recent years the UNGA has been actively engaged in R2P's implementation. For instance, the UNGA has convened informal, and since 2018, formal dialogues on R2P, which serve as a point for open debate, norm clarification, and consensus building on R2P. In May 2021, the UNGA also voted to include R2P on its annual agenda (UNGA, 2021b), and during this debate 74 member states expressed concern over UNSC inaction (GCR2P, 2021b). The UNGA has also passed resolutions pertaining to specific cases. Relying on explicit textual invocation of UfP, therefore, does not serve as a clear indicator of the influence UfP's core tenets have had on UNGA practice (Richardson, 2014, p. 138).

The example of Syria is especially significant here given the extent of UNSC deadlock and multiple vetoed draft resolutions. In December 2016, Human Rights Watch joined with 223 civil society organisations to call on the UNGA to invoke UfP (Human Rights Watch, 2016). While the UNGA has not explicitly invoked UfP over Syria, it has still taken action over the case and utilised its Charter powers to 'fill the gap' left by UNSC failure (Richardson, 2014, p. 139). Schmidt (2016, pp. 277–278) argues that the UNGA has been the main UN body for discharging its R2P over the Syria crisis by passing resolutions condemning UNSC failure and mass human rights violations committed by Syrian authorities.[10] As Russo (2020) has highlighted, UNSC failures have spurred the international community to act on its R2P in different ways; in the case of the UNGA, this has included the establishment of the International, Impartial, and Independent Mechanism on Syria (IIIMS) as an attempt at fostering accountability for atrocity crimes committed in Syria since the outbreak of the civil war.

The UNGA has also been active more recently in response to the military coup in Myanmar. In June 2021, the Assembly passed resolution A/75/L.85 by 119-1, which called for the 'immediate release of all those detained arbitrarily', for the armed forces to 'stop all violence against peaceful demonstrators', and for the 'suspension of the direct and indirect supply, sale or transfer of all weapons, munitions and other military-related equipment to Myanmar' (UNGA, 2021c).

While UfP had lain dormant for 25 years, Russia's invasion of Ukraine on 24 February 2022, and then subsequent veto of a UNSC draft resolution which sought to condemn the invasion, resulted in prompt action from the UN to invoke UfP. The UNSC referred the situation to the UNGA following the Russian veto, with the procedural vote passing by 11-1 (with three abstentions) (UN News, 2022b). Three days later, on 2 March 2022, the UNGA convened an Emergency Special Session under the UfP mechanism, adopting a resolution by vote of 141-5 which, among other things, deplored the aggression carried out by Russia against Ukraine, condemned all violations of international humanitarian law and human rights, and demanded unfettered access for humanitarian aid to reach those in need (UNGA, 2022b).

What the Ukraine case shows is that the UNGA can spring into life to quickly take action in response to pressing crises of international peace and security, including situations directly relevant to atrocity crimes under the R2P. It is clear that the R2P's core tenets have been evident in the international response to Russia's invasion of Ukraine. As Orchard (2022) has written, 'the failure of states to literally say "this is a violation of the Responsibility to Protect" discounts the range of other actions that have already occurred and will occur in future'. This includes the fact that the UNGA resolution condemned violations of international law relevant to atrocity crimes, the fact that the ICJ and ICC have ongoing cases pertaining to mass atrocity in Ukraine, and the fact that the UN Human Rights Council has established a Commission of Inquiry to investigate allegations of atrocity crime.

The invocation of UfP here has not then just been political spectacle. The ICJ's provisional ruling on 16 March 2022, in reference to the ongoing case pertaining to allegations of genocide under Convention on the Prevention and Punishment of the Crime of Genocide, that Russia should immediately halt its military operation in Ukraine, drew on the UNGA's vote of 2 March in order to establish that there was 'urgent risk of irreparable harm to the rights at issue' (ICJ, 2022). The UNGA also voted on 7 April 2022 to suspend Russia's membership of the UN Human Rights Council by a vote of 93-24 (UN News, 2022c). At the time of writing, these responses have not stopped Russia from waging its war, or curtailed atrocities committed in Ukraine.[11] They have, however, demonstrated a willingness for UN member states to take some action relevant to their R2P responsibilities, action which should not be discounted. The fallout from Ukraine remains to be seen, but the case has highlighted that there is value in the UNGA acting in response to UNSC failure.

Any fear among UNSC members that referring a case to the UNGA would not actually lead to the UNGA making any recommendations would likely be misplaced. The UNGA's recent adoption of Lichtenstein's 'veto initiative' (under resolution 76/262), without the need for a vote, reflects this fact. It should also be a point of optimism that the UNGA has always taken a recommendatory action whenever the UNSC has referred a case to it via UfP (Barber, 2019a, p. 575).

Recent statements made in the UNGA's formal debates on the R2P also support the idea that the international community is displaying increasing willingness to utilise the powers of the UNGA in response to mass atrocity. Notably, this support comes from a diverse range of state actors. Qatar, for instance, has commended 'the role of the General Assembly in … ensur[ing] accountability for the perpetrators of atrocity' (UNGA, 2019b, p. 24). Brazil, while a noted sceptic about the potential misuse of force under the R2P, has stated that '[a]s the most democratic organ of the United Nations, the Assembly should assert ownership and shape the debate on the protection of the world's populations from the most serious crimes of international concern' (UNGA, 2019a, p. 18). Rwanda, a state with whom the memory of mass atrocity remains fresh, has said that the UNGA 'cannot remain silent when atrocity crimes are being committed and the organ responsible for the maintenance of international peace and security fails to act to prevent, stop or hold those responsible to account' (UNGA, 2021a, p. 23). Notably, in the 2022 formal debate, some states, including Costa Rica on behalf of the R2P Group of Friends, Mexico on behalf of France, and the Republic of Korea also voiced their praise for the adoption of resolution 76/262 as a way for the UNGA to better hold the UNSC to account for its use of the veto and primary responsibility.

In the UNGA's meeting at the adoption of resolution 76/262, states further emphasised how the mechanism would help strengthen, via the UNGA, the UN's response to mass atrocities. Canada stated that '[t]ogether with the rest of the United Nations Organization, we have an obligation, as a General Assembly, to step up when the Security Council has actually side-lined itself' (UNGA, 2022a, p. 22). Australia asserted that 'the Charter does not preclude the General Assembly from debate and deliberation when the Council is unable to act on behalf of the wider membership' (UNGA, 2022a, p. 28). Meanwhile, Kenya drew explicit reference to the 2005 R2P agreement in the WSOD and noted that it was for this reason that it supported resolution 76/262 (UNGA, 2022a, p. 27). Again, what these examples demonstrate is an increasing desire of UNGA members for the Assembly to take a more proactive role in acting on mass atrocity.

Perhaps a more concerning feasibility obstacle for utilising the UNGA's powers through UfP relates to the use of UNSC referrals, as there has been, at least certainly prior to the Ukraine case in 2022, an unwillingness of the Council to utilise the UfP procedure (Billington, 2003). Afterall, the mechanism has only been invoked by the UNSC on eight occasions, which seems rather low considering that there have been 172 separate resolutions vetoed in the UNSC since the UfP mechanism was adopted in 1950 (UN, Dag Hammarskjöld Library, 2023).[12] On the one hand, this may reflect the legitimacy of veto use, but it may also reflect a lack of political will to upset the P5 members by circumventing their use of the veto. Further, Western P5 members who were originally supportive (to varying degrees) of UfP, dropped off their support for the mechanism as the UNGA's membership expanded and was no longer Western-biased in its makeup (Zaum, 2008, p. 156). It is perhaps telling that a P5 state such as the UK – which is an outward supporter of a rules based international order, and of the principles promoted by the R2P – chooses to champion a so-called 'doctrine of humanitarian intervention' in response to atrocity crimes (Newman, 2021), despite widescale rejection of a norm of unilateral humanitarian intervention within international law (see Richmond, 2016; O'Meara, 2017; Butchard, 2020, pp. 7–27), and yet at the same time Britain has not often sought to champion the UNGA's established and legal Charter-based powers through the UfP mechanism as a response to the UNSC's failures.

Again, this historical unease at referring crises to the UNGA via UfP may relate to the complicated relationship between the UNSC and UNGA. As noted, there is overlap in responsibilities between the two bodies as a consequence of ambiguities contained within the UN Charter (Kelsen, 1950). The UNSC is, under Article 24(1), supposed to be the primary duty bearer of a responsibility towards international peace and security, yet UfP in its current form may be invoked by the UNGA at any time. This may, as highlighted by those as Zaum and Johnson, undermine the feasibility of UfP being utilised by the UNSC's membership, as the P5 members in particular wish to maintain their preponderance over managing issues of international peace. The Syria example serves as a case in point here. Simon Adams (2021), in February 2021 email correspondence with the present author, claims that calls to utilise UfP following UNSC vetoes over Syria were gathering momentum in UN circles around 2012-2013, but did not gain enough traction for UfP to be invoked. In particular, he notes that there was unwillingness among some P5 members to enact UfP for fears that this would provide the momentum for a shift in control of the Israel-Palestine issue to the UNGA from the UNSC. It may be concerning that, even given the noted magnitude of UNSC failure in the Syria case, UfP was not viewed as the solution to promoting effective UN action.

One might be tempted to look at the Ukraine case, as well as the fact that the US, Britain, and France co-sponsored Lichtenstein's 'veto initiative' draft in the UNGA, and say that UNSC reticence to utilise the powers of the UNGA is not as strong as scholars have previously suggested. While there is perhaps something encouraging from this, Ukraine is one case and the historical record shouldn't be discounted. It is worth noting that in the UNGA's debate on Lichtenstein's veto initiative, the representative of France said that 'the General Assembly cannot become a judge of the Security Council or of its members — elected or permanent — and it is in this spirit that France and Mexico introduced a proposal to voluntarily and collectively suspend use of the veto in the event of mass atrocity crimes' (UN News, 2022a). It is also interesting that, even though the US co-sponsored UNGA resolution 76/262, it refused to denounce the veto power entirely, stating that '[t]here are times when a Permanent Five member will conclude that a particular resolution will not advance international peace and security, and it is within the authority granted by the Charter for that member to veto that resolution' (UNGA, 2022a, p. 24).

Russia's position was naturally hostile to resolution 76/262 given that its passage was essentially a 'final straw' response to its own abuses of the veto power. Russia noted that '[t]he decision that was made today, while it comes in very pretty packaging, is without doubt an attempt to create an instrument that exerts pressure on the permanent members of the Security Council. That is an approach that we categorically reject'. China has previously stated that '[c]onsensus should be gradually forged in order to avoid forcing issues onto the agenda of the General Assembly. The persistent promotion and imposition of controversial issues will only harm the common interest of Member States' (UNGA, 2019b, p. 12). At the adoption of resolution 76/262, China was surprisingly positive about the role that the UNGA can and should play under the Charter, noting that '[u]nder the "Uniting for peace" mechanism, the General Assembly can convene emergency special sessions ... Practice over the years has shown that this arrangement allows Member States to play a role on major issues of international peace and security' (UNGA, 2022a, p. 8). Nevertheless, China still displayed scepticism about the role of Lichtenstein's veto initiative, adding that:

> in the actual work of the Council, there are a variety of specific situations in which the Council is unable to act. The resolution adopted in today's meeting gives the General Assembly a new mandate — to create a mechanism that automatically triggers the General Assembly to convene meetings, which, in practice, is likely to cause procedural confusion and inconsistency. It is difficult to determine at this time whether such an arrangement would serve the intended purpose of the resolution.
>
> (UNGA, 2022a, p. 8)

What these examples of P5 response to the veto initiative perhaps demonstrate then is a still-present reluctance of the UNSC's permanent members to the idea of the UNGA acting automatically in response to veto use, even if Lichtenstein's proposal received P3 support. As international fervour generated by the Ukraine case dies down over time, we may see this reluctance harden once more.

Reticence from some UNSC members may be a feasibility concern for UNSC-UfP referrals, but it is not a debilitating constraint that serves as a fundamental bar on the feasibility of UfP being utilised. Even if some members are sceptical of the use of UfP, it is still possible for the UNSC to refer cases to the UNGA via a 9/15 vote.[13] Achieving the requisite numbers is not a given but it is a realistically attainable number. Given the overwhelming support that many vetoed draft resolutions have received in the UNSC, support for referrals is feasible. For instance, of the 17 vetoed UNSC draft resolutions over Syria, all received at least 9 votes in favour, and over half of those resolutions received at least 12 votes in favour. Nonetheless, given the record of Council members' unease towards UfP, it would still seem prudent to ensure that UfP not undermine UNSC primacy; a concern which the proposals made below attempt to address. This may help to mitigate the problem of limited will to refer cases. What this again suggests is that the UNGA should not possess the power to invoke UfP itself over a matter in which the UNSC is actively engaged.

While there are notable feasibility concerns surrounding the will to utilise the UNGA's powers through the UfP mechanism, these are not over-problematic. Despite historical reticence among UNSC members about refer-ring cases via UfP, it is still possible that – given current trends as well as the fact that many vetoed UNSC draft resolutions have received an overwhelming support from UNSC members – the UNSC will choose to utilise UfP and refer cases to the UNGA on a more consistent basis in the future. The UNGA has also shown a willingness to act on its R2P responsibilities which suggests that the body *will* continue to utilise its Charter-based powers to act on R2P cases. The fact is that the UNGA holds the ability to recommend measures in the name of international peace and security, has utilised these powers and recently reaffirmed them, and hence it is clearly feasible that it could seek to utilise these powers more regularly.

6.4 A Revised UfP Mechanism: Overcoming the Authority Dilemma

The above analysis shows that the powers of the UNGA offer a mostly effective and feasible avenue through which to overcome R2P's authority dilemma and discharge Pillar Three in the event of UNSC failure. Nonetheless, as has also been argued, there are some issues associated with utilising these powers, particularly when framed in regard to the UfP mechanism.[14] This includes UfP's 'P5 unanimity clause' as a potential bar on action in cases where the UNSC has done little-to-nothing; the fact that the resolution's language may be outdated in its emphasis on military force; and most significantly, that the current version of UfP may present a conflict with UNSC primacy in the realm of international peace and security. With regard to the latter, this has contributed to a political reticence to deploy the UNGA's powers, with a desire to maintain UNSC preponderance and fears that UfP oversteps the UNGA's Charter powers. Hence, to try and solve these problems, improve the feasibility of utilising the UNGA's powers under UfP, and to ensure the measure can be effective, this section puts forward a revised version of UfP that seeks to safeguard UNSC primacy, while allowing the UNGA to fulfil its rightful role in discharging its R2P. Here some amendments are offered to UfP language and procedure. These could be contained within a new UfP resolution adopted by the UNGA, building off the back of the recent political momentum generated by the adoption of Lichtenstein's veto initiative.

Before proceeding, it is worth addressing a potential contention that the UfP mechanism is itself superfluous. First, one might point to the adoption of Lichtenstein's veto initiative and say that the UNGA does not need to invoke its powers under UfP. Whenever a veto is cast in the UNSC, the UNGA will now convene a special session to discuss it anyway. However, as noted above, this still raises the issue of what to do when the UNSC fails to even take a matter to a resolution vote; when this happens, the veto initiative has no bearing. Furthermore, the veto initiative can be read more as an attempt at holding the UNSC's permanent members to scrutiny, rather than a direct attempt to see the UNGA take up the matter and provide its own recommendations in the name of international peace and security. UfP therefore still has an important role to play as a mechanism for the UNGA to take action on its Charter and R2P responsibilities.

Second, Johnson (2014) has argued that because the UNGA already possesses the power to make recommendations in the name of international peace and security, as per its Charter powers, there is actually no need for the UfP mechanism to be invoked when the UNGA makes recommendations. It is true that, as we have seen, the UNGA inherits its powers from the Charter and that therefore, *legally*, UfP is not essential. However, as has also been argued, a problem with invoking the UNGA's power is that the Charter does not make it clear when responsibility is transferred from the UNSC to the UNGA. This is a consequence of the Charter being a document of political compromise that leaves the exact relationship between the UNSC and UNGA somewhat blurred; granting primacy over matters of international peace and security to the UNSC along with the power of veto to its permanent members, but also giving the UNGA recommendatory powers over similar matters (Reicher, 1981, p. 35).

The benefit of UfP is that it serves as a point of *political* clarification for the UNGA's powers (Barber, 2019b, p. 104), acting as a working mechanism for activating the secondary responsibility of the Assembly. As White (2015, p. 311) notes, the UNGA did, on the adoption of the Charter, possess the power to recommend coercive measures up to and including the use of force, but UfP has served as an example of UNGA practice which has converted this power from abstract into reality. UfP is useful because it provides a 'procedural due process' that allows the UNGA to invoke its powers without the need for contentious Charter debate, and clarifies what the UNGA can do within a normatively accepted framework (Reicher, 1981, p. 40). Furthermore, as a recent report from Barber (2021, p. 13) on behalf of the Asia-Pacific Centre for the R2P notes:

> There may be political value in the UNGA invoking the [UfP] Resolution and convening an "emergency special session". Such a course could assist

to convey the UNGA's assessment of the gravity of a situation, strengthen the political legitimacy of the UNGA's recommendations, and increase political pressure on the UNSC to fulfil its responsibilities.

UfP could, therefore, serve an important political role in galvanising the UN membership to take action on the UNGA's Charter-based responsibilities for the maintenance of international peace and security, and is mechanism that could be more readily utilised to promote action under the R2P's third pillar. However, in order to rectify some of its deficiencies, some revisions are required.

The first recommendation made here is to alter the trigger mechanism in place for UfP. Currently, the mechanism can be activated by either UNSC referral, or by a majority of UNGA members at their own discretion following UNSC failure to exercise its primary responsibility in any case where there is a threat to the peace, breach of the peace, or act of aggression (including evidence of atrocity crime). The first of these – when the UNSC refers a matter formerly on its agenda to the UNGA through a procedural vote – presents no issues and should remain a mechanism through which UfP can be triggered. It is the trigger procedure of the UNGA that the recommendation here seeks to change. Rather than allowing the UNGA to trigger UfP entirely at its own discretion, this recommendation should allow for a version of UfP that does not supersede the UNSC's primary authority, but which also allows the UNGA to fulfil its secondary responsibility in instances where the UNSC has failed to act. This trigger mechanism would operate thus: the UNGA would recommend, via a two-thirds majority vote, that the UN Secretary-General determine whether a situation is one that may threaten international peace and security;[15] following that determination, any lack of UNSC resolution vote within a 30-day period would enable the UNGA to trigger UfP and make recommendations in the name of maintaining international peace and security.

The second recommendation is that the 'permanent members unanimity' clause be removed from UfP. The UfP resolution of 1950 calls for the UNGA to make recommendations only 'if the Security Council, because of lack of unanimity of the permanent members, fails to exercise its primary responsibility' (UNGA, 1950, section A). Removing this clause would better align the UfP mechanism with the UN Charter, which only requires UNSC failure in order for the UNGA to step in, and does not necessarily require a lack of great power unanimity (Reicher, 1981, p. 42).

The third and final recommendation made here is that UfP language be altered to place less emphasis on the use of armed force, and instead emphasise the need to make appropriate recommendations which are more in line with the broad array of responses available under the UNGA's powers, which includes those in the R2P response toolkit, such as diplomatic and peaceful measures, the deployment of accountability mechanisms, and the use of coercive measures short of force (UN, 2012). In light of the unease that exists over the use of UfP for fears of its links with military enforcement (Johnson,

2014; Melling and Dennett, 2017), it would seem prudent to attempt to disassociate UfP as primarily a means for authorising the use of force, and instead refocus the mechanism as a means for discharging Pillar Three of R2P via whichever means are most appropriate in a given case.

6.4.1 Test of Effective Progress

Let us now assess whether these recommendations can help to enhance the effectiveness and feasibility of utilising the UNGA's powers through the UfP mechanism. While it has been argued that there are not any significant hindrances to the effectiveness of the current UfP measure, the alteration to UfP's trigger procedure provided here would keep in place the power of the UNSC to refer cases to the UNGA where a majority of its members decide that the Council itself has been unable to effectively discharge its primary responsibility. The recommendation would also provide a way for the UNGA to act on its secondary responsibility in instances of UNSC inaction without overstepping its Charter powers.

A new UfP resolution adopted by the UNGA could serve to politically galvanise the UNGA into acting on its responsibilities where the UNSC has failed. As Carswell (2013, p. 478) puts it, '[i]f states choose a new and constitutional path for the resolution, with strong checks and balances against abuse at both the Council and Assembly levels, the resolution's positive image may indeed be restored'. A new UfP resolution would provide an up-to-date statement on the UNGA's powers, a clarification of contemporary understandings of the overlapping role of the UN's two principle organs, and one which reflects the Assembly's increasingly active role in discharging its R2P. Such a resolution would demonstrate that the UNGA is committed to upholding its responsibilities, including its R2P obligations, and send a strong political message that the Assembly will not stand idly by in the wake of UNSC failure. In this way, a new UfP resolution could help to strengthen the norm of the R2P by supporting a means for discharging Pillar Three, and enabling dialogue and potential action in response to mass atrocity crises.

Beyond the general advantages that a new UfP resolution would bring, the recommendations made here can enhance UfP's procedural effectiveness. First, establishing a clear set of criteria for when the UNGA can rightfully step in to trigger UfP following UNSC failure would make it clearer as to when UfP can be triggered by the UNGA. One might observe that a 30-day timeframe reflects something of an arbitrary value and one that precludes the UNGA from acting on its secondary responsibility within this noted timeframe. Indeed, this may be the case, and any given timeframe could be accused of representing an arbitrary figure. The 30-day timeframe recommended here has been offered though because it would arguably give the UNSC a reasonable amount of time to put forward a draft resolution over a crisis, without giving such a wide timeframe that after which the UN might be accused of having failed in its R2P Pillar Three duty to provide *timely and decisive* response.[16] A timeframe would also allow the UNGA to invoke UfP for a matter on which the UNSC has previously attempted or passed a resolution, but may not have done so for a long time. In such cases, the Council could no longer be said to be actively exercising its responsibilities.

Furthermore, establishing criteria to determine when the UNSC is not exercising its responsibilities – in this case, a UNGA vote, followed by UN Secretary-General determination that a situation threatens international peace and security, and then lack of UNSC resolution vote within a 30-day period – would give a clear trigger point for when the UNGA can activate UfP. This is a necessary step that would enhance the effectiveness of the mechanism because currently, without a clear timeframe, it is impossible to determine when the UNGA can rightfully decide that the UNSC is not actively exercising its functions. A UNGA vote, Secretary-General determination of R2P concern, and a 30 day timeframe gives a clear standard to judge this. When these criteria have been satisfied, this would indicate that the UNSC is not actively exercising its functions and provide a clear trigger point to permit the UNGA to activate UfP.

At this point, the astute readership is already likely to have noted the parallel between the recommendation made here for altering the UNGA's triggering procedure for UfP, and the recommendation made in the previous chapter for triggering the 'Responsible Veto Restraint' mechanism. Indeed, having both mechanisms triggerable via a UNGA vote and Secretary-General determination would be beneficial as it would promote coherence between the two proposals. This would enable both mechanisms to be triggered simultaneously, which would help ensure that either i) the UNSC can discharge its R2P through passing resolutions on the use of non-coercive mechanisms or by referring the case to the UNGA via UfP, or ii) that the UNGA would be able to step in following the failure of the UNSC to take any form of adequate R2P response. It should also be noted though that both proposals could work independently; while stronger transitional cosmopolitan progress would be made by adopting both, adopting just one of these reform recommendations would help strengthen states' R2P.

Second, removing the 'permanent members unanimity' clause would also serve to enhance the procedural effectiveness of UfP. Currently, UfP requires a lack of P5 unanimity to be demonstrated, which most likely refers to those situations in which a permanent member has cast a veto (Johnson, 2014, p. 107). Yet, as discussed in section 6.3, a lack of P5 unanimity is not a requisite for activating the UNGA's secondary responsibility to international peace and security under the Charter, rather, only UNSC failure is required (Reicher, 1981, p. 42). It should, therefore, not be the case that there needs to be an explicit demonstration of a lack of unanimity between the P5 in order for UfP to become applicable. Making this a requirement for UfP may be seen to preclude the applicability of the mechanism to situations that have failed to make it to a UNSC vote, even if they are quite obvious examples of the UNSC failing to fulfil its responsibilities. As noted in section 6.1, there are multiple examples of where crises which have failed to make it to a formal resolution vote, despite being some of the most extreme and protracted instances of atrocity crimes in recent years. Notably, this includes the Rohingya crisis in Myanmar where an estimated 1.3 million were left in need of assistance following a military operation targeting Rohingya communities (UNICEF); the persecution of Uyghur Muslims in Xinjiang province where at least one million ethnic Uyghur Muslims are reported to have been arbitrary detained by the Chinese state (Uyghur Human Rights Project, 2020, p. 1); and ethnic violence committed in Ethiopia since November 2020, which may amount to war crimes and crimes against humanity (GCR2P, 2021a). Removing the requirement of 'lack of P5 unanimity' to be demonstrated before UfP can be triggered would further support the UNGA to legitimately trigger UfP in instances of UNSC failure where matters have not made it to a formal vote on a resolution.

6.4.2 *Test of Moral Hazard*

The recommendation to modify UfP's procedural trigger would help foster a mechanism that allows the UNGA to act on its secondary responsibility after the UNSC, but which does not undermine the Council's primary authority. Again, Article 12(1) of the UN Charter precludes the UNGA from discussing a matter for which the UNSC is actively seized, and while the ICJ did in *Construction of a Wall* note that practice has evolved so that UNGA and UNSC do often discuss issues in tandem, there is still an unclear relationship between the two organs in terms of overlapping responsibilities which may undermine the centrality of the UNSC as it is meant to be taken under Article 24(1). It does therefore seem prudent to ensure UNSC primacy by placing primary triggering power with the UNSC when it has recently at least attempted to pass a resolution over a crisis.

The proposal offered here is relevant to the problem highlighted by some scholars that the current version of UfP has potential to allow the UNGA to supersede the power of the UNSC. Indeed, it is this problem which has led those such as Carswell (2013), Ramsden (2016), and Melling and Dennett (2017) to argue that sole UfP triggering power should be left with the UNSC, while the UNGA should simply not be permitted to trigger UfP at all. But the recommendation made here differs from these authors. As Reicher (1981, pp. 41–42) argues, UNSC inaction cannot shackle the UNGA from acting on its own Charter powers. Were it the case that the UNSC completely failed to address a crisis, then a version of UfP which only allowed the UNSC to trigger the mechanism would leave the UNGA unable to act on its secondary responsibility in the wake of Council failure. It therefore seems inappropriate to promote a version of UfP that is only applicable when activated by the UNSC, or else such a version would undermine the very purpose for which UfP was created.

By favouring UNSC primacy through referral on matters for which the Council is actively seeking to exercise its responsibilities, but allowing the UNGA to activate UfP in instances of total UNSC paralysis, in this way, the version of UfP offered here is a more nuanced one. It serves as a compromise between the version of UfP which was passed in 1950, and the version of UfP which favours sole UNSC triggering power as has been recommended by several authors in recent years. What this can help to achieve is a balance in which the UNGA cannot overstep its powers by superseding the authority of the UNSC through determining when Article 12(1) no longer applies, but also in which UNSC paralysis – because an item has not recently made it to a formal vote, or perhaps not even made it onto the UNSC's formal agenda at all – does not inhibit the UN's response to an atrocity case.

Providing clear criteria for when the UNGA can rightfully trigger UfP may help prevent the UNGA from overstepping its Charter powers by acting on a case before the UNSC has been given fair opportunity to exercise its primary responsibility. As noted above, the ICJ (2004, p. 17) in the *Wall Case* drew on the interpretation of the Legal Counsel of the United Nations that the words 'is exercising the functions' contained in Article 12(1) refer only to whether the UNSC 'is exercising the functions at this moment'. If the Security Council has not recently taken a matter to a resolution vote, this would suggest that the Council is not actively exercising its responsibilities as per Article 12(1). In contrast, if a matter has recently been put to a resolution vote, the UNSC is clearly seeking to exercise its responsibilities, even if that vote resulted in a veto. This would rightly preclude the UNGA from stepping in since, as noted, veto use does not automatically denote responsibility failure, and hence only the UNSC itself can rightly determine in such a circumstance whether it is adequately fulfilling its duties, and hence, refer a case itself to the UNGA via UfP. The recommendation made here would prevent the UNGA from being able to take items on which the UNSC is actively exercising its responsibilities, but it would also prevent cases of total UNSC inaction from barring the UNGA from acting. It would also prevent the UNGA from being able to act prior to the UNSC having had fair opportunity to discharge its primary responsibility; for example, in new and emerging cases of mass atrocities. In all, the recommendations made here would allow for an effective version of UfP, but one which does not present a potentially damaging moral hazard that undermines the delicate balance of the UN system.

6.4.3 *Test of Practical Potential*

As discussed in section 6.3, it is feasible that, given the UNGA's increasingly proactive role, UfP could be more readily utilised going forward. Nonetheless, the recommendations made here attempt to bolster this feasibility. One issue that the proposals made here attempt to address is the concern of states who have distanced themselves from UfP due to a desire to maintain UNSC pre-ponderance over matters deemed to be essentially within the primary remit of the Council, and the fear that UfP may overstep the UNGA's Charter powers (Zaum, 2008, pp. 164–166).

The recommendations for an updated UfP mechanism aim to ensure the Council's primary status in the realm of international peace and security. This could, for instance, assuage the fears of some Council members that the use of UfP over one case would serve as an automatic prelude to the use of UfP over others. If the UNSC chooses to refer a particular case to the UNGA, this would not automatically equate to UfP being utilised over other issues. Any matter for which the Council is actively exercising its responsibilities, demonstrated by its attempt to pass a formal resolution within the previous month, would require a UNSC referral from a majority of its members. Hence, fear that the use of UfP would lead to the circum-vention of UNSC primacy should be allayed given that the UNGA would only possess the power to activate UfP for cases in which the UNSC is paralysed.

The recommendations offered here also attempt to enhance the feasibility of UfP's application by promoting a more normatively acceptable use of language, less centralised on military enforcement action. The current iter-ation of UfP refers to the UNGA's willingness to recommend 'armed force when necessary' (UNGA, 1950 Sect. A). It is argued here that this use of lan-guage should be altered in order to place less emphasis on armed force, and a greater emphasis on making appropriate recommendations in line with the UNGA's powers, which includes a plethora of responses available in R2P's Pillar Three toolkit. For instance, there are a wealth of available non-military responses to atrocity crimes at the disposal of the UN (including the UNGA), with the use of targeted sanctions, asset freezes, mediation and arbitration, or even simple condemnations of irresponsible actions at the organisation's disposal (UN, 2012). UfP should not be taken solely as a means to authorise military enforcement, and in emphasising this, it might ease those fears highlighted by Johnson (2014, p. 114) that some UN members are concerned UfP would provide a 'slippery slope' towards an over-readiness to apply military force.

Military enforcement ought to remain an available response under UfP as a means for the UNGA to rightfully act on its Charter responsibilities to inter-national peace and security, which includes a duty to tackle mass atrocity. At the same time, however, the version of UfP adopted in 1950 is reflective of the political realities of the time, where armed enforcement over the Korea issue was deemed the necessity. For the present context of seeking to utilise UfP as a response to mass atrocity crises, it ought to be emphasised that there are a host of available Pillar Three responses available to the UNGA short of force that may be more effective or politically viable for addressing a crisis (Pattison, 2018; Barber, 2021).

6.5 Conclusion

The version of R2P adopted in 2005 failed to resolve the 'authority dilemma' (Gallagher, 2013, pp. 111–115) of intervention to protect fundamental human rights. Where the UNSC fails to act on atrocity crises, Pillar Three of R2P is left significantly weakened, and cosmopolitan responsibilities left wanting. UfP provides us with a solution to this authority dilemma. UfP is a clarification of the powers held by the UNGA under the UN Charter, which furnishes the body with a secondary duty towards the maintenance of international peace and security. The mechanism offers the international community a mostly effective and feasible means through which to discharge its R2P Pillar Three duty even in the advent of UNSC failure.

However, the version of UfP that was adopted by the UNGA in 1950 may contain an unnecessary barrier in the form of a 'lack of P5 unanimity clause', be outdated in its focus on military enforcement, and may also overstep the UNGA's constitutional mandate by allowing the Assembly to effectively usurp UNSC primacy over matters for which the Council is still exercising its responsibilities. Regarding the latter point, given the damage this may cause to the relationship between the UN's two principle organs, as well as the way in which this weakens the desirability and ergo feasibility that the UfP mechanism will be utilised, this chapter does favour calls in the scholarship to place the UNSC front and centre to the operationalisation of UfP (Carswell, 2013, p. 472; Ramsden, 2016, p. 298; Melling and Dennett, 2017, pp. 300–303; Barber, 2019b, p. 107). Yet, while others have argued that it would be prudent to entirely discard the UNGA's power to invoke UfP itself, this chapter, in contrast, favours an approach that ensures UNSC primacy, but does not inhibit the UNGA in acting on its secondary responsibility.

The chapter has called for UfP language and procedure be reformed in such ways as would enhance the transitional cosmopolitan effectiveness and feasibility of the mechanism. It has called for a procedural tweak which would maintain the UNSC's power to trigger UfP by referring a case to the UNGA, but which would also allow the UNGA to trigger the mechanism for matters over which the UNSC is not actively exercising its responsibilities, once specific criteria are met. The chapter also called for the removal of the P5 unanimity clause in UfP: to emphasise that UfP can rightfully be triggered in instances where there is no explicit indication of a lack of P5 unanimity. Finally, the chapter recommended that UfP language be altered to place less emphasis on the use of military force, and instead emphasise that there is a wealth of international responses available to the UNGA.

The proposals offered in this chapter can better align UfP with the transitional cosmopolitan approach, providing a more effective and feasible alternative for discharging cosmopolitan responsibilities in the wake of UNSC failure. The UNGA has the power to recommend a host of possible measures that would allow the international community to better discharge R2P and meet cosmopolitan protection demands. It is high time that these powers were more consistently utilised.

Notes

1 Such reasons may include a clash of national interests between members of the P5 and/or a conflict between the UNSC's special responsibilities for maintaining international peace and security, and their responsibilities under R2P (see Morris, 2015).

2 Some notable exceptions include works by Carswell (2013), Barber (2021), and Butchard (2020).

3 The first two examples have not even made it onto the UNSC's formal agenda.

4 UfP has been invoked in 13 instances if one counts the UNSC's removal of the Korea item from its agenda in 1951 before the issue was taken up by the UNGA.

5 A caveat to acknowledge here is that not all scholars believe the UNGA has the authority to recommend that member states take measures involving *the use of force* (see Orakhelashvili, 2011, p. 48; Talmon, 2014, p. 128; Johnson, 2014, pp. 114–115). Nonetheless, the present author favours arguments which support the UNGA's power to recommend military force (see White and Tsagourias, 2013, p. 292; Ramsden, 2016, pp. 285–288; Butchard, 2020, pp. 108–120).

6 Trahan (2020, p. 95) has also argued that veto use that obstructs international response to genocide, war crimes, and crimes against humanity is a breach of international law by the vetoing member/s as per Articles 1, 2, and 24(2) of the UN Charter.

7 This, again, relates to the tension between the UNSC's 'dual responsibility' discussed in Chapter 5 (see Morris, 2015).

8 This relates to the matter discussed in Chapter 5 on the normative purpose of the veto power.

9 UfP has only been invoked once since R2P was adopted in 2005.

10 See for instance the UNGA's July 2012 resolution 'deploring the failure of the Security Council to agree on measures to ensure the compliance of Syrian authorities with its decisions' (UNGA, 2012).

11 The ongoing war in Ukraine has mostly likely involved the commission of atrocity crimes, including potential war crimes and crimes against humanity (ICC, 2022).

12 As of 1 January 2023.

13 Gifkins (2021, p. 10) has highlighted that there is a general desire to ensure unanimity in UNSC decision making, and so while attaining 9/15 votes is mathematically quite possible, there may be a reluctance to pursue referral if anything less than Council unanimity is possible (excluding the member/s that vetoed the original resolution).

14 Many of these issues also apply to Lichtenstein's 'veto initiative', including its trigger point requiring an explicit use of the veto, as well as the potential circumvention of UNSC primacy.

15 Such a determination is consistent with Article 99 of the UN Charter, which permits the Secretary-General to 'bring to the attention of the Security Council any matter which in his opinion may threaten the maintenance of international peace and security'. This call for a determination could also explicitly reference R2P / mass atrocities, such as by declaring whether there are either likely atrocities occurring, or serious concern that they could occur.

16 Notably, the UNSC could also choose to be proactive and attempt to pass a resolution during the process at which the UNGA seeks a determination from the UN Secretary-General that a situation is one concerning a threat to international peace and security. The UNSC would certainly have ample opportunity to act on its primary responsibility.

References

Adams, S. 2021. Email Inquiry About Uniting for Peace and its Lack of Use Over Syria.

Andrassy, J. 1956. Uniting for Peace. *The American Journal of International Law.* 50(3), pp. 563–582.

Barber, R. 2019a. Accountability for Crimes Against the Rohingya: Possibilities for the General Assembly Where the Security Council Fails. *Journal of International Criminal Justice.* 17(3), pp. 557–584.

Barber, R. 2019b. Uniting for Peace Not Aggression: Responding to Chemical Weapons in Syria Without Breaking the Law. *Journal of Conflict and Security Law.* 24(1), pp. 71–110.

Barber, R. 2021. *The Powers of the UN General Assembly to Prevent and Respond to Atrocity Crimes: A Guidance Document* [Online]. Asia-Pacific Centre for the Responsibility to Protect. [Accessed 6 May 2021]. Available from: https://r2pasia pacific.org/files/6710/UNGA_2021%20%283%29.pdf.

Barber, R. 2022. Does International Law Permit the Provision of Humanitarian Assistance Without Host State Consent? Territorial Integrity, Necessity and the Determinative Function of the General Assembly *In*: T. D. Gill, R. Geiß, H. Krieger and R. Mignot-Mahdavi, eds. *Yearbook of International Humanitarian Law 2020.* New York: Springer, pp. 85–121.

Billington, M. 2003. UN "Uniting for Peace" Resolution Could Demand an End to US War in Iraq. *Executive Intelligence Review.* 11, pp. 42–44.

Bourantonis, D. and Magliveras, K. 2002. Anglo-American Differences Over the UN During the Cold War: The Uniting for Peace Resolution. *Contemporary British History.* 16(2), pp. 59–76.

Buchanan, A. and Keohane, R.O. 2011. Precommitment Regimes for Intervention: Supplementing the Security Council. *Ethics & International Affairs.* 25(1), pp. 41–63.

Butchard, P.M. 2020. *The Responsibility to Protect and the Failures of the United Nations Security Council.* Oxford: Hart Publishing.

Carswell, A.J. 2013. Unblocking the UN Security Council: The Uniting for Peace Resolution. *Journal of Conflict and Security Law.* 18(3), pp. 453–480.

Erskine, T. 2019. Coalitions of the Willing and the Shared Responsibility to Protect *In*: R. Beardsworth, G.W. Brown and R. Shapcott, eds. *The State and Cosmopolitan Responsibilities.* Oxford: Oxford University Press, pp. 61–87.

Fabre, C. 2012. *Cosmopolitan War.* Oxford: Oxford University Press.

Gallagher, A. 2013. *Genocide and its Threat to Contemporary International Order.* London: Palgrave Macmillan.

Gaston, E. 2022. The Ukraine War Could End Up Revitalizing Humanitarian Law. *World Politics Review.* [Online]. [Accessed 4 February 2022]. Available from: www. worldpoliticsreview.com/articles/30506/for-the-united-nations-ukraine-could-mark-a-new-era-of-accountability.

GCR2P 2021a. Populations at Risk: Ethiopia. [Accessed 18 May 2021]. Available from: www.globalr2p.org/countries/ethiopia/.

GCR2P 2021b. Summary of the 2021 UN General Assembly Plenary Meeting on the Responsibility to Protect. [Accessed 14 June 2021]. Available from: www.global r2p.org/publications/summary-of-the-2021-un-general-assembly-plenary-meeting-on-the-responsibility-to-protect/.

Gifkins, J. 2021. Beyond the veto: Roles in UN Security Council decision-making. *Global Governance: A Review of Multilateralism and International Organizations.* 27(1), pp. 1–24.

Gowan, R. 2021. *The Security Council and Conflict Prevention: Entry Points for Diplomatic Action.* New York: United Nations University: Centre for Policy Research.

Gowan, R. 2022. The UN Is Another Casualty of Russia's War: Why the Organization Might Never Bounce Back. *Foreign Affairs.* [Online]. [Accessed 11 March 2022]. Available from: www.foreignaffairs.com/articles/west-africa/2022-03-10/un-anot her-casualty-russias-war?utm_source=twitter_posts&utm_medium=social&utm_c ampaign=tw_daily_soc.

Hailbronner, K. and Klein, E. 2002. Article 10 *In*: B. Simma, ed. Oxford: Oxford University Press.

Hehir, A. 2012. *The Responsibility to Protect: Rhetoric, Reality and the Future of Humanitarian Intervention.* Basingstoke: Palgrave Macmillan.

Heinbecker, P. 2004. Kosovo. *In*: D. Malone, ed. *The UN Security Council: From the Cold War to the 21st Century.* Boulder CO: Lynne Rienner Publishers, pp. 537–550.

Henderson, C. 2014. Authority Without Accountability? The UN Security Council's Authorization Method and Institutional Mechanisms of Accountability. *Journal of Conflict and Security Law.* 19(3), pp. 489–509.

Higgins, R., Webb, P., Akande, D., Sivakumaran, S. and Sloan, J. 2017. *Oppenheim's International Law: United Nations.* Oxford: Oxford University Press.

Human Rights Watch 2016. Uniting for Peace in Syria: Global Civil Society Appeal to UN Member States. [Accessed 26 March 2021]. Available from: https://www. hrw.org/news/2016/12/01/uniting-peace-syria-global-civil-society-appeal-un-mem ber-states.

Hunt, C.T. 2020. The Responsibility to Protect and the Protection of Civilians in UN Peace Operations: Interaction, Feedback and Co-evolution *In*: C. T. Hunt and P. Orchard, eds. *Constructing the Responsibility to Protect: Contestation and Consolidation.* London: Routledge, pp. 89–112.

ICJ 1962. *Certain Expenses of the United Nations (Article 17, paragraph 2, of the Charter). Summary of the Advisory Opinion of 20 July 1962* [Online]. [Accessed 15 March 2021]. Available from: www.icj-cij.org/en/case/49/summaries.

ICJ 2004. *Legal Consequences of the Construction of a Wall in the Occupied Palestinian Territory* [Online]. [Accessed 18 March 2021]. Available from: www. icj-cij.org/public/files/case-related/131/131-20040709-ADV-01-00-EN.pdf.

ICJ 2022. *Allegations of Genocide Under the Convention on the Prevention and Punishment of the Crimes of Genocide (Ukraine v. Russian Federation). Request for the Indication of Provisional Measures* [Online]. [Accessed 13 April 2022]. Available from: www.icj-cij.org/public/files/case-related/182/182-20220316-ORD-01-00-EN.pdf.

Independent International Commission on Kosovo 2000. *The Kosovo Report: Conflict, International Response, Lessons Learned*. Oxford: Oxford University Press.

International Commission on Intervention and State Sovereignty 2001. The Responsibility to Protect: Report of the International Commission on Intervention and State Sovereignty. [Accessed 14 December 2018]. Available from: http://resp onsibilitytoprotect.org/ICISS%20Report.pdf.

Johnson, L.D. 2014. "Uniting for Peace": Does it Still Serve Any Useful Purpose? *AJIL Unbound*. **108**, pp. 106–115.

Kelsen, H. 1950. Is the Acheson Plan Constitutional? *Western Political Quarterly*. **3**(4), pp. 512–527.

Khan, M.T. and Ahmed, S. 2020. Dealing with the Rohingya Crisis: The Relevance of the General Assembly and R2P. *Asian Journal of Comparative Politics*. **5**(2), pp. 121–143.

Krasno, J. and Das, M. 2008. The Uniting for Peace Resolution and Other Ways of Circumventing the Authority of the Security Council *In*: B. Cronin and I. Hurd, eds. *The UN Security Council and the Politics of International Authority*. London: Routledge, pp. 173–195.

Mamlyuk, B.N. 2014. Uniting for "Peace" in the Second Cold War: A Response to Larry Johnson. *AJIL Unbound*. **108**, pp. 129–134.

Melling, G. and Dennett, A. 2017. The Security Council Veto and Syria: Responding to Mass Atrocities Through the "Uniting for Peace" Resolution. *Indian Journal of International Law*. **57**(3), pp. 285–307.

Miluna, I. 2014. What Does the Uniting for Peace Resolution Mean for the Role of the UN Security Council? *AJIL Unbound*. **108**, pp. 118–122.

Morris, J. 2015. The Responsibility to Protect and the Great Powers: The Tensions of Dual Responsibility. *Global Responsibility to Protect*. **7**(3–4), pp. 398–421.

Morris, J. 2016. The Responsibility to Protect and the Use of Force: Remaking the Procrustean Bed? *Cooperation and conflict*. **51**(2), pp. 200–215.

Morris, J. and Wheeler, N.J. 2016. The Responsibility Not to Veto *In*: A.J. Bellamy and T. Dunne, eds. *The Oxford Handbook of the Responsibility to Protect*. Oxford: Oxford University Press, pp. 227–248.

Nahlawi, Y. 2019. Overcoming Russian and Chinese vetoes on Syria Through Uniting for Peace. *Journal of Conflict and Security Law*. **24**(1), pp. 111–143.

Nanda, V.P. 2020. The Security Council Veto in the Context of Atrocity Crimes, Uniting for Peace, and the Responsibility to Protect. *Case Western Reserve Journal of International Law*. **52**, pp. 119–141.

Newman, E. 2021. Exploring the UK's Doctrine of Humanitarian Intervention. *International Peacekeeping*. **28**(4), pp. 632–660.

OHCHR 2021. Statement by Thomas H. Andrews UN Special Rapporteur on the Situation of Human Rights in Myanmar United Nations Human Rights Council. [Accessed 12 March 2021]. Available from: www.ohchr.org/EN/NewsEvents/Pages/ DisplayNews.aspx?NewsID=26884&LangID=E.

O'Meara, C. 2017. Should International Law Recognize a Right of Humanitarian Intervention. *International and Comparative Law Quarterly*. **66**, p. 441.

Orakhelashvili, A. 2011. *Collective Security*. Oxford: Oxford University Press.

Orchard, P. 2022. The Responsibility to Protect in Ukraine: 'Another False Success' Or an Imperfect But Ongoing Response? *Fresh Perspectives*. [Online]. [Accessed 13 April 2022]. Available from: https://ecr2p.leeds.ac.uk/the-responsibility-to-protect-in-ukraine-another-false-success-or-an-imperfect-but-ongoing-response/.

Pattison, J. 2018. *The Alternatives to War: From Sanctions to Nonviolence.* Oxford: Oxford University Press.

Pedersen, M.B. 2021. The Rohingya Crisis, Myanmar, and R2P 'Black Holes'. *Global Responsibility to Protect.* **1**(aop), pp. 1–30.

Petersen, K.S. 1959. The Uses of the Uniting for Peace Resolution Since 1950. *International Organization.* **13**(2), pp. 219–232.

Ramsden, M. 2016. Uniting for Peace and Humanitarian Intervention: The Authorising Function of the UN General Assembly. *Pacific Rim Law and Policy Journal.* **25**, pp. 267–305.

Reicher, H. 1981. The Uniting for Peace Resolution on the Thirtieth Anniversary of its Passage. *Columbia Journal of Transnational Law.* **20**, pp. 1–49.

Richardson, H. 2014. Comment on Larry Johnson, "Uniting for Peace". *AJIL Unbound.* **108**, pp. 135–140.

Richmond, S. 2016. Why Is Humanitarian Intervention so Divisive? Revisiting the Debate Over the 1999 Kosovo Intervention. *Journal on the Use of Force and International Law.* **3**(2), pp. 234–259.

Russo, J.B. 2020. R2P in Syria and Myanmar: Norm Violation and Advancement. *Global Responsibility to Protect.* **12**(2), pp. 211–233.

Schmidt, M. 2016. UN General Assembly *In*: A.J. Bellamy and T. Dunne, eds. *The Oxford Handbook of the Responsibility to Protect.* Oxford: Oxford University Press, pp. 269–287.

Security Council Report 2013. Security Council Deadlocks and Uniting for Peace: An Abridged History. [Accessed 15 April 2021]. Available from: www.securityco uncilreport.org/atf/cf/%7B65BFCF9B-6D27-4E9C-8CD3-CF6E4FF96FF9%7D/Security_Council_Deadlocks_and_Uniting_for_Peace.pdf.

Talmon, S. 2014. The Legalizing and Legitimizing Function of UN General Assembly Resolutions. *AJIL Unbound.* **108**, pp. 123–128.

Trahan, J. 2020. Questioning Unlimited Veto Use in the Face of Atrocity Crimes. *Case Western Reserve Journal of International Law.* **52**, pp. 73–100.

Udoh, A. 2015. Case Study: Invoking the 'Uniting for Peace' Resolution of 1950 to Authorize the Use of Humanitarian Military Intervention and Prevent Mass Atrocities in Syria. *Willamette Journal of International Law and Dispute Resolution.* **23**(1), pp. 187–232.

UN 1945. Charter of the United Nations. [Accessed 5 June 2018]. Available from: www.un.org/en/charter-united-nations/.

UN 2012. Responsibility to protect: timely and decisive response. Report of the Secretary-General. A/66/874–S/2012/578. [Accessed 9 August 2021]. Available from: https://undocs.org/A/66/874.

UN 2022. Security Council Vote Sets Up Emergency UN General Assembly Session on Ukraine crisis. [Accessed 2 March 2022]. Available from: Security Council vote sets up emergency UN General Assembly session on Ukraine crisis.

UN, Dag Hammarskjöld Library 2023. Security Council Veto List. [Accessed 16 March 2023]. Available from: https://research.un.org/en/docs/sc/quick.

UN News 2022a. General Assembly Adopts Landmark Resolution Aimed at Holding Five Permanent Security Council Members Accountable for Use of Veto. [Accessed 4 May 2022]. Available from: www.un.org/press/en/2022/ga12417.doc.htm.

UN News 2022b. Security Council vote sets up emergency UN General Assembly session on Ukraine crisis. [Accessed 28 February 2022]. Available from: https://news.un.org/en/story/2022/02/1112842.

UN News 2022c. UN General Assembly Votes to Suspend Russia from the Human Rights Council. [Accessed 13 April 2022]. Available from: https://news.un.org/en/story/2022/04/1115782.

UNA-UK 2022. Security Council Veto Use: the UK Should Champion Action for Accountability. [Accessed 6 April 2022]. Available from: https://una.org.uk/news/security-council-veto-use-uk-should-champion-action-accountability.

UNGA 1950. Uniting for Peace. A/RES/377(V). [Accessed 22 July 2018]. Available from: www.un.org/en/sc/repertoire/otherdocs/GAres377A(v).pdf.

UNGA 1956a. Resolution 1000 (ES-I). [Accessed 12 March 2021]. Available from: https://digitallibrary.un.org/record/208417?ln=en.

UNGA 1956b. Resolution 1004 (ES-II). [Accessed 12 March 2021]. Available from: https://digitallibrary.un.org/record/208408?ln=en.

UNGA 1967. A/RES/2252/ES-V – A/RES/2257/ES-V. [Accessed 12 March 2021]. Available from: www.un.org/en/ga/search/view_doc.asp?symbol=A/RES/2252 (ES-V).

UNGA 1980. A/RES/ES-7/2 – A/RES/ES-7/9. [Accessed 12 March 2021]. Available from: https://research.un.org/en/docs/ga/quick/emergency.

UNGA 1981. A/RES/ES-8/2. [Accessed 12 March 2021]. Available from: www.un.org/en/ga/search/view_doc.asp?symbol=A/RES/ES-8/2.

UNGA 1982. A/RES/ES-9/1. [Accessed 12 March 2021]. Available from: www.un.org/en/ga/search/view_doc.asp?symbol=A/RES/ES-9/1.

UNGA 1997. A/RES/ES-10/2 – A/RES/ES-10/17. [Accessed 12 March 2021]. Available from: https://research.un.org/en/docs/ga/quick/emergency.

UNGA 2005. Resolution adopted by the General Assembly on 16 September 2005. A/RES/60/1. [Accessed 15 November 2018]. Available from: www.un.org/en/development/desa/population/migration/generalassembly/docs/globalcompact/A_RES_60_1.pdf.

UNGA 2012. The Situation in the Syrian Arab Republic. A/66/L.57. [Accessed 26 March 2021]. Available from: https://undocs.org/A/66/L.57.

UNGA 2019a. 93rd plenary meeting. The Responsibility to Protect and the Prevention of Genocide, War Crimes, Ethnic Cleansing and Crimes Against Humanity. A/73/PV.93. [Accessed 31 July 2019]. Available from: https://digitallibrary.un.org/record/3812131?ln=en.

UNGA 2019b. 94th plenary meeting. The Responsibility to Protect and the Prevention of Genocide, War Crimes, Ethnic Cleansing and Crimes Against Humanity. A/73/PV.94. [Accessed 31 July 2019]. Available from: https://digitallibrary.un.org/record/3812513?ln=en.

UNGA 2021a. 64th plenary meeting. The Responsibility to Protect and the Prevention of Genocide, War Crimes, Ethnic Cleansing and Crimes Against Humanity. A/75/PV.64. [Accessed 8 September 2022]. Available from: https://documents-dds-ny.un.org/doc/UNDOC/GEN/N21/121/10/PDF/N2112110.pdf?OpenElement.

UNGA 2021b. The Responsibility to Protect and the Prevention of Genocide, War Crimes, Ethnic Cleansing and Crimes Against Humanity. A/75/L.82. [Accessed 5 July 2021]. Available from: https://undocs.org/en/A/75/L.82.

UNGA 2021c. The Situation in Myanmar. A/75/L.85. [Accessed 19 June 2021]. Available from: https://undocs.org/en/A/75/L.85.

UNGA 2022a. 69th plenary meeting. Strengthening of the United Nations System. A/76/PV.69. [Accessed 23 September 2022]. Available from: https://documents-dds-ny.un.org/doc/UNDOC/GEN/N22/330/25/PDF/N2233025.pdf?OpenElement.

UNGA 2022b. A/RES/ES-11/1. [Accessed 18 March 2022]. Available from: https://documents-dds-ny.un.org/doc/UNDOC/GEN/N22/293/36/PDF/N2229336.pdf?OpenElement.

UNICEF n.d. Rohingya Crisis. [Accessed 18 May 2021]. Available from: www.unicef.org/emergencies/rohingya-crisis.

UNSC 2022. Resolution 2669. S/RES/2669. [Accessed 10 January 2023]. Available from: https://documents-dds-ny.un.org/doc/UNDOC/GEN/N22/767/33/PDF/N2276733.pdf?OpenElement.

Uyghur Human Rights Project 2020. LOI Submission to the UN Committee on Economic, Social and Cultural Rights (66th Pre-Sessional Working Group). [Accessed 31 March 2021]. Available from: https://docs.uhrp.org/pdf/CESCR_Submission_FINAL_2020-12-18.pdf.

Walzer, M. 1995. The Politics of Rescue. *Social Research*. **62**(1), pp. 53–66.

WBFO 2021. More Than 700 Civilians Killed By Myanmar Junta Since Coup. [Accessed 13 April 2021]. Available from: https://news.wbfo.org/post/more-700-civilians-killed-myanmar-junta-coup.

Webb, P. 2014. Deadlock of Restraint? The Security Council Veto and the Use of Force in Syria. *Journal of Conflict & Security Law*. **19**(3), pp. 471–488.

Welsh, J.M. 2021. The Security Council's Role in Fulfilling the Responsibility to Protect. *Ethics & International Affairs*. **35**(2), pp. 227–243.

Wenaweser, C. and Alavi, S. 2020. Innovating to restrain the use of the Veto in the United Nations security council. *Case Western Reserve Journal of International Law*. **52**, pp. 65–72.

Wheeler, N.J. 2000. Reflections on the Legality and Legitimacy of NATO's Intervention in Kosovo. *The International Journal of Human Rights*. **4**(3–4), pp. 144–163.

White, N.D. 2015. The Relationship between the UN Security Council and General Assembly in Matters of International Peace and Security *In*: M. Weller, ed. *The Oxford Handbook of the Use of Force in International Law*. Oxford: Oxford University Press, pp. 293–313.

White, N.D. and Tsagourias, N. 2013. *Collective Security: Theory, Law and Practice*. Cambridge: Cambridge University Press.

Woolsey, L.H. 1951. The 'Uniting for Peace' Resolution of the United Nations. *American Journal of International Law*. **45**(1), pp. 129–137.

Zaum, D. 2008. The Security Council, the General Assembly, and War: The Uniting for Peace Resolution *In*: V. Lowe, A. Roberts, J. M. Welsh and D. Zaum, eds. *The United Nations Security Council and War*. Oxford: Oxford University Press, pp. 154–174.

7 Holding States to Account
An R2P Commission

7.1 Introduction

The previous two chapters proposed reform measures that operate within currently existing structures: namely, the three pillar R2P approach with the UNSC and UNGA as mediums for its operationalisation. This chapter, however, in promoting a transitional cosmopolitan approach to R2P reform, proposes the creation of an entirely new and supplementary mechanism to assist in the R2P's implementation. The chapter calls for the creation of an 'R2P Commission'. This is a suggestion for a body composed of elected experts that would serve in an independent capacity. The R2P Commission would scrutinise state practice across the R2P's three pillars via determinations of where manifest R2P failures have occurred, review international practice vis-à-vis atrocity prevention and response, and make recommendations for altering practice and potential state action.

UN Secretary-General António Guterres noted in his 2020 R2P report that 'ensuring justice and accountability for atrocity crimes are essential to advancing the responsibility to protect agenda' (UN, 2020, para. 16). However, as Chapter 3 argued, holding states accountable to their R2P commitments is difficult due to the politicisation of the norm and the international institutions for implementing it. This means that states are under no obligation to act, and scrutiny of state practice is limited.[1]

There is an urgent need to find ways to hold states accountable to their R2P commitments and to promote more consistent compliance moving forward. There are a few scholars who have advocated institutions that would strengthen the implementation of R2P duties (under Pillar Three), better enforce the norm, and hold states accountable to the commitments they made in 2005 (Tesón, 2006; Archibugi, 2008; Hehir, 2012; Roff, 2013). Yet, as is discussed below, the suggestions of these scholars are likely too idealistic, and come with practical drawbacks, meaning that they do not align with the transitional cosmopolitan approach promoted in this book.

Given the difficulties with enforcing R2P compliance, equating accountability with guaranteed enforcement would likely be too ambitious, at least in the short term. However, if we take a less stringent view of what

DOI: 10.4324/9781003394105-7

accountability means, then transitional cosmopolitan progress may well be attainable.

In his 2017 annual report on the R2P, *Implementing the Responsibility to Protect: Accountability for Prevention*, UN Secretary-General Guterres highlighted a need to close the gap between R2P rhetoric and practice, and that '[o]ne of the principal ways in which we can do this is by strengthening accountability and ensuring the rigorous and open scrutiny of practice, in the light of agreed principle' (UN, 2017, para. 5). When taken in this way, accountability is about whether the actions of states are critiqued against accepted standards, including the standards to which states have themselves consented. In 2005, *all* UN member states committed to the responsibility to protect, meaning that this commitment implies accountability (Šimonović, 2019, p. 251), and that all states should rightly see their practice scrutinised against that (moral and political) commitment.

Increased accountability in this way, while short of direct enforcement, can help to influence state actions over time by clarifying expected standards of behaviour, raising the social costs of R2P breaches (Glanville, 2016, pp. 186–187; Bellamy and Luck, 2018, pp. 48–49), and providing guidance for state practice moving forward. As Strauss (2019, p. 193) has argued, accountability can focus discussion of an at-risk situation to appropriate action and whether a situation is one of R2P-relevance, adding legitimacy to determinations of situations of a state's 'manifest failing' under the R2P, which can then help promote greater consistency of action taken by the international community when implementing R2P responses. Jacob (2021) has argued that the international community has witnessed a recent 'accountability turn' in an attempt to prevent mass human rights violations via the deterrent effect of accountability efforts. She claims that there are increasing demands from the international community, including civil society, to strengthen mechanisms for protecting vulnerable populations and to hold perpetrators accountable, even when the UNSC won't cooperate to this end. Jacob sees evidence of evolving efforts to develop the UN's regulatory architecture to improve preventive capacity and strengthen mechanisms for holding states accountable to their human rights commitments (Jacob, 2021, p. 1354). In this way, accountability efforts should be viewed as means through which the implementation of norms like the R2P can be made more consistent, helping to promote a deeper understanding of where and why protection duties fail, and how this can be redressed through reparative efforts such as criminal prosecution and international intervention (whether coercive or not).

A recent report by D'Alessandra et al. (2022, pp. 14–19) on the need to 'anchor accountability' for mass atrocity prevention efforts at the UN argues that investigative and accountability efforts further normative commitments to human rights norms and international law by legitimising or de-legitimising the behaviour of actors, and that this deters the future repetition of serious human rights violations. As they note, 'UN investigations play a crucial role in prompting international action in response to serious violations of international law that might amount to atrocity crimes and in galvanising political and legal accountability for such atrocities' (D'Alessandra et al., 2022, p. 97). However, they also acknowledge that there is currently an accountability gap in the conduct of atrocity prevention efforts, as the deployment of investigative mechanisms remains ad hoc and prone to political manoeuvring, which in turn fuels accusation of inconsistency, hypocrisy, and politicisation (D'Alessandra et al., 2022, p. 19). As a result, they argue in favour of greater institutional and operational support for investigative efforts in order to promote more consistent establishment of investigative mandates (D'Alessandra et al., 2022, p. 102).

There are many parts of the UN system with a role to play in accountability efforts for the R2P. This includes both principle organs like the UNSC and UNGA, as well as subsidiary organs like the UN Human Rights Council (UNHRC), and the joint UN Office on Genocide Prevention and the Responsibility to Protect (Strauss, 2015). The joint office, for instance, was singled out by the UN Secretary-General in his 2021 annual report on the R2P as holding significance in 'analysing risk, providing early warning and encouraging Member States to take effective action in response to situations' (UN, 2021, para. 11).

Yet these accountability mechanisms tend to focus their attention on monitoring host state compliance with human protection norms (i.e. whether there are violations being committed in a particular territory), and generally ignore questions of how the wider international community should be held accountable for its responsibility to assist in prevention (i.e. where states' international practices contribute to underlying conditions of violence), or to respond when immediate crises present themselves (i.e. where the international community is faced with a mass atrocity situation and ought to discharge available tools). Moreover, with the exception of the joint office, none of the UN's mechanisms are specifically mass atrocity focused, with atrocity prevention often viewed as a by-product of conflict prevention, peacebuilding, development, or human rights work (Strauss, 2015, p. 82).

Before proceeding, it is worth noting that the proposal offered in this chapter would not infringe on the work of the joint office, as the two bodies would serve largely separate functions that would complement, rather than interfere with one-another. The joint office has an important role to play in the R2P's implementation via general R2P advocacy, assessing national risk factors, and providing early warning of impending crises. The joint office has also been identified as an agent of the R2P's norm development through the contribution of the special advisers' conceptualisation of the R2P, as well as their political advocacy for the concept in practice (Prokhorova, 2022). This is evident in particular through the work of the special advisers in drafting the Secretary-General's annual R2P reports, which focus on particular thematic issues surrounding the R2P, helping to shape the subsequent annual debates in the UNGA.

One might look at the role of the joint office of the special advisers and argue that, given their established position in the UN's architecture and the legitimacy that comes with this, a transitional cosmopolitan might be better focused on looking to expand the mandate of the joint office, rather than calling for a new body like the one recommended in this chapter. However, to reiterate, the joint office and the R2P Commission proposed here would serve complementary but differentiated roles. While the joint office is focused on the conceptualisation of, and general political advocacy for the R2P,[2] the proposal made here in the present chapter is aimed at strengthening the UN's accountability architecture, holding states to their R2P commitments via authoritative determinations of where atrocity crimes have occurred, and through scrutinising the actions of states in the context of their atrocity prevention and response efforts under the R2P's three pillars. Where the work of the joint office may overlap with this new institution is in efforts to provide proactive recommendations for how to address ongoing atrocity situations. However, this does not necessarily indicate a conflict, as here both the R2P Commission and the joint office could draw on and support each other's work. The joint office, for instance, could look to 'action' recommendations from the R2P Commission by utilising its diplomatic tools to encourage member states to act on the Commission's recommendations. In this way, the work of the special advisors can be enhanced by drawing on the dedicated accountability efforts of the R2P Commission, thus strengthening the base from which the advisers conduct their political advocacy efforts for the R2P.

Beyond the role of the joint office, the work of the UNHRC is especially relevant to the R2P in the context of raising awareness of human rights abuses and atrocity cases, fact-finding, and reporting. This may suggest that the UNHRC should be taken as an essential component of the UN's efforts to tackle mass atrocity by 'promot[ing] greater unity among the members of the international community on the protection of populations against those crimes' (UN, n.d.). Given the relevance of the UNHRC's work to accountability for atrocity prevention efforts, the body is given specific attention in this chapter. However, as is discussed below, the political biases inherent to the UNHRC mean that it cannot be relied on as the main institution for promoting accountability under the R2P.

The weaknesses and / or differentiated roles of current institutions suggests that there is a gap in the UN's atrocity prevention architecture, and thus, a necessity to establish a new body with a specific mass atrocity focus, aimed at promoting stronger state accountability to duties under the R2P.

The chapter proceeds as follows. Section 7.2 examines proposals for an independent body charged with the authority to enforce the R2P in practice. This argues that establishing a new institution with legal authority over states and the UNSC would be neither an effective nor feasible solution to the problem of holding states accountable to their R2P. This leads to the suggestion that instead of seeking a new enforcement body for the R2P, we should seek an institution to promote state accountability through expert-based independent fact-finding, scrutiny of state practice, and recommendations for action. Recommendations would not compel state compliance, thus making such an institution more palatable for states. Yet, review and recommendations can help by providing valuable 'lessons learned' in the context of appropriate R2P practice, impose political costs on states by highlighting R2P breaches, and offer useful recommendations for practice going forward. Section 7.3 discusses the UNHRC as the body which might be argued to be best suited for this role. This section argues, however, that the UNHRC is not appropriate for serving this function due to problems of political bias inherent to its state-based makeup. Finally, section 7.4 offers the 'R2P Commission'. This is a proposal for an entirely new, independent body of elected experts, uniquely charged with holding states to account under the full range of their R2P commitments across the three pillars.

7.2 A New Institution for Discharging the R2P?

Other scholars have previously called for the creation of new institutions to hold states accountable to their responsibilities to halt mass atrocities. While not writing explicitly on the R2P, Tesón (2006, p. 766), for instance, criticises the UNSC, arguing that the political interests of its members often conflict with cosmopolitan aspirations. To rectify this, he proposes the creation of a new institution: 'The Court of Human Security'. The Court's role would be to hear the evidence for any proposed intervention and determine where international response, including the use of military measures, is permissible (Tesón, 2006, p. 772). Under his proposal, this would permit the unilateral application of force by a state or coalition of states. Meanwhile, Archibugi (2008, p. 194) has proposed the creation of an elected UN 'World Parliament' that would, among other things, be charged with the responsibility for determining where humanitarian intervention should take place (Archibugi, 2008, p. 198). For him, this should be supplemented with a commission of military and civilian humanitarian organisations to decide on appropriate intervention methods, and whether military action would be efficacious (Archibugi, 2008, p. 200). He further proposes that a UN standing force be established that would be ready for rapid deployment as required (Archibugi, 2008, pp. 201–202).

Hehir (2012, chap. 8) has called for the creation of an 'international judicial body', with the role of stepping in when the UNSC fails to act on atrocity crises: utilising fact-finding missions to first determine whether an atrocity crime has been committed and then what international response should follow (Hehir, 2012, pp. 233–235). For him, the judicial body would help ensure consistency of response, as well as act as a guard against spurious intervention by delegitimising R2P enforcement response taken outside the UNSC or this judicial body (Hehir, 2012, pp. 239–243). A similar proposal comes from Roff (2013). She argues that the international system lacks the means to uphold rights, with treaties and courts politicised in favour of the powerful (Roff, 2013, pp. 100–101). In this way, the R2P promotes a kind of vicious cycle that empowers the UNSC with the primary authority to respond robustly to atrocity crimes, but does nothing to change the way the UNSC responds to situations. In response, Roff (2013, p. 122) proposes the creation of an 'R2P Institution' to promulgate public rules of when, where, and how the R2P should be discharged in practice.

While these recommendations offer useful perspectives, in particular, highlighting problems with relying on the UNSC to implement the R2P, they ultimately suffer from considerable effectiveness and feasibility restraints that render them unsatisfactory from a transitional cosmopolitan perspective.

Regarding the effectiveness of such proposals, a first problem is that they relate only to Pillar Three enforcement action taken in response to ongoing crises. This ignores a vital question of how to hold the international community accountable for the duty of *assistance* under Pillar Two and its relevance to atrocity prevention. This overlooks the interlinked concept of cosmopolitan negative duties to avoid the imposition of harm (Linklater, 2001; Shapcott, 2008) and the actions of international actors – such as arms sales, regime ties, and damaging trade policies – which have been argued to weaken state resilience and contribute to outbreaks of mass atrocity crime (Shaw, 2012; Dunford and Neu, 2019; Bohm and Brown, 2021), and thus which undermine the Pillar Two duty of the R2P (see section 3.6). Given that the three pillars are meant to be taken as equal under the R2P concept (Bellamy and Drummond, 2011, p. 181), it is important that attention is paid not just to holding states accountable to response to mass atrocity under Pillar Three, but also that states are held accountable for their responsibility to assist others, and not undermine this duty of assistance, under Pillar Two.

Second, there appears a problem relating to the delivery of *timely and decisive* response in those most extreme cases where events unfold at a dramatic pace. The idea that a panel of independent legal experts could deliver conclusions on timely and decisive enforcement action required in response to fast-moving atrocity crises is doubtful, given the time that would be required to first determine whether crimes are being committed, *and* second to determine what enforcement action should follow.[3] Atrocities and mass suffering would occur long before such an institution could deliver a verdict on appropriate response.

This is an important reason as to why an independent expert panel should not replace the UN's political bodies as the primary means for passing enforcement action under R2P Pillar Three. For instance, while the UNSC's politicised nature is problematic in that it brings inconsistent response to crises, it does allow for the UNSC to act quickly in situations which may necessitate a rapid response. Over the Libya case in 2011, only 19 days separated the passage of UNSC Resolutions 1970 and 1973.[4] It seems highly unlikely that the level of legal deliberation required for an independent panel of experts to respond to a crisis would allow timely and decisive decisions in this way. As an example, the UNHRC's Independent International Fact-Finding Mission on Myanmar (IIFFMM) was established in March 2017. It took 18 months to deliver its first full account of violations by the Myanmar military in Rakhine, Kachin, and Shan States. Further, a subsequent legal case brought to the ICJ in November 2019 by The Gambia in relation to Myanmar's possible breach of the Genocide Convention in November 2019 remains ongoing as of early 2023.[5] This point is not to ignore the crucial fact that the UNSC far too often fails to deliver timely and decisive responses to rapidly developing R2P crises, but merely that it is unlikely that a legal institution with power over or beyond the UNSC would be able to deliver timely response either.

As argued further below, an independent panel of experts dedicated to monitoring and promoting accountability under the R2P could have a useful role to play in shaping response to atrocity crises. However, it would not be appropriate to place preponderance of decision making for enforcement response in the hands of such a body, due to the problem of delivering a timely and decisive response for those most rapidly unfolding emergencies where quick decisions need to be made.

Regarding concerns about the feasibility of such suggestions, previous chapters have already covered numerous arguments related to the unwillingness of states to bind themselves to commitments to act under the R2P, the currently challenging political environment within which the R2P exists, and the desire of the P5 states to maintain UNSC primacy and freedom of decision making. What this suggests is that establishing a new institution with authority over states and the P5 is a step too far, one which is unfeasible and unlikely to be accepted by states in the foreseeable future.

For instance, Roff (2013, p. 123) claims that it would be the duty of the UNSC to establish the R2P Institution in the first place. Yet it seems overly ambitious to expect the UNSC and the P5 to willingly agree to forfeit their primacy in decision making over matters of international peace and security to a separate body in which they have no control. Such a suggestion seems *even less* feasible than calling for the abolishment of the P5's veto power as discussed in Chapter Five (section 5.2). Tesón's suggestion – which despite his claim that it is not overly utopian – appears problematic from a feasibility standpoint, as a Human Rights Court, active in decision making surrounding an ongoing crisis, would certainly challenge the authority of the UNSC as the primary body for determining threats to international peace and security and making recommendations to respond to those under Article 39 of the UN Charter. Consequently, it would seem highly unlikely that the P5 would consent to such a proposal. Archibugi (2008, p. 203) does note that his own proposal is 'unrealistic' in the current political climate.

The problems identified above show that we need to temper expectations for what a new institution to promote accountability under the R2P could and should deliver. For effectiveness and feasibility reasons, to better align with the transitional cosmopolitan approach, any such body: i) cannot hold preponderance in decision making for ongoing crisis which require timely and decisive response, and ii) cannot hold supreme authority over states and the UNSC.

Given these two requirements, in addition to the less stringent framing of accountability noted in the introduction to this chapter (UN, 2017), it is argued here that instead of framing the R2P's accountability deficit as requiring a new *enforcement* body, we should instead seek an institution to promote accountability for R2P commitments via *review and scrutiny* of state practice. As will be argued in section 7.4, while (perhaps) less desirable than an independent body with power over states to demand action or punish violations, an institution dedicated to reviewing compliance under the R2P's three pillars could meet transitional cosmopolitan requirements and aid atrocity prevention efforts. This can be achieved through consistent investigative action, calling out actions unaligned with R2P commitments and the three pillars, and making expert recommendations to rectify practice. This may help to influence state practice over time by helping to clarify what the R2P demands in terms of expected state behaviour; raising the social costs of R2P breaches as malpractice becomes scrutinised; and providing useful guidance for state practice moving forward.

7.3 The UN Human Rights Council: An Unsuitable Body for Monitoring R2P Compliance

This section explores the UNHRC as the institution that may seem *prima facie* best suited to the role of scrutinising human rights practice and holding states accountable for their R2P. However, as will be outlined – while there is a theoretical connection between the UNHRC's work in fostering state accountability, dialogue, and cooperation in the field of human rights and the R2P (UN, 2017, paras 33–34) – the UNHRC cannot provide an independent mechanism to reliably scrutinise state practice across the R2P's three pillars.

The UNHRC is the UN's primary body for the discussion of human rights issues, promoting dialogue and cooperation among member states (Scannella and Splinter, 2007). The UNHRC can fulfil numerous roles to aid in the R2P's implementation, such as field monitoring, fact-finding, and technical assistance for states (Strauss, 2016, pp. 315–317). The UNHRC adopted its first thematic resolution on the R2P in July 2020 (GCR2P, 2020a), and prior to this had adopted 50 resolutions referencing the R2P (GCR2P, 2020b), which suggests that the UNHRC can be a vehicle for driving mass atrocity prevention efforts. It may appear then that the UNHRC shows promise as a body for holding states to account for their R2P pledges.

Pramendorfer (2020, p. 7) argues that, despite its faults, the UNHRC 'is uniquely suited to address atrocities by mandating a variety of mechanisms to raise awareness, collect information, and provide recommendations'. Similarly, Jacob (2021, pp. 1362–1364) has argued that the UNHRC's mechanisms help encourage human rights compliance through state engagement and reporting, fact-finding, and contribution to international criminal proceedings. The 'Universal Periodic Review' (UPR) and the 'special procedures mandates', as two examples of this, encourage compliance with human rights law, and therefore promote goals sympathetic with the R2P.[6] The UPR is a process of state-to-state peer review, whereby countries are reviewed every four and half years on their human rights record, while the special procedures mandate holders are established by UNHRC members and are made up from special rapporteurs and experts who undertake country visits. The UPR and the special procedures mandates exist to hold states to account for their human rights records, and can be viewed as an attempt to influence state practice and internalise human rights issues over time (Etone, 2019, pp. 49–50). They encourage states to improve their international standing on human rights via reporting, recommendations, and the provision of capacity building and technical support to state actors willing to engage (Jacob, 2021, p. 1362).

Yet, while such mechanisms help frame human rights discussion at the UN level, they are, however, politically flawed. Geopolitics and conflicts of interest over human rights persist through the UNHRC as a state-based organ of the UN (Chané and Sharma, 2016). This hampers the effectiveness of such mechanisms. For example, UPR recommendations are largely heralded for their 'realistic' ambitions but the majority of recommendations are vague and undemanding in their attempts to alter state practice (Carraro, 2019b, p. 1090). Charlesworth and Larking (2015) argue that the UPR process reflects a 'rights ritualism' approach wherein states engage with human rights language to deflect criticism of their actual practice. This allows states to claim that they are following appropriate behaviour when the reality may be very different (Charlesworth and Larking, 2015, pp. 14–15). Recommendations made through the UPR system are largely determined based on political relationships between the reviewer and reviewee, both being sovereign states (Terman and Voeten, 2018). This means that recommendations will often be political trade-offs based on states' competing interests between promoting human rights and other policy areas.

Even though recommendations are tempered in this way, their impact is also questionable. An example of this comes from the Philippines, where the Duterte regime conducted a campaign of extrajudicial killings and systematic violations of human rights during its 'war on drugs' (Gallagher, Raffle, and Maulana, 2019). The 2017 UPR of the Philippines resulted in 257 recommendations, but the Philippines rejected 154 of these (CNN Philippines, 2017). The UPR process appeared to have little impact on the Duterte regime. In May 2020, Human Rights Watch submitted a 48-page report to the UNHRC outlining grievous human rights abuses and calling for an inquiry into the situation in the Philippines (Human Rights Watch, 2020a). This was followed by a June 2020 report from the UN Office of the High Commissioner for Human Rights which condemned the Philippines' human rights record (OHCHR, 2020). In July 2021, Duterte, while taunting the ICC, stated that '[w]e still have long way in our fight against the prolif-eration of drugs' (Reuters, 2021), which suggests that the UNHRC's efforts were not fruitful in altering Duterte's policy.[7]

Of the special procedures mandates, Ramcharan (2019, p. 163) notes that Afro-Asian states are unwilling to discuss highlighted human rights violations of the states they ally with; while Freedman and Mchangama (2016) find that state alliances play a significant role in influencing which human rights are focused on and what special procedures mandates are established by the UNHRC. Linked with this problem, states will also cooperate with which-ever special procedures mandates are favourable to their interests. Syria, for instance, prior to the Assad regime's violent repression of civilian protests in 2011, received praise for work in its healthcare system while refusing to cooperate with the special rapporteur on both arbitrary detention and enforced disappearance (Freedman and Mchangama, 2016, p. 191).

One important mechanism through which the UNHRC can promote accountability for human rights commitments are 'commissions of inquiry' (CoIs). CoIs are ad hoc fact-finding missions deployed to investigate specific cases. They 'assist in ensuring accountability for serious violations [of human rights], which is fundamental in order to deter future violations' (OHCHR, 2015, p. 7). CoIs are representative of the movement towards international monitoring of human rights (Kim, 2019, p. 99), providing a means for testing facts, scrutinising actors, and holding perpetrators to account (Chinkin, 2011). Although it is not the exclusive purview of the UNHRC to mandate CoIs, the UNHRC has increasingly taken a proactive role in authorising them. This has especially been the case in situations where the UNSC has failed to act. For example, the UNHRC has launched CoIs for Gaza, Syria, Myanmar, and Ukraine, where any attempt to launch a fact-finding investi-gation through the UNSC would have been vetoed by one or more of the P5 members. D'Alessandra et al. (2022, p. 14) note that it is UNHRC-mandated investigations that have made the greatest contribution to UN efforts to foster accountability for atrocities by raising awareness, generating public attention, and fostering support for subsequent judicial proceedings. In this sense, by making the most significant contribution of any UN body to accountability efforts and the deployment of investigative mandates, espe-cially in cases where the UNSC will not act, the UNHRC seems to be seizing the mantle of responsibility from the UNSC.

CoIs are usually focused on finding evidence of the atrocity crimes of genocide, crimes against humanity, and war crimes (Nesbitt, 2017, p. 88). This naturally aligns them with the goals of the R2P as a means of gen-erating accountability for the commission of mass atrocity. CoIs provide an impartial way of generating knowledge of atrocity crises that can help shape international responses to these situations. The previously mentioned UNHRC-mandated IIFFMM (Myanmar) serves as an illustrative example, as it was this fact-finding mission which provided the basis of evidence for The Gambia, in November 2019, to bring its case against Myanmar to the

ICJ under the Genocide Convention. Following the 1 February 2021 military coup in Myanmar, the UNHRC, on 24 March 2021, passed a resolution which condemned the deposition of the elected civilian government and use of lethal force against civilians by the Myanmar military, and also called for the Independent Investigative Mechanism for Myanmar (IIMM) to continue to discharge its mandate (UNHRC, 2021).

Other examples include the September 2020 report of the fact-finding mission on Venezuela, and the September 2019 report of the CoI on Burundi; both of which employed a 'preventative lens' to identify the need for system-wide institutional change, as well as the need for continued international engagement with the situation, in order to tackle the conditions of mass atrocity (Pramendorfer, 2021). In the case of Burundi, the work of the CoI is accredited for keeping the situation under 'intense international scrutiny', which may have contributed to the prevention of post-election violence in May 2020 (Pramendorfer, 2021). Further, on 4 March 2022, the UNHRC voted to establish a fact-finding mission to investigate all violations of human rights in the context of Russia's invasion of Ukraine. Such practice has demonstrated that UNHRC-launched CoIs support the implementation of the R2P.

While UN CoIs serve a vital function, there are weaknesses related to the political processes by which cases are acted upon. Discussing this problem with reference to UNHRC-mandated CoIs, Farrell, and Murphy (2017, p. 13) argue that the makeup of the UNHRC, which contains an Asian-African majority, is vulnerable to accusations of bias, as certain issues deemed more significant by these members are more likely to see action conducted by the UNHRC. Van Den Herik (2014, p. 536) claims that this makes UNHRC-mandated CoIs inflammatory and predisposed to condemning actors even before sufficient evidence has been gathered. Others such as Devaney (2016, p. 102) and Freedman (2013, p. 243) highlight that the UNHRC dispro-portionately focuses on some situations over others. Likewise, Frulli (2012, pp. 1334–1335) – highlighting the 2009 example of the first UNHRC Gaza CoI which was tasked with only investigating possible breaches of inter-national humanitarian law by Israeli forces – observes that a 'mandate with a one-sided focus … has serious negative consequences in terms of credibility and impartiality, which are key factors for a successful investigation' (Frulli, 2012, p. 1335).

Perceived bias can weaken the legitimacy of the UNHRC-mandated CoIs, which may subsequently reduce state compliance with investigations, as well as their findings. For instance, lack of compliance may lead to an unwill-ingness of states to grant CoIs territorial access to conduct investigations (Chinkin, 2011, p. 488), as was the case in Libya, Syria, North Korea, Myanmar, and partially with Gaza. A lack of territorial access undermines the thorough investigation of the facts of a case and makes the work of CoIs more difficult. Russia and China, for instance, cited the lack of territorial access for the fact-finding mission on Myanmar as a reason to doubt the veracity of the report's claims (UN, 2018). Further, while a lack of territorial access does not prevent a CoI from conducting its work entirely, a lack of target state cooperation restricts access to sources of investigation, such as persons, locations, and documentation (OHCHR, 2015, pp. 64–65). A lack of compliance may also undermine the potential for future criminal prosecution as target states will be less likely to cooperate with international courts. It is notable, for instance, that Israel rejects the jurisdiction of the ICC, with former Prime Minister, Benjamin Netanyahu, calling for sanctions to be directed 'against the international court, its officials, its prosecutors, everyone' (The Guardian, 2020).

Selectivity in what cases are acted on is also problematic because it means that the UNHRC cannot serve as an impartial mechanism for reviewing state compliance with human rights and connected R2P commitments. If accountability for cosmopolitan positive and negative duties adopted under R2P is the goal, it is unlikely that an institution heavily influenced by state interests will be able to deliver this goal in a way that minimises bias and selectivity. While the UNHRC has established CoIs for cases like Syria and Myanmar, it has failed to do so in some other notable cases, such as the ongoing abuse of Uyghur Muslims in China. Violence commencing in the Tigray region of Ethiopia in November 2020 also did not draw a significant response from the UNHRC until July 2021 (Human Rights Watch, 2021).

Relatedly, politicisation can prevent the UNHRC from delivering timely and decisive action. Deliberation and clashes of interest are liable to delay action over whether an investigative mission is launched. So for instance, while the UNHRC can act quickly, as it did when establishing its CoI for Ukraine,[8] in contrast it was a full five months after the violent crackdown against the Rohingya began before the UNHRC launched its fact-finding mission for Myanmar in March 2017. Delayed response is perhaps more likely in those situations which occur outside more tangible 'crisis points' of armed conflict, such as the Uyghur crisis in China. This has been described by former Executive Director of the Global Centre for the Responsibility to Protect, Simon Adams (2020), as a 'slow-motion genocide', yet, as of the time of writing, no UNHRC investigative inquiry has been launched into Chinese state actions in Xinjiang province. Furthermore, while the Office of the High Commissioner for Human Rights published a report in August 2022 detailing that crimes against humanity may have occurred in Xinjiang (OHCHR, 2022), the UNHRC voted against adopting a decision to even discuss the human rights situation in Xinjiang, with 17 votes in favour, 19 against, and 11 abstentions (Amnesty International, 2022).

Beyond the issue of bias and partisanship in its state review and fact-finding, another issue with the UNHRC is that flagrant human rights abusers regularly attain elected memberships. The election of states such as Venezuela in October 2019 – which had itself been subject to an independent fact-finding mission mandated by the UNHRC only shortly prior – undermines the normative purpose of the UNHRC. Human Rights Watch has issued calls to deny UNHRC seats to major human rights violators such as China, Saudi Arabia, and Russia (Human Rights Watch, 2020b). However, all three were elected in October 2020. According to Pramendorfer (2020, p. 5), 'there has never been a time where all 47 of its members fulfilled the minimum requirements for UNHRC candidacy'.

Relying on the UNHRC as the main body for promoting state accountability under human rights places responsibility with states themselves. In this sense, states sit in their own judgement. Again, the example of China – which has 'persistently block[ed] human rights investigations in its own country and has failed to answer outstanding requests and reminders from at least 17 UN experts or Working Groups for official visits' (World Uyghur Congress, 2020) – demonstrates the problem associated with relying on states with poor human rights records to scrutinise global human rights practices (Hehir, 2012, p. 228). Clearly, this is not a sound basis for an independent accountability mechanism charged with scrutinising state actions vis-à-vis the R2P.

The UNHRC, while *prima facie* suited to the role, is not the solution to the problem of holding states accountable to their R2P. Interestingly, states themselves have not sought to utilise the UNHRC as a primary body for shaping the implementation of the R2P, with the UNHRC choosing instead to '[follow] the statements of other UN entities rather than leading the discussion on its application' (Strauss, 2019, p. 183). Regardless, state-based organs inevitably involve members protecting their own sovereignty and agendas, hampering their effectiveness in promoting accountability for human rights commitments. This is why any mechanism for reviewing state practice under the R2P needs to try and minimise the influence of partisanship and state bias. Given the problems identified with previous recommendations and currently existing institutions, the next section proposes the creation of an entirely new body dedicated to monitoring state compliance with the R2P.

7.4 An R2P Commission: A Proposal for Holding States Accountable to Their R2P

Following the transitional cosmopolitan approach, this final section proposes the creation of a new UN institution dedicated to holding states accountable to their commitments under the R2P. This proposal fits with calls for increasing accountability and scrutiny of state practice as a means of strengthening international protection norms: 'public reporting has been important towards shining a light on the suffering of countless victims of abuse, putting perpetrators on notice, and reminding the international community of its responsibility to halt and remedy violence' (D'Alessandra et al., 2022, p. 13). However, this proposal is about more than just holding domestic actors accountable who are directly responsible for the commission of atrocities. Instead, it seeks to build on calls for increased scrutiny of state practice in light of agreed principled (UN, 2017, para. 5; Šimonović, 2019, p. 251) by expanding R2P accountability to include all aspects of states' three pillar responsibilities. What this means is that the body proposed here would provide a mechanism to scrutinise state practice in light of their duties to assist others under Pillar Two, and to respond timely and decisively when atrocity situations have commenced under Pillar Three. This would help to evolve the notion of state accountability under the R2P, appreciating that – as the three pillars are meant to be taken as equal under the concept (Bellamy and Drummond, 2011, p. 181) – the doctrine is meant to be one of universal and international commitment, in addition to its domestic responsibilities. The proposal here, therefore, offers a unique contribution, as the UN's accountability efforts to date have largely focused on the role of scrutinising states' domestic practices, and generating data to support the criminal prosecution of actors directly complicit in atrocities. On top of a contribution to these accountability efforts relevant to R2P Pillar One, the proposal offered here would also help generate scrutiny of states' international practices vis-à-vis the prevention of mass atrocity crime under Pillar Two and Pillar Three of the R2P. This would provide useful channels to scrutinise state practice and identify windows for shaping more positive behaviour, appreciating that mass atrocity is bound up in international webs of activity (Shaw, 2012) and not merely a phenomenon that occurs or persists because of domestic actors.

It is recommended here that the UNGA establish an 'R2P Commission' as a permanent mechanism to determine where manifest R2P failings have occurred, to review international practice vis-à-vis atrocity prevention and response, and to make recommendations for altering practice and potential further action. The authority of the UNGA to establish such a body comes from Article 22 of the UN Charter, which states that the UNGA may establish 'such subsidiary organs as it deems necessary for the performance of its functions'. The UNGA has utilised this power in the past, for instance, when establishing the Human Rights Council 'as a subsidiary of the General Assembly' (UNGA, 2006). This power is also reflected in the Assembly's recent establishment of pre-prosecutorial investigative bodies in Syria (2016) and Myanmar (2017; 2018) (Barber, 2021, pp. 28–29).

It is envisioned that the R2P Commission would be comprised of 15 individuals, elected by the UNGA, with each given an equal vote and deliberative voice on the Commission. These individuals would be nominated by UN member states for election and should be experts in the field of international human rights and/or humanitarian law so that they possess knowledge relevant to the R2P and atrocity crimes. This could include former high level civil society leaders, academics, international legal experts, or those with experience working on judicial or quasi-judicial bodies. Individuals who have served high level political roles for their domestic government such as former leaders, government ministers, or UN representatives must be excluded in order to help reduce political bias within the Commission. Experts would be elected on a rotational basis with terms of six years, and elections staggered every two years.[9] A quota system would be required for candidate selections to promote equitable geographical and gender distribution of the R2P Commission, to ensure a legitimate institution is created that is fairly representative of the international community and the UN's membership. The institution's funding should be conducted through a pooled or 'basket fund' mechanism, whereby donors (be they state or private) contribute on an annual basis, with funds directed by the Commission into its investigative and report work.

Regarding its functions: the Commission would be responsible for bringing cases onto its own agenda. When a case is raised, the first task of the R2P Commission would be to vote on whether to launch an investigation into a potential atrocity crimes case.[10] For the R2P Commission to launch an inquiry, a super majority vote of 10/15 members would be required. The R2P Commission would be able to draw on support from the OHCHR when establishing these investigations (e.g. recruiting appropriate personnel), as has become customary practice by other UN bodies when launching fact-finding missions (OHCHR, 2015, p. 3). Upon hearing the evidence presented by the inquiry, the R2P Commission would then be tasked with voting to determine whether the case is reflective of a manifest failing of a state's R2P under Pillar One.[11] This should once again require a super majority of 10/15 Commission members. Upon determining that a breach of R2P Pillar One has taken place, the R2P Commission would then be tasked to review both international assistance to the target state prior to the outbreak of atrocity violence under Pillar Two, as well as international response to the crisis under Pillar Three. Here, the Commission would be tasked with delivering a written report directly to the UNGA where its findings and recommendations would be subject to debate (and potential actioning) by member states.

Regarding Pillar Two, the R2P Commission's report would investigate whether the international community had adequately fulfilled its responsibility to assist the target state in preventing mass atrocity crimes, highlighting strengths and weaknesses of international engagement with the target state. Crucially, this aspect of the Commission's report would also concern whether international practice may have undermined the goal of atrocity prevention through damaging state actions. Regarding Pillar Three, the R2P Commission would scrutinise international response to the crisis. This would amount to a review of whether the international community had successfully discharged its responsibility in a timely and decisive manner, with particular reference to the UNSC. Here, the commission would also be entitled to offer recommendations going forward, potentially including but not limited to: the adoption of targeted sanctions; a call for states to meet refugee obligations as part of R2P response; referral to the ICC; and UNSC veto restraint over the case. The R2P Commission would be able to offer further updates on its case reports as time progresses, ensuring that atrocity cases remain under enduring scrutiny.

7.4.1 *Test of Effective Progress*

The R2P Commission would provide a new institutionalised mechanism specifically devoted to holding states to account for their R2P commitments. As discussed shortly, this would help to strengthen cosmopolitan duties to prevent and respond to mass atrocities under the R2P in a number of ways.

Yet one might question the value of establishing a new UN-based institution for the R2P, given that current institutions have thus far often failed to prevent atrocities. However, the R2P Commission would differ from anything that currently exists. The Commission would be centred on the work of independent experts and a benefit this would bring in terms of effectiveness would be to mitigate state partisanship and bias, preventing scrutiny of R2P practice from becoming a political exercise devoid of meaningful review. Commission members should serve free and independently from state interests, allowing for scrutiny of R2P practice to be generated in a more even and universalised way, rather than only in specific cases where political will and interests are favourable. As a dedicated body aimed at holding actors to account, the R2P Commission would help transcend the problem of the UN accountability regime's selective nature. D'Alessandra et al. (2022, p. 19) have argued that the current politicised deployment of investigative mandates undermines the accountability regime as a whole, as it leads to accusations of bias, selectivity, and prejudice. As an independent institution acting under a dedicated mandate, the R2P Commission would be far less prone to problems of selectivity, instead helping to facilitate accountability for mass atrocities in response to appropriate cases.

Independent experts provide knowledge and assessments which are authoritative and more objective than those provided by state representatives seeking to further their country's interests (Boswell, 2008; Rodley, 2013; Carraro, 2019b; Strauss, 2019). As Rodley (2013, p. 624) argues, 'individual experts are more apt than government representatives to be able to bring independent judgement to bear on the neuralgic issue of states' respect (or otherwise) for their human rights obligations'. The UN treaty bodies, as just one example of the use of independent experts and their contribution to the work of the UN,[12] highlight the value of using elected experts to review state practice vis-à-vis human rights commitments. The treaty bodies are committees of elected independent experts which work to monitor state compliance with specific UN human rights treaties.

Scholars have shown how the work of the treaty bodies influences state practice (Rodley, 2013; Ploton, 2017; Meier and Gomes, 2018). For example, the recent development of follow-up on recommendations grading systems by the Human Rights Committee and other treaty bodies – whereby states are graded from A-E based on a follow-up review of their implementation of treaty body recommendations – is testament to the developing norm of accountability towards international commitments fostered by the treaty bodies. This is evidenced by examples such as Mongolia, which has, following the recommendations of the Human Rights Committee, achieved a 'Grade A' by making substantial reform to its criminal justice system (Ploton, 2017, p. 222). The value of independent experts, reflected in the work of the treaty bodies, demonstrates how the findings of an R2P Commission, similarly composed of independent experts, could have an effective role in influencing R2P practice.

Now, an important caveat to acknowledge here is that the R2P Commission would not be *wholly* independent or free from political bias. As Warren (2002, p. 181) notes, politics operates among 'power and conflict', and institutions should be designed in ways as to mitigate the impact of this power. This is necessary for such institutions to fulfil their normative purpose in a way which lessens the impact of political bias.

The most obvious way state power and interests may leech into the R2P Commission is the candidate nomination and election process. Empowering the UNGA, a political body, with the power to elect the members of the R2P Commission will naturally infuse state interests with the election process, as states may attempt to pursue their own ends through nominations and voting. However, this would not necessarily hamper the effectiveness of the Commission. The deliberation and voting procedure of the Commission should help mitigate issues of political bias with individual members. Commission members would hold equal voting power and opportunity for equal deliberation ought to be ensured. The requirement of a super majority of 10/15 members in the body's decisions can promote consensus building via group deliberation and expressed reason giving (see Brown, 2010, p. 521). This would ensure that decisions are only taken where a large group consensus exists, thus reducing the likelihood that individual state interests could have any notable effect on the body's decisions. As Carraro has argued in relation to the UN treaty bodies, politicised electoral processes do not automatically result in the actual conduct of expert bodies becoming politicised (Carraro, 2019a). Expert committees function as an independent group dynamic, with their deliberative processes helping to filter out the politicisation of individuals, preventing states from being able to control the work of such bodies (Carraro, 2019a, p. 843).

Another way power and interests could potentially leech into the R2P Commission is through funding. In anticipating this concern, a 'basket fund' mechanism has been advocated. This follows a common approach in the field of global health, where funding has been identified as an area which may undermine the accountability, coordination, and cooperation of global health efforts as donors seek to direct funding to fulfil their own interests (Buse and Harmer, 2007). However, basket funds ensure that donor funding from multiple sources is pooled and allocated to appropriate channels by institutions themselves (Meghani et al., 2015, p. 4). This allows an institution to ring-fence donations, meaning that donor interests will counteract each other, and reduces the potential for individual donors to hold to ransom organisations to further their own interests.

The above procedures attempt to mitigate partisan biases within the R2P Commission, though they cannot remove them entirely. Nonetheless, electing experts to serve in an independent capacity can provide a more effective way of promoting state accountability than an institution explicitly made up from state representatives working to further their state's interests, often at the expense of cosmopolitan human rights commitments.

The R2P Commission can effectively promote accountability across the R2P's three pillars, providing an institutionalised UN entity for coordinating atrocity prevention efforts; something which the UN system has not effectively addressed to date (Šimonović, 2019, pp. 259–260). Regarding Pillar One, the R2P Commission would provide an expert and impartial body to launch UN investigative inquiries to determine the facts of a case and whether manifest breaches of a state's R2P are evident. This would be advantageous in three ways: i) the UN would no longer be (mostly) dependent on fact-finding inquiries being launched by state-based bodies, where investigative action may be rejected by member states; ii) in not having to rely on initiation through other UN bodies, the R2P Commission, dedicated to the *specific* purpose of monitoring R2P compliance, would be better placed to launch investigations in a timely and decisive manner, consistent with R2P pledges (UNGA, 2005, para. 139), so that investigative action is prompt, and findings can be fed back into UN institutions for deliberation and potential action; iii) the R2P Commission would also provide a means for generating 'lessons learned' from past atrocity cases. Regarding this third point, Strauss (2015, pp. 71–75) has identified in the context of the UN treaty bodies that review procedures can make valuable contributions to atrocity prevention by identifying risk factors and avenues for mitigation measures in future cases. Tacheva (2021) has recently put forward a substantive list of nine determinants for a state's 'manifest failing' to protect its populations against the four mass atrocity crimes under the R2P. These relate to areas such as the gravity and imminence of atrocities, as well host state intent, capacity, and cooperative willingness. These criteria could go a long way to addressing the current 'ambiguity and inconsistency' (Gallagher, 2014, p. 435) that surrounds understandings of what constitutes a manifest failing. The R2P Commission could utilise the criteria put forward by Tacheva as a means of determining where Pillar One failures have occurred, serving as a useful means for review of state practice, developing understandings of how manifest failure criteria apply in practice, and in generating accountability for where manifest R2P failings have occurred/are occurring.

As noted above, in addition to serving as a permanent institution to determine manifest failures of R2P Pillar One, what is particularly novel about the R2P Commission is that it would also promote accountability for the R2P's international responsibilities under Pillar Two and Three. This is where the work of the R2P Commission would go beyond that of fact-finding by UN CoIs. While CoIs are focused on finding evidence of the commission of atrocity crimes domestically, the reports submitted by the R2P Commission to the UNGA would involve scrutiny of international state practice in atrocity prevention and response efforts. This is an attempt to move away from looking at mass atrocity crises as simply 'problem state' issues (see section 3.6), to instead appreciate that the R2P is multifaceted, with its success dependent not just on states meeting domestic obligations but also in their commitments to preventing atrocity crimes abroad. This is appropriate to the R2P as a multi-layered norm of both domestic and international responsibilities (Welsh, 2013). The R2P Commission would provide the international community with a mechanism to scrutinise international practices which are conducive to the outbreak of atrocities, as well as a means to hold UN actors to account for Pillar Three response efforts. The R2P Commission would exist to highlight malpractice, provide recommendations for altering practice, and pressure states into compliance. The findings of the R2P Commission could provide useful contributions to enhance the normative development of the R2P through Secretary-General reports, as well as R2P debates within the UNGA, which are now a formal item on the UNGA's agenda. Going forward, this would offer valuable lessons in how practice ought to be altered in order to better meet states' responsibilities.

Regarding Pillar Two duties of assistance, the R2P Commission could provide a means for holding states to account for their negative duties to atrocity prevention and damaging practices linked to the commission of atrocities – such as arms sales and support for oppressive regimes – which scholars have argued undermine the Pillar Two duty of assistance within the R2P (Dunford and Neu, 2019; Bohm and Brown, 2021). For example, there is scope for complementarity between the R2P Commission and scrutiny of the international arms trade. The R2P Commission can provide an independent mechanism for monitoring state practice with regard to the global arms trade, which is something currently lacking with international arms regulation.

A link has been made between the need for better arms regulation and achieving the goals of the R2P (Henderson, 2017). In May 2020, the Journal *Global Responsibility to Protect* even produced a special issue dedicated to the Arms Trade Treaty (ATT). The ATT exists to regulate the flow of conventional arms internationally, with part of its aim to promote human security interests by helping to curb arms flows to situations where atrocity crimes may occur (UN, 2013, ATT Article 6). The ATT requires that states transferring arms pay consideration for the potential of arms transfers to undermine peace and security or violate international law (UN, 2013, ATT Article 7).

However, problems exist with the enforcement of the ATT, weakening its ability to serve R2P goals. States parties to the ATT continue to supply arms to human rights abusers (Stavrianakis, 2016); for example, instrumental ties between the UK and Saudi Arabia are significant, with UK aircraft making up half of the Saudi Air Force strike force. From 2009–2018, 38 per cent of total UK arms exports were to Saudi Arabia (Perlo-Freeman, 2020, p. 184). This relationship endures between both states despite the Saudi campaign of war in Yemen and reported breaches of international humanitarian law and an ongoing humanitarian crisis (UNHCR).

Breaches of the ATT may in part be attributable to the weakness of the treaty's accountability mechanisms (Whang, 2015; Pytlak, 2020). For Coppen (2016, p. 373), 'review mechanisms', such as the ATT's Conference of State Parties (CSP), have the potential to provide clarity to legal agreements, which can develop their implementation over time. What this suggests is that dialogue and debate on the scope of treaty provisions and their practical implementation through accountability mechanisms can help alter state practice in the long term by establishing norms of expected practice. Yet, ATT CSPs have thus far failed to systematically address treaty violations; references to real-world cases in need of attention, or to potential breaches by ATT states parties, have rarely occurred. Pytlak (2020, pp. 174–175) suggests that if CSPs are unable to fulfil this scrutinising function then an alternative mechanism is likely necessitated.

This is a function that the R2P Commission could step in to fill.[13] The R2P Commission could provide a means for scrutinising arms transfers that may have contributed to outbreaks of atrocity violence. This may raise the political costs of ATT breaches, which as noted, relate directly to R2P commitments. Perlo-Freeman (2020, p. 197) argues that major arms exporters have little interest in upholding ATT regulations because '[t]he impetus to export as a strategic necessity for maintaining domestic technological capabilities … override[s] the concerns for the impact of the arms trade'. Increased accountability for states' commitments to curb arms flows that risk undermining atrocity prevention, and the subsequent political pressure that ensues from having one's actions directly linked to atrocity violence, may force states to reconsider this balance of interests in favour of upholding commitments to curb arms flows, even if only for the instrumental reason of maintaining a favourable public image. The R2P Commission could provide the means for scrutinising state practice for this purpose.

Regarding the R2P Commission's role in scrutinising international response under Pillar Three of the R2P, there are also useful avenues for transitional cosmopolitan progress. Review of international response or recommendations for future practice from an independent expert body can provide legitimacy to calls for R2P-based action. This may open up the potential for influencing future UNSC action if the international community were to increase pressure on the P5 members as a result of the R2P Commission's findings. This may, for instance, be one way of increasing pressure on the P5 to employ veto restraint on matters of R2P concern.

Here a link can be drawn with Chapter 5 and the recommendation for 'Responsible Veto Restraint'. The R2P Commission could lend some authority to a determination of whether employing veto restraint is an appropriate action. One could contend that the R2P Commission may be unlikely to determine in a timely and decisive manner whether P5 veto restraint is appropriate in response to an ongoing crisis. However, had RVR been previously adopted and triggered at the same time a case was being assessed by the R2P Commission, then a future recommendation by the R2P Commission to employ veto restraint would at least add further normative weight to the call for veto restraint, potentially influencing whether the P5 continue to respectfully adhere to the RVR mechanism in that case and in future cases.

The R2P Commission's recommendations may also help influence the UNSC to discharge its positive duty of response and take further action on an R2P case, such as political condemnation, the employment of sanctions, or referral of a case to the ICC. As Mills and Bloomfield (2018, p. 107) note, 'the Rome Statute empowers the Council to both refer a situation in a non-party to the Prosecutor (Article 15) and to also defer any ICC investigation or prosecution for a renewable term of 12 months (Article 16)'. This only empowers the UNSC to refer cases, meaning that the R2P Commission could only recommend that the UNSC to do this, rather than refer cases itself. Nevertheless, a recommendation by an impartial, internationally legitimate R2P Commission for a case to be referred to the ICC could help to provide added legitimacy to UNSC case referrals and reduce accusations of political bias. This may subsequently increase the likelihood of state compliance with the ICC's follow-up demands, which is something that the politicisation of ICC case referrals has thus far negatively affected as many states, especially those in Africa, have perceived the ICC to be a Western tool used to punish its political enemies (Mills and Bloomfield, 2018; Pattison, 2018; Saba and Akbarzadeh, 2020). Increasing state compliance with ICC demands would likely be a positive contribution to implementing an anti-impunity norm for atrocity crimes, thus promoting the implementation of R2P goals in the long term.

Furthermore, even if pressure resulting from the R2P Commission's findings is not enough to influence UNSC practice, recommendations issued from an independent and legitimate international review body could help legitimise R2P action taken through other channels, such as the UNGA via its own Charter responsibility for upholding international peace and security or the Uniting for Peace mechanism as was discussed extensively in Chapter 6. Given that the R2P Commission is envisioned here as a subsidiary organ of the UNGA, the Commission could have an important relationship with the Assembly and its power to pass recommendatory resolutions in the name of maintaining international peace and security. The R2P Commission would provide an authoritative and legitimate expert body to make recommendations that the UNGA could choose to act on in instances of UNSC failure.

Finally, it is worth addressing some concerns over the effectiveness of the R2P Commission which may have arisen. First is the problem of enforcement capability. As noted, the Commission would only have the power to recommend, not demand, compliance, and thus it would not be a guarantee for overcoming lack of political will to act on crises. However, as argued in section 7.2, any attempt to enshrine a body with the capacity to enforce itself upon states, above or separate to the UNSC, would not be a feasible recommendation for transitional cosmopolitan progress. Therefore, for now at least, we must rely on the socialisation of states into adhering to the demands of an R2P Commission as a result of political pressure and self-interest. The scrutiny that comes about from the R2P Commission's work would be unlikely to influence the will to act in all cases, but it may be enough to shame and/or influence states into taking action in some situations. The Commission would not be a panacea for the R2P's ills, but it would be an iterative, transitional mechanism, which can offer some effective avenues for progress. Over time, state practice may become more conducive to following the demands of the R2P Commission as the legitimacy of its decisions develop. At the very least, the Commission would provide an international body to scrutinise all aspects of states' R2P, preventing practice which runs anathema to R2P from being ignored, and providing a window of opportunity to discuss and shape practices of expected state behaviour.

Second is the likely problem of the R2P Commission's limited ability to serve timely and decisive response due to the high level of deliberation required to deliver recommendations on how to address complex crises. However, the Commission would still provide a dedicated body for monitoring R2P that would be able to i) authorise investigative action promptly in response to unfolding crises, and ii) deliver findings and recommendations to the UNGA through expert-based scrutiny. The R2P Commission would provide a devoted R2P Institution that actively works to identify atrocity cases and provide solutions for how to ameliorate them. The R2P Commission may not be an ideal solution to the issue of timely and decisive R2P response, but it would still provide a nuanced and transitional mechanism for improving current practice. Its work may be particularly useful for slower, more drawn-out cases, where atrocities have occurred against a backdrop of human rights abuses developed over a longer period of time; such as has been the case with the Uyghur case in China, the Israeli occupation of Palestinian territories, and the large-scale human rights violations in Burundi. Furthermore, even if an atrocity case has been one which has necessitated and led to immediate response prior to the R2P Commission being able to launch an inquiry and report findings, the later findings of the R2P Commission could still lend expert guidance on what further action could be taken on an atrocity case to ensure that R2P responsibilities continue to be adequately discharged. The R2P Commission is not intended to serve as the body responsible for determining how response to all mass atrocity cases will proceed, and if a case necessitates immediate response, then it is still very much the duty of the international community, particularly the UNSC, but also the UNGA, to act appropriately.

7.4.2 *Test of Moral Hazard*

While there does not appear to be any striking moral hazard presented by the creation of an R2P Commission that would significantly reduce the transitional cosmopolitan value of the proposal, there is one particular concern which should be flagged. This relates to the potential negative fallout that can ensue from criticising state practice. Gallagher (2021), for instance, aware of the backlash that can result when state actors react negatively to the shaming of their actions, argues in favour of a 'pragmatic approach' when attempting to name and shame actors, which takes account of both the potential intended and unintended consequences of such actions. Discussing the value of the UNHRC's UPR process, Etone (2019, pp. 42–45) is outright sceptical of the value of attempts to force compliance or name and shame. He claims that these can actually reduce compliance by harming cooperation between states and weakening human rights implementation overall. This argument can also be linked to that of Welsh (2013, p. 395), who claims that the remedial duty of the international community under the R2P is highly contentious, and therefore we ought to avoid the 'spectre of external enforcement' through responses to mass atrocity. For some, it may appear then that a focus on softer forms of state engagement and cooperation are more appropriate for achieving compliance with cosmopolitan human rights and R2P commitments than attempts to name and shame or criticise state practice.

This line of argument is perhaps an important one to acknowledge when framed in the context of bodies, such as the UNHRC, which are purposely designed to promote state cooperation. The UNHRC is, after all, a political body designed to promote dialogue and engagement over human rights. Yet, the recommendation of an R2P Commission would not infringe on the UNHRC's political role for state cooperation and softer engagement with human rights issues. Instead, the recommendation made here would provide a point for criticism of state practice, which is necessary to shape standards of expected behaviour by clarifying what appropriate action is. Research, which is backed by examples of successful atrocity prevention like Kenya (2009; 2013), Guinea (2009), and Kyrgyzstan (2010) (Bellamy and Luck, 2018, chap. seven) has shown that diplomatic pressure can help in altering actor's behaviour and reducing mass atrocity risk and scope (DeMeritt, 2012; Krain, 2012).

Crucially though, the fact that the R2P Commission would exist to scrutinise the full range of R2P commitments relating to domestic *and* international responsibilities would prevent naming and shaming from becoming a practice simply channelled at (typically non-Western) 'problem states'. Indeed, it is the increasing evidence of Western hypocrisy – present in its own practices such as arms sales, regime ties, irresponsible use of military technology, and neglection of refugee responsibilities – which has partly contributed to an erosion of the usefulness of naming and shaming as a tool for the R2P in recent years, as human rights abuses, or those who shield them, have simply deflected criticism back at Western states (Glanville, 2021, p. 157). Calling out the practice of the wider international community, including that of Western states, would provide an unbiased approach, which current institutions like the UNHRC have been accused of lacking. The R2P Commission is about monitoring the full range of R2P commitments, including international duties of assistance and response, and not just that of individual state compliance with domestic obligations. This would result in a more universalised critique of the practice of the international community, reducing the possibility for claims that the R2P Commission would simply be a liberal-Western tool designed to infringe on the interests of non-Western states. This should help allay fears that a new body for reviewing the implementation of the R2P's three pillars would become politicised to the point that it actually hindered state compliance with human rights and R2P obligations.

Furthermore, to reiterate the point made above, the R2P Commission would operate in a way that avoids ad hoc and selective responses to atrocity violations, helping facilitate accountability for violations in a more universalised way, rather than just where political will has been favourable enough to establish an accountability mandate. Again, this would help avoid fuelling accusations of political bias which hamper accountability efforts and normative commitments to the R2P more generally.

7.4.3 Test of Practical Potential

Before assessing whether the R2P Commission satisfies the transitional cosmopolitan test for practical potential, it should be noted that reform recommendations made in the previous two chapters have covered numerous arguments related to feasibility in the context of achieving the requisite state will to achieve reform. Such arguments have related to: a lack of state will to enact R2P-based action; an unwillingness to alter the current R2P consensus; a wish to avoid being shamed for malpractice; and a desire to maintain state preponderance (particularly of the UNSC's P5) in the implementation of R2P. Many of these points may apply here and there is no need to run over these again in detail. Suffice to say, there are a number of feasibility constraints in the way of establishing the R2P Commission, and in achieving state compliance with its findings, that would need to be overcome if the recommendation is to be successful.

One vital point to reiterate here in response to these concerns is that the R2P Commission would reflect a hybrid system. The Commission would be dependent on states for its existence and for electing its composition, but it would be independent once elected. This hybridity may partially weaken the independence of the R2P Commission as a body charged with promoting state accountability, but such hybridity fits with the statist approach inherent to the R2P, and it is a necessary requirement in an attempt to attain state 'buy-in' to the proposal. To return to the conceptualisation of feasibility in Chapter 4, trade-offs must be made when applying normative demands to practical contexts (Erman and Möller, 2018, p. 127), with feasibility and desirability requiring balancing in order for recommendations for change to hold political value (Gilabert and Lawford-Smith, 2012, p. 819).

A degree of state buy-in will be necessary for attainting the requisite will to establish the R2P Commission, and for the body to achieve practical impact through state compliance with its findings. Again, it should be emphasised that in addition to its scrutiny function, the R2P Commission would only be entitled to make recommendations for further action on an R2P case. The R2P Commission would not supplant the power of states (or the UNSC) in decision making. Furthermore, the fact that the R2P Commission would scrutinise the full range of states' three pillar commitments should contribute to the feasibility of the recommendation by alleviating fears that such an institution would exist only to target particular states.

It is not possible to claim with certainty that the R2P Commission could receive the requisite votes in the UNGA to be established. Yet the increasingly active role that the UNGA has shown in discharging its R2P offers scope for optimism (see Chapter 6). The UNGA has now also placed discussion of the R2P on its formal agenda as of May 2021. Further, the support that P5 veto restraint measures have now garnered (see Chapter 5) demonstrates that the vast majority of UN member states wish to see more consistent and effective R2P implementation, which offers promise that member states could one day establish an R2P Commission.

What this also shows is that, while the UNSC has often failed to discharge its R2P, suggesting that the feasibility of the UNSC acting on the R2P Commission's findings would be limited, the UNGA perhaps offers a more promising route. While positive UNGA receptiveness to the findings of the R2P commission would not be a given, the examples of UNGA action and its generally favourable attitude to R2P and related normative efforts offers a point for tempered optimism.

In the 2017 Informal Interactive Dialogue on the Responsibility to Protect that followed the Secretary-General's report on *Implementing the Responsibility to Protect: Accountability for Prevention*, member states expressed the 'importance of continuing efforts to fully integrate the responsibility to protect within the United Nations' (UNGA, 2017, para. 8), while they also 'emphasized the primary role of the General Assembly in advancing the principle' (UNGA, 2017, para. 9). Member states also implied a desire for greater accountability for the international community's role under Pillar Three of the R2P when a 'significant number' of states re-affirmed calls for P5 veto restraint in the face of mass atrocity; called in support for UNSC open debates on atrocity prevention; and 'reiterated their invitation to the Secretary-General and to the Special Advisers on the Prevention of Genocide and on the Responsibility to Protect to bring situations of concern to the attention of the Council' (UNGA, 2017, para. 11). This latter point is especially interesting for the purposes of this chapter, as it could be interpreted to reflect an increasing desire of UN member states to see situations of mass atrocity more consistently highlighted and acted on by the UN system. This may imply that there could be feasible support for the establishment of an R2P Commission by the UNGA, dedicated to promoting accountability for mass atrocity as a means of supporting this very goal. The R2P Commission would, after all, provide a mechanism for more consistently investigating potential R2P breaches and generating additional pressure for states (either the UNSC or the UNGA) to take concerted action to support their duty of international assistance and / or response.

Numerous states have voiced frustration at the inconsistency in the way that the R2P is applied in practice. Pakistan, for instance, during the 2019 formal UNGA debate on R2P claimed that 'what is needed is to summon our collective resolve and our collective will and to act in a consistent and uniform manner towards all transgressions' (UNGA, 2019a, p. 16). Similarly, Turkey noted that '[p]ursuing a non-selective approach vis-à-vis the implementation of the [R2P] concept is relevant if we are to achieve the widest possible consensus among the membership on this important issue' (UNGA, 2019b, pp. 26–27). Such sentiment was reiterated by some states during the 2021 formal UNGA debate on R2P; Slovakia stated that 'we have seen far too often how the actions of the international community and Member States fall short of adequately deterring or preventing atrocity crimes' (UNGA, 2021, p. 13), while Qatar emphasised the need for 'more determined and consistent measures on the part of the international community as it assumes its responsibility to protect civilians' (UNGA, 2021, p. 16). During the 2021 debate, 35 out of 59 states and groupings that delivered a statement also explicitly acknowledged their support for more consistency in efforts to hold perpetrators to account for their atrocities.

What the UNGA's annual debates on the R2P continue to demonstrate then is that there is wide-ranging support at the UN for more rigorous response to all instances of mass atrocity, which aligns with cosmopolitan demands. This position would therefore also seem to align with the demand for (and therefore feasibility of) establishing stronger institutionalised means at the UN for investigating atrocities, and holding all actors to account for the full range of their commitments under the R2P's three pillars. This is not at all to suggest that this is a universal position, for if it were, then there would be no need for a book such as the one you're currently reading, and mass atrocities would be far less likely to occur than they now are. Nevertheless, the point is that, given the number of outspoken states in the UNGA, there may be sufficient political will for establishing a body with the stated goals of the R2P Commission; one that would help reinforce more consistent responses to cases of mass atrocity through a dedicated scrutinising function that would provide additional legitimacy to calls for concerted R2P action.

It has been argued here that the UNGA should establish the R2P Commission as a UN body and subsidiary organ of the Assembly. It would be favourable for the UNGA to establish the R2P commission due to the potential for readily utilising other elements of the UN system to assist in its work, for instance, support from the OHCHR in designing fact-finding missions. Further, as noted, as a subsidiary organ of the UNGA, the R2P Commission would also have a direct link to the use of UfP and the recommendatory powers of the General Assembly to act on R2P crises in instances where the UNSC has failed to exercise its responsibilities. The political capital of the UNGA also points to the favourability of establishing the Commission within the UN system, given that were the body established, this would mean that it was supported by the world's universally representative state body, providing the R2P Commission with international legitimacy and a clear mandate to hold UN member states accountable to their R2P commitments.

However, should it be deemed politically unfeasible for the UNGA to establish the R2P Commission, then it would be desirable for states to establish the Commission through another channel. This would essentially require that states forego the UN route and instead seek to establish the R2P Commission through separate treaty law. This would weaken the efficiency and legitimacy of the R2P Commission in comparison to if it were established as a UN body, but it would at least bring the advantage of circumventing the feasibility concern of requiring widespread support from UN member states.

This would mean that *mass* state buy-in to the R2P Commission would not be *essential*, at least not in the short term.[14] Arguing for the creation of a representative and democratic UN Parliament, Archibugi claims that formal constitutional reform of the UN is very difficult. More realistically, he argues, would be the formation of such a body through treaty law, signed by like-minded states, with the hope that other states would follow suit over time as the institution demonstrates success (Archibugi, 2008, p. 174). Notably, this is the approach that has been taken with the ICC; another ambitious international institution which would have doubtlessly seemed unfeasible in the decades prior to its creation. Should the UN route be closed off, it would therefore be logical for a small group of willing states to establish the R2P Commission, in the hope that its membership and legitimacy would develop over time.

It is worth ending here by highlighting a quote from Rodley (2013, p. 647), eloquently noting that '[o]ccasionally, a catalytic event or chain of events occurs that makes radical institutional change, considered unrealistic yesterday, become tomorrow's necessity'. For him, institutional developments such as the ICC provide evidence of how quickly something which seems *prima facie* unfeasible in the immediate short term can become a living reality. Even if it is the case that the R2P Commission may seem an improbable recommendation in the short term, this does not render it fundamentally unfeasible. Given the normative and instrumental challenges – such as state failure, mass refugee crises, and the damage to human rights – presented by R2P failures, it may very well be the case that 'radical institutional change' is indeed necessary.

7.5 Conclusion

A key problem with the implementation of the R2P is that there is a lack of means for enforcing state compliance with the norm in practice. This means that states can too often get away with committing atrocities; to continue damaging practices that contribute to atrocity cases; and means that the response and scrutiny of the international community to unfolding atrocity crises is limited. However, it is unfeasible to suggest that a new institution could be created with authority over states to determine where R2P action must take place or where state practice must change. Such a recommendation would also face practical drawbacks, as an independent body would be unlikely to deliver timely and decisive enforcement action in response to unfolding crises. Furthermore, states, and certainly the P5, would not readily consent to the establishment of such a body.

Consequently, to better align with the transitional cosmopolitan approach, while favouring the UN Secretary-General's less stringent view of what R2P accountability should entail (consistent critique of state practice against accepted standards), it has been argued here that we need to seek ways to promote state accountability under the R2P, but in ways which would not infringe on timely and decisive response, or on the vital interests of states themselves. The UNHRC was discussed as one potential avenue for this, through its ability to highlight malpractice, pressure states, and enhance the work of other institutions. However, as argued, the UNHRC is not an appropriate body for holding states to account for the full range of their R2P commitments due to problems of bias and partisanship inherent to its state-based makeup.

In response to these challenges, the chapter proposed the creation of an 'R2P Commission'. This is a suggestion for a body comprised of experts elected by the UNGA, uniquely charged with scrutinising the implementation of the R2P. It was argued that the R2P Commission can effectively promote state accountability under the three pillar R2P approach by highlighting breaches across the pillars and offering recommendations for shaping state practice. The fact that the R2P Commission would exist to scrutinise both the domestic and international aspects of the R2P would provide for a more holistic approach that seeks to go beyond merely highlighting 'problem states'. This would allay fears that such an institution would present a moral hazard by damaging state cooperation by simply calling out domestic R2P breaches and becoming perceived as a Western tool. Further, the fact that the R2P Commission would be a hybrid system, involving states in its maintenance and not possessing power above them, helps to promote its feasibility by maintaining state buy-in. While the recommendation for an R2P Commission may not be as revolutionary as establishing an institution with power to enforce the R2P, since it would only possess a review and recommendatory function; such an institution nevertheless offers a new, transitional cosmopolitan step for promoting state accountability under the R2P. The impact of such a body could be enough to affect state practice and contribute to an application of the R2P more aligned with cosmopolitan protection responsibilities as standards of appropriate behaviour are reinforced, malpractice more consistently drawn to attention, and proactive recommendations are offered for addressing atrocity crises.

Notes

1 The ICC may be argued to provide a legal and impartial accountability mechanism for generating compliance with atrocity prevention at the domestic level, which at least relates to Pillar One responsibilities under the R2P. The ICC does not, however, have any mandate to hold states to account for their Pillar Two and Three responsibilities under the R2P. Further, the ICC suffers from a number of problems that hamper its effectiveness and political independence (see Ainley, 2015; Mills and Bloomfield, 2018; Pattison, 2018; Saba and Akbarzadeh, 2020). These factors mean that the ICC cannot function as an independent review body to hold states to account for the full range of their R2P commitments.

2 Prokhorova (2022, pp. 294; 307–308), for instance, has highlighted how recent special advisers have sought to more deeply politicise their role by not merely providing objective clarifications of facts, but through enhancing attention to specific situations, including through the use of emotive and politically charged language.

3 Archibugi's suggestion is stronger in this regard, for his World Parliament proposal would be a political institution more likely able to deliver fast-paced response than a panel of independent legal experts.

4 This is not a comment on the efficacy of the UNSC's actions in the Libya case but merely highlights that the Council can act quickly when its members are not (overly) divided.

5 The ICJ was relatively quick in passing provisional measures, however, and in January 2020, just two months after The Gambia had initiated the case, the ICJ delivered provisional measures in order to preserve certain rights claimed by The Gambia for the protection of the Rohingya in Myanmar. The ICJ noted that 'there is a real and imminent risk of irreparable prejudice to the rights invoked by The Gambia, as specified by the Court' and outlined a series of demands for Myanmar to comply with (International Court of Justice, 2020). While the ICJ did deliver this preliminary verdict quickly, it must be noted that this was possible due to the lengthy fact-finding and evidence delivered by the IIFFMM and its successor, the Independent Investigative Mechanism for Myanmar (IIMM). Further, the provisional measures listed essentially amounted to a decree that Myanmar must uphold the Genocide Convention and preserve evidence to aid the investigation; they did not allude to enforcement action.

6 Another useful component of the UNHRC comes from the work of the UN treaty bodies, which is discussed below.

7 On 15 September 2021, the ICC Prosecutor's request to commence investigation into the war on drugs was granted by the Pre-Trial Chamber I (ICC, 2021).

8 Notably, the Ukraine case has seen accountability initiatives established at a rate near-unprecedented in the history of international response to mass atrocity crimes (Barber, 2022, p. 164). This case is very much an exception to the rule.

9 This election system roughly corresponds to that of the Human Rights Committee UN treaty body. Staggered elections allow for a 'balance between continuity and change' to be maintained in composition (OHCHR) which allows for those with experience to work alongside those newly elected.

10 Logistically, it would be impossible for the R2P Commission to itself conduct CoIs. CoIs typically involve a small number of panel members which would make the R2P Commission inappropriate for carrying out this function. Furthermore, the R2P Commission is likely to have several investigations underway at any one time, making it logistically impossible for its members it to carry out its own fact-finding work.

11 It is beyond the scope of this chapter to determine exactly how this determination of manifest R2P Pillar One failing could be made. There has, however, been excellent research on this matter, which is complementary to the proposal made in this chapter (see Tacheva, 2021).

12 Beyond the UN treaty bodies, there are many other examples, including judges of the International Court of Justice, the members of the International Law Commission, as well as other commissions that operate as subsidiary organs of the General Assembly.

13 Note, this does not mean that the R2P Commission would directly serve as a treaty monitoring body for the ATT, but merely that the Commission's function would be complementary to efforts to curb international arms flows.

14 Of course, if the Commission were established this way, attaining greater state buy-in would still be a desirable goal to work at over time in order to promote the legitimacy of, and compliance with, its findings.

References

Adams, S. 2020. Twitter post on Uyghur crisis. [Accessed 16 October 2020]. Available from: https://twitter.com/SAdamsR2P/status/1316765730952679424?s=20.

Ainley, K. 2015. The Responsibility to Protect and the International Criminal Court: Counteracting the Crisis. *International Affairs*. **91**(1), pp. 37–54.

Amnesty International 2022. China: Xinjiang Vote Failure Betrays Core Mission of UN Human Rights Council. [Accessed 7 October 2022]. Available from: www.amnesty.org/en/latest/news/2022/10/china-xinjiang-vote-failure-betrays-core-mission-of-un-human-rights-council/.

Archibugi, D. 2008. *The Global Commonwealth of Citizens: Toward Cosmopolitan Democracy*. Princeton, NJ: Princeton University Press.

Barber, R. 2021. *The Powers of the UN General Assembly to Prevent and Respond to Atrocity Crimes: A Guidance Document* [Online]. Asia-Pacific Centre for the Responsibility to Protect. [Accessed 6 May 2021]. Available from: https://r2pasia pacific.org/files/6710/UNGA_2021%20%283%29.pdf.

Barber, R. 2022. What Does the 'Responsibility to Protect' Require of States in Ukraine? *Journal of International Peacekeeping*. **25**(2), pp. 155–177.

Bellamy, A.J. and Drummond, C. 2011. The Responsibility to Protect in Southeast Asia: Between Non-interference and Sovereignty as Responsibility. *The Pacific Review*. **24**(2), pp. 179–200.

Bellamy, A.J. and Luck, E.C. 2018. *The Responsibility to Protect: From Promise to Practice*. Cambridge: Polity Press.

Bohm, A. and Brown, G.W. 2021. R2P and Prevention: The International Community and Its Role in the Determinants of Mass Atrocity. *Global Responsibility to Protect*. **13**(1), pp. 60–95.

Boswell, C. 2008. The Political Functions of Expert Knowledge: Knowledge and Legitimation in European Union Immigration Policy. *Journal of European Public Policy*. **15**(4), pp. 471–488.

Brown, G.W. 2010. Safeguarding Deliberative Global Governance: The Case of the Global Fund to Fight AIDS, Tuberculosis and Malaria. *Review of International Studies*. 36(2), pp. 511–530.

Buse, K. and Harmer, A.M. 2007. Seven Habits of Highly Effective Global Public–Private Health Partnerships: Practice and Potential. *Social Science & Medicine*. 64(2), pp. 259–271.

Carraro, V. 2019a. Electing the Experts: Expertise and Independence in the UN Human Rights Treaty Bodies. *European Journal of International Relations*. 25(3), pp. 826–851.

Carraro, V. 2019b. Promoting Compliance with Human Rights: The Performance of the United Nations' Universal Periodic Review and Treaty Bodies. *International Studies Quarterly*. 63(4), pp. 1079–1093.

Chané, A.-L. and Sharma, A. 2016. Universal Human Rights: Exploring Contestation and Consensus in the UN Human Rights Council. *Human Rights & International Legal Discourse*. 10(2), pp. 219–247.

Charlesworth, H. and Larking, E. 2015. *Human Rights and the Universal Periodic Review: Rituals and Ritualism*. Cambridge: Cambridge University Press.

Chinkin, C. 2011. UN Human Rights Council Fact-Finding Missions: Lessons from Gaza *In*: M. H. Arsanjani, J. Cogan, R. Sloane, and S. Wiessner, eds. *Looking to the Future: Essays on International Law in Honor of W. Michael Reisman*. Leiden: Martinus Nijhoff, pp. 475–498.

CNN Philippines 2017. PH Rejects Over Half of Human Rights Recommendations of UN. [Accessed 4 March 2021]. Available from: https://cnnphilippines.com/news/2017/09/23/Philippines-human-rights-report-United-Nations.html.

Coppen, T. 2016. The Evolution of Arms Control Instruments and the Potential of the Arms Trade Treaty. *Goettingen Journal of International Law*. 7, pp. 353–382.

D'Alessandra, F., Rapp, A.S.J., Sutherland, K., and Ashraph 2022. *Anchoring Accountability for Mass Atrocities: The Permanent Support Needed to Fulfil UN Investigative Mandates* [Online]. the Oxford Institute for Ethics, Law, and Armed Conflict. [Accessed 25 August 2022]. Available from: www.bsg.ox.ac.uk/sites/default/files/2022-05/Anchoring%20Accountability%20for%20Mass%20Atrocities%20Report.pdf.

DeMeritt, J.H. 2012. International Organizations and Government Killing: Does Naming and Shaming Save Lives? *International Interactions*. 38(5), pp. 597–621.

Devaney, J.G. 2016. *Fact-Finding before the International Court of Justice*. Cambridge: Cambridge University Press.

Dunford, R. and Neu, M. 2019. The Responsibility to Protect in a World of Already Existing Intervention. *European Journal of International Relations*. 25(4), pp. 1080–1102.

Erman, E. and Möller, N. 2018. *The Practical Turn in Political Theory*. Edinburgh: Edinburgh University Press.

Etone, D. 2019. Theoretical Challenges to Understanding the Potential Impact of the Universal Periodic Review Mechanism: Revisiting Theoretical Approaches to State Human Rights Compliance. *Journal of Human Rights*. 18(1), pp. 36–56.

Farrell, M. and Murphy, B. 2017. Hegemony and Counter-Hegemony: The Politics of Establishing United Nations Commissions of Inquiry *In*: C. Henderson ed. *Commissions of Inquiry: Problems and Prospects*. Oxford: Hart Publishing, pp. 34–64.

Freedman, R. 2013. *The United Nations Human Rights Council: An Early Assessment*. London: Routledge.

Freedman, R. and Mchangama, J. 2016. Expanding or Diluting Human Rights: The Proliferation of United Nations Special Procedures Mandates. *Human Rights Quarterly*. **38**, pp. 164–193.

Frulli, M. 2012. Fact-Finding or Paving the Road to Criminal Justice? Some Reflections on United Nations Commissions of Inquiry. *Journal of International Criminal Justice*. **10**(5), pp. 1323–1338.

Gallagher, A. 2014. What Constitutes a 'Manifest Failing'? Ambiguous and Inconsistent Terminology and the Responsibility to Protect. *International Relations*. **28**(4), pp. 428–444.

Gallagher, A. 2021. To Name and Shame or Not, and If So, How? A Pragmatic Analysis of Naming and Shaming the Chinese Government Over Mass Atrocity Crimes against the Uyghurs and Other Muslim Minorities in Xinjiang. *Journal of Global Security Studies*. **6**(4), pp. 1–16.

Gallagher, A., Raffle, E. and Maulana, Z. 2019. Failing to Fulfil the Responsibility to Protect: The War on Drugs as Crimes Against Humanity in the Philippines. *The Pacific Review*. **33**(2), pp. 247–277.

GCR2P 2020a. UN Human Rights Council Adopts First Thematic Resolution on the Responsibility to Protect. [Accessed 17 May 2021]. Available from: www.global r2p.org/publications/un-human-rights-council-adopts-first-thematic-resolution-on-the-responsibility-to-protect/.

GCR2P 2020b. UN Human Rights Council Resolutions Referencing R2P. [Accessed 21 August 2020]. Available from: www.globalr2p.org/resources/un-human-rights-council-resolutions-referencing-r2p/.

Gilabert, P. and Lawford-Smith, H. 2012. Political Feasibility: A Conceptual Exploration. *Political Studies*. **60**(4), pp. 809–825.

Glanville, L. 2016. Does R2P Matter? Interpreting the Impact of a Norm. *Cooperation and Conflict*. **51**(2), pp. 184–199.

Glanville, L. 2021. *Sharing Responsibility: The History and Future of Protection from Atrocities*. Princeton, NJ: Princeton University Press.

Hehir, A. 2012. *The Responsibility to Protect: Rhetoric, Reality and the Future of Humanitarian Intervention*. Basingstoke: Palgrave Macmillan.

Henderson, S. 2017. The Arms Trade Treaty: Responsibility to Protect in Action? *Global Responsibility to Protect*. **9**(2), pp. 147–172.

Human Rights Watch 2020a. Philippines: Lasting Harm to Children from 'Drug War': UN Human Rights Council Should Promote Justice for Killings. [Accessed 30 June 2020]. Available from: www.hrw.org/news/2020/05/27/philippines-lasting-harm-children-drug-war.

Human Rights Watch 2020b. UN: Deny Rights Council Seats to Major Violators. [Accessed 9 October 2020]. Available from: www.hrw.org/news/2020/10/08/un-deny-rights-council-seats-major-violators.

Human Rights Watch 2021. NGOs Call for UN Human Rights Council Resolution on Tigray. [Accessed 12 June 2021]. Available from: www.hrw.org/news/2021/06/11/ngos-call-un-human-rights-council-resolution-tigray.

International Court of Justice 2020. Application of the Convention on the Prevention and Punishment of the Crime of Genocide (The Gambia v. Myanmar): Request for the indication of provisional measures. [Accessed 23 January 2020]. Available from: www.icj-cij.org/files/case-related/178/178-20200123-SUM-01-00-EN.pdf.

International Criminal Court 2021. Situation in the Philippines: ICC Pre-Trial Chamber I Authorises the Opening of an Investigation. [Accessed 21 September 2021]. Available from: www.icc-cpi.int/Pages/item.aspx?name=PR1610.

Jacob, C. 2021. Regulatory Contestation: Steering Toward Consistency in International Norm Implementation. *International Studies Review.* **23**(4), pp. 1349–1369.

Kim, H.J. 2019. Are UN Investigations into Human Rights Violations a Viable Solution? An Assessment of UN Commissions of Inquiry. *Journal of Human Rights Practice.* **11**(1), pp. 96–115.

Krain, M. 2012. J'accuse! Does Naming and Shaming Perpetrators Reduce the Severity of Genocides or Politicides? *International Studies Quarterly.* **56**(3), pp. 574–589.

Linklater, A. 2001. Citizenship, Humanity, and Cosmopolitan Harm Conventions. *International Political Science Review.* **22**(3), pp. 261–277.

Meghani, A., Abdulwahab, A., Privor-Dumm, L., and Wonodi, C. 2015. Basket Funds: A Pooled Arrangement to Finance Primary Health Care Delivery and Address the Funding Flow in Nigeria. *Baltimore, MD: International Vaccine Access Center (IVAC). Johns Hopkins Bloomberg School of Public Health.*

Meier, B.M. and Gomes, V.B. 2018. Human Rights Treaty Bodies: Monitoring, Interpreting, and Adjudicating Health-Related Human Rights *In*: B.M. Meier and L.O. Gostin, eds. *Human Rights in Global Health: Rights-Based Governance for a Globalizing World.* Oxford: Oxford University Press, pp. 509–536.

Mills, K. and Bloomfield, A. 2018. African Resistance to the International Criminal Court: Halting the Advance of the Anti-impunity Norm. *Review of International Studies.* **44**(1), pp. 101–127.

Nesbitt, M. 2017. Re-Purposing UN Commissions of Inquiry. *Journal of International Law & International Relations.* **13**, pp. 83–121.

OHCHR 2015. *Commissions of Inquiry and Fact-Finding Missions on International Human Rights and Humanitarian Law: Guidance and Practice* [Online]. New York: Unites Nations. [Accessed 25 August 2020]. Available from: www. ohchr.org/Documents/Publications/CoI_Guidance_and_Practice.pdf.

OHCHR n.d. Elections of Treaty Body Members. [Accessed 7 July 2020]. Available from: www.ohchr.org/EN/HRBodies/Pages/ElectionsofTreatyBodiesMembers. aspx.

OHCHR 2020. Philippines: UN Report Details Widespread Human Rights Violations and Persistent Impunity. [Accessed 21 August 2020]. Available from: www.ohchr. org/EN/NewsEvents/Pages/DisplayNews.aspx?NewsID=25924&LangID=E.

OHCHR 2022. *OHCHR Assessment of human rights concerns in the Xinjiang Uyghur Autonomous Region, People's Republic of China* [Online]. [Accessed 1 September 2022]. Available from: www.ohchr.org/sites/default/files/documents/ countries/2022-08-31/22-08-31-final-assesment.pdf.

Pattison, J. 2018. *The Alternatives to War: From Sanctions to Nonviolence.* Oxford: Oxford University Press.

Perlo-Freeman, S. 2020. The ATT and War Profiteering: The Case of the UK. *Global Responsibility to Protect.* **12**(2), pp. 178–201.

Ploton, V. 2017. The Implementation of UN Treaty Body Recommendations. *SUR International Journal on Human Rights.* **25**, pp. 219–235.

Pramendorfer, E. 2020. The Role of the Human Rights Council in Implementing the Responsibility to Protect. *Global Responsibility to Protect.* **12**(3), pp. 239–245.

Pramendorfer, E. 2021. How and Why We Should Utilise HRC Investigative Mechanisms to Prevent Recurrence of Atrocities. *ECR2P Fresh Perspectives Blog.* [Online]. [Accessed 1 December 2021]. Available from: https://ecr2p.leeds.ac.uk/ how-and-why-we-should-utilise-hrc-investigative-mechanisms-to-prevent-recurre nce-of-atrocities/.

Prokhorova, A. 2022. The Special Adviser on the Responsibility to Protect: Performing Norm Leadership. *Global Responsibility to Protect.* **14**(3), pp. 281–312.

Pytlak, A. 2020. Are Arms Trade Treaty Meetings Being Used to Their Full Potential? *Global Responsibility to Protect.* **12**(2), pp. 156–177.

Ramcharan, B.G. 2019. *Modernizing the UN Human Rights System.* Leiden: Brill.

Reuters 2021. Philippines' Duterte Taunts ICC, Saying War on Drugs Far from Over. [Accessed 21 September 2021]. Available from: www.reuters.com/world/asia-paci fic/philippines-duterte-taunts-icc-saying-war-drugs-far-over-2021-07-26/.

Rodley, N.S. 2013. The Role and Impact of Treaty Bodies *In*: D. Shelton, ed. *The Oxford Handbook of International Human Rights Law.* Oxford: Oxford University Press, pp. 621–648.

Roff, H. 2013. *Global Justice, Kant and the Responsibility to Protect: A Provisional Duty.* London: Routledge.

Saba, A. and Akbarzadeh, S. 2020. The ICC and R2P: Complementary or Contradictory? *International Peacekeeping.* **28**(1), pp. 84–109.

Scannella, P. and Splinter, P. 2007. The United Nations Human Rights Council: A Promise to Be Fulfilled. *Human Rights Law Review.* 7(1), pp. 41–72.

Shapcott, R. 2008. Anti-cosmopolitanism, Pluralism and the Cosmopolitan Harm Principle. *Review of International Studies.* 34(2), pp. 185–205.

Shaw, M. 2012. From Comparative to international Genocide Studies: The International Production of Genocide in 20th-century Europe. *European Journal of International Relations.* 18(4), pp. 645–668.

Šimonović, I. 2019. R2P at a Crossroads: Implementation or Marginalization *In*: C. Jacob and M. Mennecke, eds. *Implementing the Responsibility to Protect: A Future Agenda.* London: Routledge, pp. 251–267.

Stavrianakis, A. 2016. Legitimising liberal Militarism: Politics, Law and War in the Arms Trade Treaty. *Third World Quarterly.* 37(5), pp. 840–865.

Strauss, E. 2015. Institutional Capacities of the United Nations to Prevent and Halt Atrocity Crimes *In*: S. K. Sharma and J. M. Welsh, eds. *The Responsibility to Prevent: Overcoming the Challenges of Atrocity Prevention.* Oxford: Oxford University Press, pp. 38–82.

Strauss, E. 2016. UN Human Rights Council and High Commissioner for Human Rights *In*: A. J. Bellamy and T. Dunne, eds. *The Oxford Handbook of the Responsibility to Protect.* Oxford: Oxford University Press, pp. 315–334.

Strauss, E. 2019. Linking Human Rights Accountability and Compliance with R2P Implementation *In*: C. Jacob and M. Mennecke, eds. *Implementing the Responsibility to Protect: A Future Agenda.* London: Routledge, pp. 179–196.

Tacheva, B. 2021. 'Manifest Failing': Investigating the Substantive Threshold for Collective International Action in Response to Mass Atrocity Crimes. University of Leeds.

Terman, R. and Voeten, E. 2018. The Relational Politics of Shame: Evidence from the Universal Periodic Review. *The Review of International Organizations.* **13**(1), pp. 1–23.

Tesón, F.R. 2006. The Vexing Problem of Authority in Humanitarian Intervention: A Proposal. *Wisconsin International Law Journal.* **24**, pp. 761–772.

The Guardian 2020. Netanyahu calls for sanctions over ICC war crimes investigation. [Accessed 4 September 2020]. Available from: www.theguardian.com/world/ 2020/jan/21/netanyahu-calls-for-sanctions-over-icc-war-crimes-investigation-israel.

UN 2013. The Arms Trade Treaty. [Accessed 19 June 2019]. Available from: https://unoda-web.s3-accelerate.amazonaws.com/wp-content/uploads/2013/06/English7.pdf.

UN 2017. Implementing the Responsibility to Protect: Accountability for Prevention. Report of the Secretary-General. A/71/1016–S/2017/556. [Accessed 2 August 2021]. Available from: https://undocs.org/A/71/1016.

UN 2018. Head of Human Rights Fact-Finding Mission on Myanmar Urges Security Council to Ensure Accountability for Serious Violations against Rohingya. [Accessed 4 September 2020]. Available from: www.un.org/press/en/2018/sc13552.doc.htm.

UN 2020. Prioritizing Prevention and Strengthening Response: Women and the Responsibility to Protect. Report of the Secretary-General. A/74/964 – S/2020/501. [Accessed 8 September 2020]. Available from: www.un.org/en/genocideprevention/documents/2009954E.pdf.

UN 2021. *Advancing Atrocity Prevention: Work of the Office on Genocide Prevention and the Responsibility to Protect. Report of the Secretary-General. A/75/863–S/ 2021/424* [Online]. [Accessed 14 June 2021]. Available from: https://undocs.org/en/A/75/863.

UN n.d. Human Rights Council. [Accessed 21 September 2021]. Available from: www.un.org/en/genocideprevention/human-rights-council.shtml.

UNGA 2005. Resolution adopted by the General Assembly on 16 September 2005. A/RES/60/1. [Accessed 15 November 2018]. Available from: www.un.org/en/development/desa/population/migration/generalassembly/docs/globalcompact/A_RES_60_1.pdf.

UNGA 2006. Resolution adopted by the General Assembly. 60/251. Human Rights Council. [Accessed 4 January 2022]. Available from: www2.ohchr.org/english/bodies/hrcouncil/docs/A.RES.60.251_En.pdf.

UNGA 2017. President's Summary: Informal, Interactive Dialogue of the 71st Session of the General Assembly on the Responsibility to Protect: Implementing the responsibility to protect: accountability for prevention. [Accessed 6 September 2022]. Available from: www.un.org/pga/71/wp-content/uploads/sites/40/2015/08/informal-interactive-dialogue-on-the-Responsibility-to-Protect.pdf.

UNGA 2019a. 93rd Plenary Meeting. The Responsibility to Protect and the Prevention of Genocide, War Crimes, Ethnic Cleansing and Crimes Against Humanity. A/73/PV.93. [Accessed 31 July 2019]. Available from: https://digitallibrary.un.org/record/3812131?ln=en.

UNGA 2019b. 94th Plenary Meeting. The Responsibility to Protect and the Prevention of Genocide, War Crimes, Ethnic Cleansing and Crimes Against Humanity. A/73/PV.94. [Accessed 31 July 2019]. Available from: https://digitallibrary.un.org/record/3812513?ln=en.

UNGA 2021. 64th Plenary Meeting. The responsibility to Protect and the Prevention of Genocide, War Crimes, Ethnic Cleansing and Crimes Against Humanity. A/75/PV.64. [Accessed 8 September 2022]. Available from: https://documents-dds-ny.un.org/doc/UNDOC/GEN/N21/121/10/PDF/N2112110.pdf?OpenElement.

UNHCR n.d. Yemen Humanitarian Crisis. [Accessed 1 March 2021]. Available from: www.unrefugees.org/emergencies/yemen/.

UNHCR 2021. Situation of Human Rights in Myanmar. A/HRC/46/L.21. [Accessed 6 April 2021]. Available from: https://undocs.org/A/HRC/46/L.21.

Van den Herik, L.J. 2014. An Inquiry into the Role of Commissions of Inquiry in International Law: Navigating the Tensions between Fact-Finding and Application of International Law. *Chinese Journal of International Law.* **13**(3), pp. 507–537.

Warren, M. 2002. Deliberative Democracy *In*: G. Stokes and A. Carter, eds. *Democratic Theory Today: Challenges for the 21st Century.* Cambridge: Polity Press, pp. 173–202.

Welsh, J.M. 2013. Norm Contestation and the Responsibility to Protect. *Global Responsibility to Protect.* 5(4), pp. 365–396.

Whang, C. 2015. The Challenges of Enforcing International Military-Use Technology Export Control Regimes: An Analysis of the United Nations Arms Trade Treaty. *Wisconsin International Law Journal.* 33(1), pp. 114–139.

World Uyghur Congress 2020. #VoteNoChina: 70 Uyghur Organizations Call on Governments to Vote Against China's Election to UN Human Rights Body. [Accessed 8 October 2020]. Available from: www.uyghurcongress.org/en/votenoch ina-70-uyghur-organizations-call-on-governments-to-vote-against-chinas-election-to-un-human-rights-body/.

8 Conclusion

The R2P – Let's Stay Critical Friends

8.1 Taking Stock

Twenty-two years on since the ICISS first coined the term 'Responsibility to Protect', and 18 years since the international community agreed to uphold (some form) of the principle at the 2005 UN World Summit, it is evident that the R2P has not successfully imparted a standard of cosmopolitan human protection. Persistent cases of atrocity violence, many of which have been flagged in the preceding chapters – such as Syria, Myanmar, China, Ukraine, CAR, Yemen, and many others (see GCR2P) – make it clear that the consistent fulfilment of a right to protection, and obligations to act on mass atrocity crimes, are areas in which practice falls well short of a cosmopolitan ideal. As a norm of atrocity prevention and response, the R2P is not working as well as proponents of cosmopolitan human protection would wish.

The R2P has often been unfairly criticised for failing to end mass atrocity violence entirely, something which it could never achieve, given that it is dependent on actors with little altruistic motivation, and especially in a lifespan of under two decades (Gallagher, 2015). However, the rise in the outbreak of mass atrocities is seriously concerning, as is the fact that international response has often been weak where atrocity violence has occurred. What this necessitates, therefore, is proactive attempts to improve the conceptualisation and implementation of the R2P. This is something which can only be achieved by reform.

In responding to these challenges, the main contribution of this book was to offer the first ever systematic attempt at analysing reform measures to strengthen the R2P. Critiques of the R2P, its practical impact, and its norm status, are important for understanding its worth and for identifying failings; they, however, exist in abundance, while far fewer scholars have sought to analyse the means through which the R2P norm can be enhanced.

8.2 Strengthening the Responsibility to Protect

This book has espoused a cosmopolitan vision for the R2P: an aspirational demand that can be used to both critique the current state of mass atrocity

DOI: 10.4324/9781003394105-8

prevention efforts, as well as serve as the normative compass to point us in the direction of potential reform. There is, after all, a *prima facie* link between the R2P and cosmopolitan demands for fundamental human rights protection, suggesting that there is conceptual value in linking the R2P and cosmopolitanism together as a means of understanding what the R2P ought to, as a moral norm, promote.

Chapter 2 therefore addressed the question of what a cosmopolitan view of fundamental human protection morally obliges from actors operating at the international level. The chapter argued that a cosmopolitan view of global justice supports the existence of both positive and negative duties to secure fundamental rights at a universal level. If international actors hold these duties, they must, by extension, hold a duty to intervene in foreign states if this is necessary to secure the fundamental rights of peoples within that state. Ideally, this duty can be met through non-forceful measures, but if that is not possible, then it is morally permissible to exercise the use of coercive measures (including military force) to this end.

This cosmopolitan reading of the R2P demands: i) an appropriate international response to any given case of mass atrocities, and to promote the conditions within which this is possible; and ii) a duty to take meaningful commitments to prevent atrocity crises from arising in the first place. In providing a cosmopolitan reading of the R2P, the chapter contributes to our current understandings of what the R2P norm ought to morally entail. It has been argued that, moving forward, it is this cosmopolitan standard which should be aimed at if the R2P is to successfully serve protection against mass atrocity.

Chapter 3 examined the extent to which mass atrocity prevention efforts currently meet these cosmopolitan demands. This was essential for understanding where the R2P currently fails from a cosmopolitan perspective, and what cosmopolitan elements are missing which can be brought in to critique and reinforce the R2P through reform efforts. It argued that the R2P promotes fundamental cosmopolitan demands of individualism, egalitarianism, and universality. Beyond this, the R2P also holds a deeper theoretical connection with ethical maxims of cosmopolitan human protection. This is reflected in the norm's relationship with conditional sovereignty, collective responsibility, and its attempt to delineate criteria for when intervention is morally permissible (Wyatt, 2019), as well as in its relationship with structural and operational levels of atrocity prevention (Bohm and Brown, 2021).

Despite this theoretical alignment between the R2P and cosmopolitanism, the R2P currently represents a norm with weak compliance pull, and as a consequence, has a limited influence on state behaviour. The result is frequent failures to realise the implementation of cosmopolitan positive and negative duties through the R2P. The statist focus of the R2P, *combined* with the weaknesses of institutionalised means to implement the norm, has meant that R2P has ultimately served as a matter of self-regulation for states. This has upheld the discretionary power of the state to act on cases of mass atrocities as it sees fit, as well as allowing states to pay lip-service to atrocity prevention.

The R2P aims to set a standard of appropriate behaviour in relation to tackling atrocity crimes and is therefore representative of having what could be considered a cosmopolitan aspiration. However, the related failures of the current R2P approach stand in the way of meeting cosmopolitan protection goals. What this shows is that reform is necessary in order to promote cosmopolitan progress.

The issue of how to go about analysing potential reforms was taken up in Chapter 4. This set a foundation for subsequent chapters to analyse the practical value of reforms. Cosmopolitan demands to curb mass-scale egregious suffering may, on the face of it, seem to be making an overly ambitious demand of states operating in a heavily politicised international environment. If the state system is viewed only as a force for self-interest, incapable of promoting moral goals of human protection, then this would almost certainly be the case. Yet, it would be far too fatalistic to simply determine that cosmopolitan demands of human protection are unreachable and of no value. Halting mass atrocities is a normative demand which ought to be aspired to, regardless of its difficulty. However, while the importance of making normative demands should never be underplayed, there is value in not attempting to demand too much change at once, and instead adopting a transitional approach to achieving progress. Missing this point may result in advocacy for unobtainable change, demand too much from actors, and achieve little in the way of progress.

With this in mind, Chapter 4 argued for a transitional cosmopolitan (Brown and Jarvis, 2019; Brown and Hobbs, 2022) approach for R2P reform. Transitional cosmopolitanism's aim is to help foster the conditions where human protection can be strengthened, working to overcome practical constraints that stand in the way of achieving ideal progress. Transitional cosmopolitanism accepts that imperfect normative progress still represents progress, and also promotes the idea that tempered progress in the short term can open up the possibility of further iterative steps and normative gains. In an important attempt to enhance the methodological application of transitional cosmopolitanism, two central criteria for assessing the practical potential of any given reform measure were developed in this chapter. These criteria are those of the *effectiveness* and *feasibility* of potential reforms. At a basic level, effectiveness is about whether a reform measure should be adopted, while feasibility is about whether a measure could be adopted. The chapter laid out a set of tests, adapted from Gilabert and Lawford-Smith's (2012) work, which can be used to assess the criteria of effectiveness and feasibility. These tests were applied in subsequent chapters when examining potential reform measures. Chapter 4 argued further that adopting a statist focus is necessary when considering reform, noting that the transitional cosmopolitan approach requires analysis of reform to work among the reality of competing state interests at the international level. By operating among a statist conception of international relations, the criteria of effectiveness and feasibility can be satisfied by attempting to better align state interest with the goals of R2P reform.

The book then turned to examining specific reform recommendations in the name of strengthening the R2P's implementation. Chapter 5 examined the UNSC P5's 'veto power' as a significant institutional obstruction to R2P action. Since the UNSC is the preponderant body for R2P response under Pillar Three, the veto and R2P are intrinsically linked. Indeed, practice has shown that the veto impinges on the UNSC's response to atrocity crises. Veto use can effectively stall Pillar Three, undermining the international community's positive responsibility to respond to atrocity crimes. Building on suggestions put forward in the Accountability, Coherency and Transparency (ACT) Group's 'Code of Conduct', and the 'France-Mexico initiative' for veto restraint, the chapter called for the adoption of a new proposal: 'Responsible Veto Restraint' (RVR). The aim of this proposal is to promote incremental progress towards desirable UNSC voting behaviour. As a transitional and politically grounded recommendation, RVR can help to promote an application of R2P response aligned with the cosmopolitan responsibilities. RVR differs from previous proposals in several key aspects: it recommends that non-consensual military force, sanctions, and criminal prosecutorial mechanisms be separated from veto restraint, calls for the removal of subjective get-out clauses for the P5, and favours a more stringent trigger system for when veto restraint should become active.

While numerous significant feasibility obstacles stand in the way of making progress on the veto issue, RVR could help in passing non-coercive and potentially useful R2P action in the Council such as but not limited to: rhetorical condemnations of actors, humanitarian access for life-saving aid, and counter-narratives to combat atrocity violence. In the short term, this could help to ensure the passage of immediate action that helps ameliorate mass atrocity crises. In the longer term, RVR can help promote the conditions in which it is possible to make iterative behavioural progress towards satisfying the goal of cosmopolitan human protection. Regarding veto restraint, this means contributing to a normative practice wherein P5 members accept the need to avoid veto use in R2P cases, or at least where certain conditions are satisfied, that veto use ought to be precluded in particular instances and for particular types of resolutions. RVR offers a new and potentially useful avenue addressing the problem of weak UNSC response to atrocity crimes.

While Chapter 5 put forward a tempered veto restraint proposal for enhancing the UNSC's working methods, Chapter 6 sought to examine an alternative channel for implementing R2P Pillar Three. Reforming the veto is difficult and unlikely to overcome institutional problems of Pillar Three implementation on its own. This is because the UNSC's failures to act on atrocity situations have presented an 'authority dilemma' in international relations (Gallagher, 2013, pp. 111–115), as the authority of the Council to serve as the only legitimate body for authorising coercive intervention has come into question. As the version of the R2P accepted by the international community in 2005 relies on an unaltered UNSC for its implementation, the authority dilemma remains, and the R2P norm fails to address a key problem of effective response to mass atrocity. The current R2P approach leaves unaddressed the questions of how the international community should proceed when the UNSC is left stalled, and if other means can be utilised for implementing Pillar Three beyond the UNSC. In response, Chapter 6 examined one potential means for implementing the R2P beyond a deadlocked UNSC: the Uniting for Peace (UfP) mechanism (UNGA, 1950) and the powers of the UNGA. This is an area that has been largely overlooked within the R2P literature, which is surprising given the potential that the UNGA has for overcoming the authority dilemma. Acting on Pillar Three through the UNGA would keep R2P response aligned with a legal and UN-centred collective international response that allows the UNGA to recommend a host of potential measures following UNSC failure, including peaceful, coercive, and military means of response. The chapter makes its own new contribution by arguing that some tweaks to both UfP language and procedure could serve to further enhance the measure's effectiveness and feasibility.

Addressing some important concerns with the current UfP mechanism, the chapter proposed a procedural tweak which would alleviate any concerns about the UNGA overstepping its constitutional powers under the UN Charter; first, by maintaining the UNSC's power to trigger UfP by referring a case to the UNGA, and second, which would also allow the UNGA to trigger the mechanism when the UNSC is not actively exercising its responsibilities. The chapter also called for the removal of the P5 unanimity clause in UfP: to emphasise that UfP can rightfully be triggered in instances lacking an explicit indication of a lack of P5 unanimity. Finally, the chapter recommended that UfP language be altered to place less emphasis on the use of military force, and instead emphasise that there are a range of measures available to the UNGA to respond to mass atrocities. The proposals offered in Chapter 6 can better align UfP with a transitional cosmopolitan approach, providing a more effective and feasible alternative for discharging the R2P in the wake of UNSC failure.

Finally, Chapter 7 proposed a new and supplementary mechanism to assist in the R2P's implementation. The means of holding states accountable to their R2P commitments are weak: states often commit atrocities without fear of punishment; states engage in damaging practices which contribute to the outbreak or perpetuation of atrocity violence; and the response of the international community to unfolding atrocity crises, and scrutiny of that response, is significantly limited. The failure to hold states accountable to their R2P means that we cannot view the norm's status as enshrining cosmopolitan standards. However, given the difficulties with enforcing R2P compliance, equating accountability with guaranteed enforcement would likely be too ambitious in the short term. Hence, the chapter adopted a less stringent view of accountability that focuses on consistent scrutiny of practice, rather than guaranteed enforcement.

The chapter suggested that instead of seeking a new enforcement body for the R2P, we should pursue an institution to promote state accountability through expert-based independent fact-finding, scrutiny of practice, and pro-active recommendations for action. While the UNHRC may appear suited to this role, its heavily politicised nature of its statist composition means that it cannot serve as a reliable body for holding states accountable to their R2P. The chapter instead recommended the creation of an 'R2P Commission'. This is a proposal for an expert body, uniquely charged with scrutinising the implementation of the R2P. The R2P Commission can effectively pro-mote state accountability under the three pillar R2P approach via determin-ations of where manifest R2P failures have occurred, review of international practice vis-à-vis atrocity prevention and response, and recommendations for altering practice and potential further action. While the R2P Commission would not be as revolutionary as establishing an institution with power to enforce the R2P, since it would only possess a review and recommendatory function, such an institution nevertheless offers a new, transitional step for promoting state accountability under the R2P.

8.3 Responding to Some Limitations

Before offering some final thoughts, it is worth addressing some points about the potential limitations of this study. A first relates to breadth and depth. This book has looked at a range of measures in the name of enhancing the implementation of the R2P. One criticism which may be levelled here is that each of these measures deserves more attention than a single chapter. It is not suggested that this book has comprehensively solved debate on the topic of R2P reform generally, or in regard to the individual reform areas covered. Further scholarly works on the measures proposed here would be welcome and likely necessary. Yet, what this book has done is provide the first ever systematic attempt at analysing measures for R2P reform, bringing together a range of crucial debates, with the hope that this will lead to further conceptu-alisation and debate within the literature, addressing a dearth in current R2P analysis. Consequently, the book has looked at several different areas for potential reform. This was necessary given the broadness of the R2P itself as both an attempt at improving domestic and international approaches to atro-city prevention, as well as international approaches to effectively responding to atrocities. The R2P suffers from a multitude of complex issues that inhibit its implementation. This book has provided a range of potential avenues to pursue for overcoming some of these issues and for better aligning the R2P with a cosmopolitan approach to human protection.

As a contrary argument, another potential criticism that may be levelled is that the book has not covered enough ground. This would be to critique the choice to focus on the three particular areas for reform progress, while other potential areas were left out. Indeed, this book has not sought to cover every potential area for R2P-enhancing reform. Some other potential avenues for reform could include themes such as (though not limited to): a UN standing force for rapid deployment to situations of high concern; the potential for utilising so-called 'coalitions of the willing' for implementing Pillar Three response action where the UN system has been highly ineffective at addressing a crisis; or the adoption of international reforms aimed at the cosmopolitanisation of global economic, legal, and political structures that may be linked with the goal of atrocity prevention.[1] Naturally, the entire range of possible R2P-enhancing reforms could not be covered here. Yet this book has nevertheless covered a range of measures – while working within a transitional cosmopolitan framework – for enhancing the R2P's implementation, which it has argued offer opportunity for real progress. The fact that there exist other potential areas for R2P reform brings scope for both concern and optimism. Concern in that there are clearly further areas in need of cosmopolitan advancement, but optimism in that they suggest that fruitful areas for cosmopolitan advancement do exist. Such themes point to areas for future study, and further areas for applying a transitional cosmopolitan lens going forward.

A final point of criticism may be that the measures proposed in this book lack the transformational potential to significantly enhance the current R2P approach. The book has not sought to offer reform measures with the transformational capacity to morph the R2P into something that can immediately meet and satisfy cosmopolitan standards. While it would certainly be possible to devise reform proposals for the R2P that would hold more transformational influence than the measures proposed within this book, it has been argued here that, given the nature of the highly competitive and unfavourable political environment that the R2P currently occupies (Glanville, 2021, p. 3), working roughly within the boundaries of the currently accepted R2P approach is favourable in terms of the feasibility of actually achieving reform progress. Maintaining the current state-centric, three pillar R2P approach that relies on UN institutions as the main means for practical implementation, is likely the most feasible way for achieving reform progress in the present.

Furthermore, it has been argued that advocating tempered reform progress within a framework of transitional cosmopolitanism does offer us scope for positive change. As Chapters 5–7 all highlighted, there are important reforms which can and should be taken up to promote effective change within this approach. Furthermore, seeking to utilise supplementary measures to enhance the R2P's implementation – such as those provided in Chapters 6 and 7 which, despite going beyond the version of the, agreed to in 2005 do not attempt to supplant the power of states or the hierarchy of the UN's core institutions – can also provide effective and feasible reform avenues. Notably, those proposals in Chapters 6 and 7 do not seek to circumvent the current R2P approach by entirely overhauling the means for responding to mass atrocity crises, such as by going beyond the UN system via ad hoc coalitions of the willing. Instead, these proposals also operate within a matrix of transitional progress, seeking to work within a state-based UN system in order to promote effective and feasible avenues for the R2P's advancement.

8.4 Looking Ahead: Choosing the Middle Path Between Fatalism and Idealism

Trends of mass violence point to a human protection regime in crisis. The R2P was designed to promote progress in preventing and responding to genocide, war crimes, crimes against humanity, and ethnic cleansing. Yet the numerous instances of these crimes, their concurrence across multiple states and regions, and their perpetuation by various state and non-state actors, as well as the complicity of the international community in the outbreak of atrocities, makes clear that the R2P has not successfully promoted anywhere near a cosmopolitan standard of human protection.

It is probably too idealistic to suggest that mass atrocity violence could be ended in its entirety. International actors, especially the UN, can perform better in their cosmopolitan positive duty to act where evidence of potential atrocities is becoming clear. At the very least, international actors can take action to stop their own practices of harm that violate their cosmopolitan negative duty. Yet, when domestic actors become intent on inflicting atrocities due to a perception of necessity, there may not be much that can be done by outside actors to stop them. Perhaps what is most troubling though is that where mass atrocities have occurred, international response has still often lacked – even when that international response has concerned something as minor as rhetorical condemnation, never mind whether the question is one of robust enforcement.

Even so, fatalism is unacceptable. Rather than lamenting failures or simply declaring the human protection regime irrevocably 'broken', this book has made a proactive attempt at addressing problems by analysing the scope for normative advancement via reform. The transitional cosmopolitan approach allows us to identify where effective and feasible change is possible, and indeed, the measures analysed through the chapters of this book have demonstrated that there are avenues for effective and feasible R2P improvement.

It is too early to say that the R2P has failed. Nonetheless, the current trajectory is not a positive one. On the one hand, it is important to not be fatalistic about the potential for achieving successful human protection. Yet, we also shouldn't be overly optimistic by assuming that this can be achieved through current mechanisms, without further and significant political struggle. This means that the status quo cannot be accepted, nor can small successes be heralded as marks of general progressiveness while ignoring wider trends. In sum, we cannot rely on the *current* R2P approach to serve the ends of cosmopolitan human protection. Instead of taking the position of outright positive advocacy, or outright cynical scepticism, this book has instead assumed the role of 'critical friend' to the R2P. This has meant rejecting fatalism, rejecting the status quo, and instead pursuing a middle line that advocates positive change. There is more that can be done than that which was proposed in this book, and it is important that moving forward we continue to identify and push for reform. Looking ahead, a challenge for R2P scholarship is to do just that, to go beyond discussion of successes and failures and instead identify where change must and can occur. This book has made the first systematic attempt at analysing the issue of R2P reform. The sooner that reform is adopted, the sooner we can begin to bend the arc of progress more favourably in the direction of protection from mass atrocity.

Note

1 For an overview of these topics see Pattison (2008) on UN standing force; Erskine (2019) on coalitions of the willing; and Held (2010) on cosmopolitan reform of global governance.

References

Brown, G.W. and Hobbs, J. 2022. Self-interest, Transitional Cosmopolitanism and the Motivational Problem. *Journal of International Political Theory.* **19**(1), pp. 64–86.

Brown, G.W. and Jarvis, S. 2019. Motivating Cosmopolitanism and the Responsibility for the Health of Others *In*: R. Beardsworth, G.W. Brown and R. Shapcott, eds. *The State and Cosmopolitan Responsibilities.* Oxford: Oxford University Press, pp. 203–223.

Erskine, T. 2019. Coalitions of the Willing and the Shared Responsibility to Protect *In*: R. Beardsworth, G.W. Brown and R. Shapcott, eds. *The State and Cosmopolitan Responsibilities.* Oxford: Oxford University Press, pp. 61–87.

Gallagher, A. 2015. The Responsibility to Protect Ten Years on from the World Summit: A Call to Manage Expectations. *Global Responsibility to Protect.* 7(3–4), pp. 254–274.

Gilabert, P. and Lawford-Smith, H. 2012. Political Feasibility: A Conceptual Exploration. *Political Studies.* **60**(4), pp. 809–825.

Glanville, L. 2021. *Sharing Responsibility: The History and Future of Protection from Atrocities.* Princeton, NJ: Princeton University Press.

Global Centre for the Responsibility to Protect n.d. Populations at Risk. [Accessed 1 January 2023]. Available from: www.globalr2p.org/regions/.

Held, D. 2010. Reframing Global Governance: Apocalypse Soon or Reform *In*: G.W. Brown and D. Held, eds. *The Cosmopolitanism Reader.* Cambridge: Polity Press.

Pattison, J. 2008. Humanitarian Intervention and a Cosmopolitan UN Force. *Journal of International Political Theory.* 4(1), pp. 126–145.

UNGA 1950. Uniting for Peace. A/RES/377(V). [Accessed 22 July 2018]. Available from: www.un.org/en/sc/repertoire/otherdocs/GAres377A(v).pdf.

Wyatt, S.J. 2019. *The Responsibility to Protect and a Cosmopolitan Approach to Human Protection.* London: Palgrave Macmillan.

Index